The Grasp That Reaches Beyond the Grave

The Grasp That Reaches
Beyond the Grave

The Ancestral Call in Black Women's Texts

Venetria K. Patton

Cover art: *Adara (ah DAH rah): Exalted One* (2008) by Delita Martin.

Published by State University of New York Press, Albany

© 2013 State University of New York

For information, contact State University of New York Press, Albany, NY
www.sunypress.edu

Production by Diane Ganeles
Marketing by Anne M. Valentine

Library of Congress Cataloging-in-Publication Data

Patton, Venetria K., 1968-
  The grasp that reaches beyond the grave : the ancestral call in black women's texts / Venetria K. Patton.
       p. cm.
  Includes bibliographical references and index.
  ISBN 978-1-4384-4737-7 (hardcover : alk. paper)
  1. American literature—African American authors—History and criticism.
2. American literature—African influences.   3. African American
women—Intellectual life.   4. African Americans in literature.   I. Title.

PS153.N5P37 2013
810.9'928708996073—dc23   2012029400

10 9 8 7 6 5 4 3 2 1

For my son, Hollis

Contents

Acknowledgments   ix

Introduction
Revising The Legacy of Kinlessness Through Elders
and Ancestors   1

Part I Preface: The Elder as Culture Bearer   27

Chapter 1
Othermothers as Elders and Culture Bearers in
Daughters of the Dust and *The Salt Eaters*   31

**Part II Preface: The Dead Are Not Dead:
The Ancestral Presence**   55

Chapter 2
Ancestral Prodding in *Praisesong for the Widow*   59

Chapter 3
Ancestral Disturbances in *Stigmata*   89

Chapter 4
Beloved: A Ghost Story with an Ogbanje Twist   119

Part III Preface: The Child and Ancestor Bond   151

Chapter 5
The Child Figure as a Means to Ancestral Knowledge
in *Daughters of the Dust* and *A Sunday in June*   153

Conclusion
Looking Backward and Forward: The Ancestral Presence
in Speculative Fiction   175

Notes   191

Bibliography   197

Index   211

Acknowledgments

This book has been a long time in coming, so I must recognize all of those who assisted me and cheered me along the way. First and foremost, is my partner, Ronald J. Stephens, who was with me before I even knew this was a book. Thank you for always believing in me, encouraging me, and for reading my work and talking things through. I have had the good fortune to have wonderful colleagues who have read portions of this project in its various stages. Much thanks to Wendy Flory, Carol E. Henderson, Maureen Honey, Bill V. Mullen, and Aparajita Sagar. I am particularly appreciative of the insightful comments provided by my English Department head, Nancy J. Peterson, because I know so well how difficult it is to balance administrative duties and scholarly activities, but Nancy has not only emulated how to do this but encouraged me in my own balancing act. I also must give special mention to my writing group, Marlo David and Jennifer Freeman-Marshall; it was a pleasure working through our manuscripts together. I must also make special mention of Viktor Gecas, former head of Purdue's Sociology Department. Viktor always encouraged me with regard to my progress on my manuscript and it was one of our conversations that led to my "aha" moment regarding Kongo cosmology and the women I was researching. I also must recognize the support I have received from my deans, Irwin Weiser, John Contreni, and Toby Parcel. They all were supportive of my work on this project in terms of course releases and the sabbatical that made all the difference. Special thanks to Delita Martin for the art that graces this cover. And of course, I must recognize James Peltz, SUNY Press' co-director, for continued faith in my research; my editor, Beth Bouloukos who kept things going; the anonymous reviewers for their excellent comments regarding the manuscript, and everyone at SUNY who brought this project to fruition.

In closing, I thank my son, Hollis, for his patience as I completed this project and my girls, Kiara and Karielle, for keeping me grounded.

My family and friends truly kept me sane, especially my mother, Hildegarde Patton, who made everything possible; my cheering section: Frederick, Pinar, Laeres, Christina, Chloe, Lyle-Jehan, Kyle-Roth, and Letiwe; and my sisters in spirit: Zenephia Evans, Carolyn E. Johnson, and Matilda Stokes.

An earlier version of Chapter 3 was originally published as "Stigmata: Embodying the Scars of Slavery" in *Imagining the Black Female Body* edited by Carol E. Henderson (Palgrave Macmillan, 2010) and is used with permission from Palgrave Macmillan.

Special thanks to the Department of English and the Office of the Vice President for Research at Purdue University for supporting the publication of my research.

Introduction

Revising the Legacy of Kinlessness Through Elders and Ancestors

Elders have traditionally played an important role within African and African American communities. Elders preserve cultural memory and help younger generations navigate the world. However, sometimes the younger generation becomes distant from traditional beliefs and elders must remind them of the importance of tradition and cultural roots. This reliance on elders as guides is particularly evident in matrilineal relationships between mothers and daughters, but also in the bonds shared with grandmothers, aunts, and othermothers. In *Black Feminist Thought*, Patricia Hill Collins discusses the importance of othermothers and woman-centered networks. She asserts, "African and African-American communities have . . . recognized that vesting one person with full responsibility for mothering a child may not be wise or possible. As a result, othermothers—women who assist bloodmothers by sharing mothering responsibilities—traditionally have been central to the institution of Black motherhood" (119). Several scholars, such as Nancy Tanner, Carol Stack, and Niara Sudarkasa, have noted that "[t]he centrality of women in African-American extended families reflects both a continuation of West African cultural values and functional adaptations to race and gender oppression" (119). However, Hill Collins admonishes that "[t]his centrality is not characterized by the absence of husbands and fathers. Men may be physically present and/or have well-defined and culturally significant roles in the extended family and the kin unit may be woman-centered" (119). Therefore, we are not talking about matriarchal families in which mothers head the household, but rather matrifocal societies that emphasize the mother–child bond. According to Deborah Gray White, in matrifocal societies, females "*in their role*

1

as mothers are the focus of familial relationships" (256). Thus texts by black women often emphasize mother–child relationships or other woman-centered bonds because of the significant roles women play in family relations.

This is the case for the texts under discussion here—men are very present in the roles of father, husband, lover, and community leader—however, the protagonists of Toni Cade Bambara's *The Salt Eaters* (1980), Paule Marshall's *Praisesong for the Widow* (1984), Phyllis Alesia Perry's *Stigmata* (1998) and *A Sunday in June* (2004), Toni Morrison's *Beloved* (1987), and Julie Dash's film, *Daughters of the Dust*[1] (1991) are very much a part of woman-centered networks of mothers and daughters and elders and ancestors serving as othermothers. However, these woman-centered networks still have not received sufficient scholarly attention. In the foreword to their book, *The Lost Tradition: Mothers and Daughters in Literature*, Cathy N. Davidson and E. M. Broner note, "We have already heard the story of fathers and sons, of mothers and sons, even of fathers and daughters. But who has sung the song of mothers and daughters?" (xi). Since the 1980 publication of their essay collection much has changed. In 1983, Alice Walker found her mother's garden—ten years after finding her literary foremother, Zora Neale Hurston. In her essay collection, *In Search of Our Mothers' Gardens*, Walker observes, "these grandmothers and mothers of ours were not Saints, but Artists; driven to a numb and bleeding madness by the springs of creativity in them for which there was no release" (233). Since these early discussions of mothers, much attention has been paid to maternity and matrilineal relations. Within the African Diaspora, mothers, motherlands, and mother tongues have tremendous symbolic force. In her 1991 essay collection, *Motherlands: Black Women's Writing from Africa, the Caribbean and South Asia*, Sushelia Nasta asserts, "The whole question of 'motherhood' is also a major concern universally in contemporary women's literature and has obvious reverberations in terms of feminist criticism—the relation between mothers and daughters, mothers mirroring and affirming identity or notions of the birth of female identity through transference to text and symbol . . ." (xix). The aim of this book is to investigate not only relationships between literal mothers and daughters, but to explore the extended woman-centered networks of mothers, daughters, and othermothers in the form of elders and ancestors.

One might ask why I chose this emphasis on mothers and daughters and matri-lineal networks. There are of course male elders and patri-lineal networks; however, my interest in African American women writers' use of elders and ancestors in their work is rooted in the womb. In my book, *Women in Chains: The Legacy of Slavery in Black Women's Fiction*, I assert that "often black women writers' articulations of gender are not the same as their white counterparts due to their different experiences as a result of race and the history of slavery" (xiv). I make a similar contention here with regard to my decision to limit my discussion to woman-centered networks. Although high regard for elders and ancestors is an important part of African and African American traditions, I believe that the experience of slavery with its concomitant view of black women as "natally dead" has had an effect on African American women writers' emphasis on elders and ancestors and familial bonds whether they are blood bonds or not. In *Playing in the Dark: Whiteness and the Literary Imagination*, Toni Morrison observes that there is an assumption "that slave women are not mothers; they are 'natally dead,' with no obligations to their offspring or their own parents" (21). Thus this emphasis on family seems to be a way to counteract notions of black women as somehow disconnected from the progeny of their wombs.

This disconnection is central to Orlando Patterson's argument in *Slavery and Social Death: A Comparative Study*. "Perhaps the most distinctive attribute of the slave's powerlessness was that it always originated (or was conceived of as having originated) as a substitute for death, usually violent death," states Patterson (5). Slaves experienced "social death" because they "had no socially recognized existence" beyond their masters (5). Patterson calls this condition, "natal alienation," because the slave is "alienated from all 'rights' or claims of birth," ceasing "to belong . . . to any legitimate social order" (5). Patterson prefers this term "because it goes directly to the heart of what is critical in the slave's forced alienation, the loss of ties of birth in both ascending and descending generations" (7). The slave is essentially orphaned—cut off from all familial ties.

Although the texts under discussion here are not all about slavery, they are all responding to the legacy of slavery. For example, *Beloved*, *Stigmata*, and *A Sunday in June* deal directly with the effects of slavery; *Daughters of the Dust* addresses the aftermath of slavery and the impact of Jim Crow; and *The Salt Eaters* and *Praisesong for the Widow* reference the role of the Civil Rights Movement in seeking to gain rights that were denied during slavery. With the exception of *A Sunday in June*, which is a prequel, all of these texts are products of the 1980s and 1990s, which I suggest is a significant sociohistorical moment as African Americans began to seriously assess the gains of the Civil Rights Movement. In making this argument, I take my lead from literary scholar, Ashraf H. A. Rushdy's study of neo-slave narratives, which he situates in the 1970s and 1980s; however, his discussion of contemporary narratives of slavery includes texts from the 1970s, 1980s, and 1990s.[2] In his *Neo-Slave Narratives: Studies in the Social Logic of a Literary Form*, Rushdy argues:

The political atmosphere of the 1980s, though, with rising
right-wing attacks on affirmative action and premature calls
for a color-blind polity, led inevitably to cultural projects
aimed precisely at masking those contradictions that cultural
workers in the 1960s had so brilliantly exposed. Just as the
Reagan administration defined its political agenda largely in
direct repudiation of the "sixties," a term right-wing politicians
used to codify a seamless monolith of permissive liberalism
they anathematized in the process of formulating a series of
reactionary policies aimed at dismantling the social programs
and civil rights legislation of the Johnson administration, so
did conservative intellectuals seek to resist what they variously
saw as the "fraying" or "disuniting" of American culture
by calling for "an all-embracing, revamped national literary
history." (10)

Thus, it is no accident that these revisionist responses to slavery and its
aftermath appear in the 1980s and 1990s. These writers are responding
to a conservative impetus to present a homogeneous view of U.S. history that tends to dismiss the residual effects of slavery and its legacy
on our national history, creating instead historical amnesia. In her essay,
"What is an American Life?," Adrienne Rich astutely notes, "Cruelty,
greed, assassination of cultures are part of all history. But we, here, have
been staggering under the weight of a national fantasy that the history
of the conquest of the Americas, 'the westward movement,' was different—was a history of bravery, enlightenment, righteous claiming, service
to religious values and civilizing spirit" (122). Michael Kammen makes
a similar point in his book, *In the Past Lane: Historical Perspectives on
American Culture*, "Abundant evidence indicates that amnesia concerning the American past afflicts those who are responsible for policy at all
levels" (214). However, African American women writers did not remain
silent in the face of this amnesia, but instead created counter-narratives.

In many ways, the analysis that follows is in dialogue with Nancy J.
Peterson's *Against Amnesia: Contemporary Women Writers and the Crises
of Historical Memory* and Gauthier Marni's *Amnesia and Redress in Contemporary American Fiction: Counterhistory* in that I see these texts as
revisionist works invested in rethinking African Americans' placement in
American history. I agree with Peterson's contention that like the writers
in her study, "Their primary impetus is not only deconstructive, but also
(re)constructive. They outline counter-histories to intervene in the painful amnesia that marks contemporary America and postmodern culture"
(16). Marni builds on Peterson's discussion while also specifically situat-
ing her study of historical novels in the 1990s by looking at a political

climate marked by "denial and a particularly American forgetting on the one hand and recent international concern with public acknowledgment and official apology on the other" (3). Marni points to the launching of truth commissions in the mid-1980s and their proliferation in the 1990s as well as the wave of official apologies to argue:

> Massive violence—and associative denial—punctuates the entire twentieth century. Yet coordinated tenacious efforts at public acknowledgment of "what really happened"—a recurrent and insistent emphasis in the context of criminal tribunals and trials, reparations, and above all, truth commissions—and ensuing redress for state sanctioned crimes is a particularly recent phenomenon, unique, in fact to the 1990s. (3)

Thus, although the texts I address are certainly part of an evolving African American literary tradition, the 1980s and 1990s provided a sociocultural backdrop that encouraged these particular types of revisionist productions.

Deborah McDowell has observed that although black men wrote most of the slave narratives, black women have written the majority of contemporary novels about slavery—novels that emphasize "not what was *done* to slave women, but what they *did* with what was done to them" (146). I would argue that the investment of black women writers in contemporary novels of slavery, such as *Beloved* and *Stigmata*, is rooted in the history of *partus sequitur ventrem*—the child follows the condition of the mother. Thus, the mother's body determined the slave status of her offspring. Through this doctrine, the mother's body serves as a border to police the purity of the nation's boundary (Patton 124). In *Bordering on the Body: The Racial Matrix of Modern Fiction and Culture*, Laura Doyle notes, "In the race-bounded economy the mother is a maker and marker of boundaries, a generator of liminality . . ." (27). This position of "maker and marker of boundaries" placed slave women in a rather precarious position. Nancy Bentley addresses the significance of the loss of kinship created through this process in her essay, "The Fourth Dimension: Kinlessness and African American Narrative." According to Bentley, "The fact that kinlessness can be transmitted *through* birth, however, suggests it is something more than a physical separation or juridical loss. Natal transmission means that kinlessness is also a heritable condition. By appropriating a woman's 'future increase,' the law relies on the facts of birth and descent even as it refuses to accord any bonds of belonging to that birth" (270–71). It is the passing on of kinlessness, which haunts these texts, as these black women revise the legacy of slavery in order to reclaim their progeny.

These women seem to tap into the possibly empowering potential that Hortense J. Spillers identifies because "slave mothers pass on more than the condition of slavery—they also continue a maternal line of descent that is in opposition to the American tradition of patrilineage" (Patton 14). Spillers argues, "motherhood as female blood-rite is outraged, is denied, at the very same time that it becomes the founding term of a human and social enactment" ("Mama's" 80). In fact in an earlier essay, Spillers asserts that black females served as "the principal point of passage between the human and non-human world. Her issue became the focus of a cunning difference—visually, psychologically, ontologically as the route by which the dominant male decided the distinction between humanity and 'other'" ("Intersticies" 76). In other words, by determining the slave status of her offspring, black females effectively determined the humanity/freedom or non-humanity/slavery of their progeny. In *Raising the Dead: Readings of Death and (Black) Subjectivity*, Sharon Holland elaborates on Spillers' articulation of black females as the passage between the human and non-human by suggesting "that this border, which is no border at all but a passageway, also encompasses the terrain between the living and the dead, between the ancestral and the living community" (43). This potential contact between the living and the dead through the process of childbirth will be addressed in greater detail during my discussion of the relationship between the ancestor and the child.

Let us now return to the notion of *partus sequitur ventrem*, which many would view as an emotionally untenable situation. However, Spillers concludes that this paradoxical position is potentially empowering. In fact, she comments on the power of feminist revisions to "at once define a new position of attack and lay claim to a site of ancestral imperative" ("Interstices" 88). I argue that the texts under discussion here should be viewed as feminist revisions of a slave past. The revisionist slant of these texts is suggested by images of rebirth as well as moments that seem to revise the notion of *partus sequitur ventrem*. According to critic Lene Brøndum, "For African American women writers, storytelling is often important as a method of revision" (156). In her essay, "'The Persistence of Tradition': The Retelling of Sea Islands Culture in Works by Julie Dash, Gloria Naylor, and Paule Marshall," Brøndum retells the history of the sea islands, but her argument may be extrapolated to the texts under discussion here as they are all telling stories—Bambara tells the story of ancient mud mothers, Marshall and Dash retell the story of the flying Africans, Perry tells the story of an enslaved woman stolen from Africa and Morrison retells the story of Margaret Garner. For these writers, "storytelling becomes a significant means of revising traditional historiography, because it gives authority to the spoken word as a historical record. In other words, storytelling disrupts the discursive history of hegemony" (156). Brøndum further asserts, "Storytelling and mythic memory are not only means of revision; they also function as means of celebration. In other words, [these writers] . . . are engaged in a pursuit of the survival of body and spirit and the triumph of their people's cultural heritage against all odds" (162). However, I argue that these revisions, although celebratory, also are a means of responding to an ancestral imperative despite the initial resistance of some of the protagonists. According to Doyle, "Because of the mother's alignment with the body and her function as reproducer of the group as a social body, the mother comes to signify, often ambivalently, a bodily and collective past" (6). It is this collective past that these black women writers are responding to with the assistance of elder and ancestor figures in their texts. These figures allow Bambara, Marshall, Perry, and Dash to illustrate the necessity of ancestral bonds in maintaining a sense of health and well-being in the face of a legacy of slavery and racial discrimination, while Morrison's text complicates our view of the ancestor through the depiction of what some would consider a malevolent ancestor.

Due to the history of slave families being disrupted, it should be no surprise that there is a particular emphasis on family within these texts. The assault on the black family epitomized by the infamous Moynihan report would have also made this a particularly germane theme for these writers. Rushdy notes, "In the seventies, [Daniel Patrick] Moynihan's critique of black family life was carried on through manifestoes and journalistic essays that appeared to be race-neutral but read as racialist discourse" (*Remembering* 13). Whereas Rushdy establishes a connection between the palimpsest narratives of the mid-1970s and the Moynihan report, I contend that this "challenge to the historiography of slavery on which the report drew, and then in the production of familial narratives attesting to the strength of the black families Moynihan had maligned" did not end with the 1970s, but continued into the Reagan era. In *Nixon's Piano*, Kenneth O'Reilly notes Ronald Reagan's tendency to speak in code, which allowed him to call for racial justice while advocating "a rollback of the civil rights movement's achievements, including any government programs smacking of welfare" (360). O'Reilly observes that one of Reagan's favorite stories was that of Linda Taylor, the Chicago welfare queen, whose story was inflated to the point of having " 'eighty names, thirty addresses, twelve Social Security cards' " in order to collect " 'veterans' benefits on four non-existing deceased husbands' " and other welfare benefits in excess of $150,000 tax-free income, not the $8,000 in public aid checks associated with her 1977 conviction. According to O' Reilly, "There was no mistaking the president's attempt to put a black face on such abuses" (360). O'Reilly concludes:

> If the liberal solution to past racial injustices not only asked working-class and middle-income whites to support black programs with their tax dollars but to offer public atonements, Reagan's message was that racial injustice no longer existed and any past injustices were not at issue. The issue was African American's behavior and self-destructive values (crime, drugs, teenage pregnancy, laziness, etc.). (362)

Numerous African American scholars criticized Reagan's administration as evidenced by *The Journal of Blacks in Higher Education* article, "Looking Back: Ronald Reagan, a Master of Racial Polarization." The article charges Reagan with using racial code to pander to southern racism as part of his election strategy, resisting the establishment of the Dr. Martin Luther King Jr. holiday, attempting to dismantle social safety net programs, endeavoring to weaken the Voting Rights Act, and vetoing a bill that would have expanded civil rights legislation (35–36). Similar criticisms are raised by Angela Davis as she takes the Reagan administration to task in two essays included in her 1989 collection, *Women, Culture, & Politics*. In "Sick and Tired of Being Sick and Tired: The Politics of Black Women's Health," Davis claims "The politics of Black women's health are also directly influenced by the general assault on the democracy in this country, which reached a high point during the Reagan years" (62–63). "Women in the 1980's: Setbacks and Victories" points to the difficulties associated with Reagan's two terms in office: "The reactionary forces that shaped Ronald Reagan's regressive policies have perpetuated dangerously high levels of unemployment and homelessness, a social climate promoting racist violence, and increased discrimination against women" (92–93). This is the sociohistorical climate in which these black women were writing—the black family, particularly the black mother, was vilified; racial injustices were denied; and social welfare programs were under attack.[3]

Thus it is in this moment that these writers created texts that foreground the black family and celebrate its non-nuclear nature. For African Americans the family unit may include non-blood relatives and extended families, but regardless of the composition elders are held in high regard. However, this honoring of elders is not just about respect for wisdom associated with a long life. Malidoma Patrice Somé, author of *The Healing Wisdom of Africa: Finding Life Purpose Through Nature, Ritual, and Community*, suggests that the "respect owed to the elder derives from the perception that the elder is at this critical junction where the natural meets the supernatural and where the ancestors and the divine intersect with the humans" (125). The elder is an ancestor in the making, and "every day brings the elder closer to the world of the Spirit and thus more distant from this world, hence this sense of increased sacredness associated with the voice of an elder" (127). Jean-Marc Ela notes in "Ancestors and Christian Faith: An African Problem," "[i]t is rare in black Africa for the dead not to be honoured [*sic*] by any cult after the funeral ceremonies" (35). The ancestor cult is linked to a cyclical view of life in which "The dead are not dead" (37). I argue that this view of life is replicated in such diverse black women's texts, as Morrison's *Beloved* and Tina McElroy Ansa's *The Hand I Fan With* in which ghosts come back to life; Marshall's *Praisesong for the Widow* in which Avey is haunted by her deceased Aunt Cuney; J. California Cooper's *Family*, which is narrated by a dead woman following four generations of her family; Perry's *Stigmata* and Octavia Butler's *Kindred*, which feature protagonists who are able to go back into time with their ancestors; or Bambara's *The Salt Eaters* in which people, memories, the "quietly dead," and "roaming spirits" have "no meaningful difference between their various states of corporeality/being/presence" (Hull 219). Although these texts have very distinctive story lines, they are linked by the notion that life does not end with the grave.

Although very different, each of these texts is illustrative of an African kinship system, in which "ancestors are still connected to their families, and continue to protect the living, to look after them and to act as their intermediaries; at the same time they are open to the interests and worries of the living" (Ela 38). Somé provides additional insight regarding the reverence of ancestors: "in the traditional view, to look to the old ways is to avoid death. The argument is that our ancestors lived thousands of years under conditions that today would be considered extremely harsh and unbearable. In honor of their wisdom, we feel a sacred approach to and reverence for, tradition, even when its dictates are not fully understood" (*Healing* 124–25). Ancestors are seen as sources of ancient wisdom, which forms the backbone of the community, as "[t]he ancestor's life crystallizes the teachings of the family, of the ethnic group and the culture" (Ela 42). In order to address the way in which black women writers tap into the power of this ancient ancestral wisdom, I have divided this book into three parts to address the role of elders, ancestors, and children within an African cyclical view of life.

In *Black Time: Fiction of Africa, the Caribbean and the United States*, Bonnie Barthold argues that people of African descent have a different relationship to time. She traces this difference to the traditions of the Guinea Coast, which she considers to be "the cultural birthplace of black fiction" because this is the area from which most

African slaves originated (9).[4] Prior to colonization, the Guinea Coast was a unified cultural area, and thus Barthold suggests that although the area represents only a small portion of the African continent we can extrapolate from Guinea traditions to discuss Africanisms or African retentions as they relate to the descendants of African slaves. Thus she asserts that "[t]here is little doubt that a mythic concept of time was part of Guinea Coast traditional culture and that the same was true of traditional Africa generally" (9). Barthold links this concept of mythic time to African religion.[5]

African religion authority John S. Mbiti notes in *Introduction to African Religion* that Africans view the universe as eternal: "In many places, circles are used as symbols of the continuity of the universe. They are the symbols of eternity, of unendingness, of continuity" (37). The circle is also an apt illustration of the African concept of time, which is synchronic or cyclical in nature rather than diachronic or linear. In addition to having a cyclical view of time, Africans tend to have a holistic view of life, which does not separate the sacred from the secular. According to Mbiti, "Because traditional religions permeate all the departments of life, there is no formal distinction between the sacred and the secular, between the religious and non-religious, between the spiritual and the material areas of life" (*African* 2). This point is reinforced by Adama and Naomi Doumbia, who argue that the "holistic understanding of the inseparability of the physical and spiritual spheres of life has been the foundation of African beliefs since the beginning of time" (xiii). Thus it should be no surprise that African beliefs also include the acceptance of spirits.

African religion often is misconstrued as ancestor worship, but Mbiti is quick to distinguish the two. He notes that while, "[i]t is true that departed relatives are believed to continue to live and to show interest in their surviving families," they "do not worship their departed relatives" (*Introduction* 18). They do, however, believe in human spirits, which Mbiti attributes to "the natural consequence of the strong belief in African Religion that human life does not terminate at the death of the individual, but continues beyond death" (75). Thus, the reach of ancestors is not terminated by the grave; they can, like Avey's Aunt Cuney, reach out through dreams or go so far as to visit the living as Beloved does with Sethe.[6]

Here, I build on Mbiti's discussion of traditional African religion and Barthold's notion of "Black Time," by drawing specifically on the traditions of a particular group of people from the Guinea Coast—the Kongo. Atlthough the Kongo people currently reside in several countries—Bas-Zaïre, Cabinda, Congo-Brazzaville, and Angola—the area was once united as the ancient kingdom of Kongo. Renowned African Art scholars, Robert Farris Thompson and Joseph Cornet note, "Kongo spelled with a *K*, refers to the unitary civilization by which Bakongo (the Kongo people) themselves refer to their traditional territory and way of life" (27). I follow their lead in using that preferred spelling. Kongo influences are readily apparent in the symbols associated with traditional African American burials throughout the southeastern United States, which seem to reflect the Kongo ancestry of African Americans (32).[7] However, other scholars have made the case for the continued influence of Africanisms and thus I do not make that case here.[8] Nor do I argue that these particular writers had knowledge of Kongo cosmology; however, I do assert that there appears to be an uncanny connection between the depictions of elder, ancestor, and child figures in these texts and Kongo cosmology.

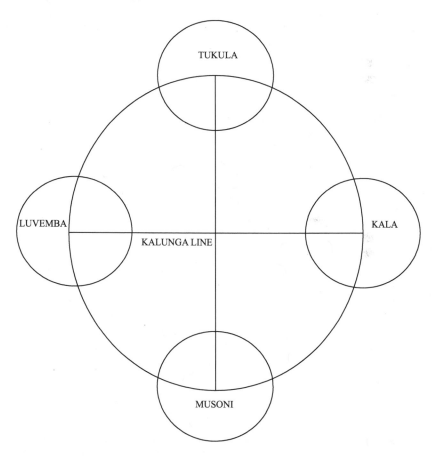

For example, *Beloved* and *Daughters of the Dust* make very specific references to the Kongo cosmogram.[9] This image of a circle with a cross is not a major moment in either text, but yet sends a significant message. In *Beloved*, Sethe knows her mother by this symbol: "Right on her rib was a circle and a cross burnt right in the skin. She said, 'This is your ma'am. This,' and she pointed. 'I am the only one got this mark now. The rest dead" (Morrison, *Beloved* 72). In *Daughters of the Dust*, young boys paint the quartered circle on a turtle's back. Perhaps viewers of the film may not recognize the significance of the symbol, but its deliberateness is apparent in the screenplay. A note in the margin reads, "use ki-kongo symbol" and a circle with a cross is drawn below (Dash, *Making* 147). According to La Vinia Delois Jennings in *Toni Morrison and the Idea of Africa*, the Yowa, "Kongo's quartered circle became one of the most discernible African survivals in the Western hemisphere" (19). One might trace these African survivals or Africanisms to the concept of Diaspora time or limbo time as developed by Sheila Smith McKoy. McKoy argues that "Time as it functions in Diaspora cultures deviates from Western notions of time and is consistent in its uses in all African Diaspora cultures" (208). Like Barthold, McKoy sees African time as cyclical and Western time as linear; however, unlike Barthold she does not envision "black time as a temporal dispossession" due to the collision of African and Western time (208). Instead, McKoy envisions Diaspora time as "a fusion of African cyclical time and the disruption of this cycle forced by the Middle Passage." She asserts, "While colonization and the Transatlantic Slave Trade undeniably brought about cultural ruptures in these communities, the persistency of Diaspora time marks a people's commitment to cultural survival" (209). According to McKoy, Diaspora time, or what she refers to as limbo time, "marks linguistic patterns, ritual processes, and is intricately tied to being in these new world cultures. It is an African contiguity that is reproduced in the literatures and films these cultures produce" (209). Thus, I argue that the references to Kongo cosmology in the texts I discuss are examples of this African contiguity.

Although Perry's novels do not include physical manifestations of the Yowa or Kongo cosmogram, the view of the life cycle that it describes is depicted in both texts. Jennings observes that the Yowa "invokes the indestructibility and circularity of the human soul" (19). This allusion to the continuity of life suggested by the circle is reflected in the words of *Stigmata*'s Ayo, "I come from a long line of forever people. We are forever. Here at the bottom of heaven we live in the circle. We back and gone and back again" (Perry, *Stigmata* 7). However, Ayo's ability to return and communicate with her descendants is not necessarily welcomed. In the prequel to *Stigmata*, *A Sunday in June*, Grace is very clear when she tells her grandmother, Ayo, " 'The dead should stay dead, you hear me?!' " (Perry, *Sunday* 67). Both of Perry's novels illustrate the circularity of life as exemplified by the cosmogram. Ayo, and later Grace, are able to reach out to their descendants because life does not end at the grave.

Another means of referencing the cosmogram is found in Marshall's *Praisesong for the Widow* in the form of the Ring Shout. According to Jennings, "In its most recognized North American, Christian manifestation, worshippers physically form the Yowa configuration in the Ring Shout, a shuffling counterclockwise sacred dance performed to remember familial ancestors and to communicate with the ultimate ancestor, God" (20). We see depictions of the Ring Shout in *Praisesong for the Widow* in both Tatem and Carriacou. Ring Shouts were held at the church in Tatem: "the handful of elderly men and women still left, and who still held to the old ways, could be seen slowly circling the room in a loose ring" (Marshall 34). During the Beg Pardon in Carriacou, Avey gradually transitions from spectator to participant as she begins "performing the dance that wasn't supposed to be dancing in imitation of the old folk shuffling in a loose ring inside the church" (248). Marshall is very explicit in representing these two different expressions of the Ring Shout as related events—Avey is able to join the dance that wasn't a dance in Carriacou because of its familiarity due to her childhood experiences of the Ring Shout in Tatem.

The Ring Shout calls attention to the essential component of the cosmogram—the circle. In *Slave Culture: Nationalist Theory & The Foundations of Black America*, Sterling Stuckey argues that in central and western Africa,

> an integral part of religion and culture was movement in a ring during ceremonies honoring the ancestors. There is, in fact, substantial evidence for the importance of the ancestral function of the circle in West Africa, but the circle ritual imported by Africans from the Congo region was so powerful in its elaboration of a religious vision that it contributed disproportionately to the centrality of the circle in slavery. The use of the circle for religious purposes in slavery was so consistent and profound that one could argue that it was what gave form and meaning to black religion and art. (11)

Stuckey describes the use of circles for singing, dancing, and storytelling, so it is no surprise to find the circle used for the healing session in

Bambara's *The Salt Eaters*. Velma and Minnie are seated on stools while circled by twelve members of The Master's Mind. Although Velma and Minnie are the focal point of the healing session, "the circle of twelve that ringed the two women" are very much a part of the session (11). Although Velma must choose to be well, the healing session is a communal act as indicated by the use of the circle format.

Thompson and Cornet describe the cosmogram, a central concept of Kongo cosmology, as the four moments of the sun—"that is dawn, noon, sunset, and midnight (when the sun, so it is believed, is shining on the kingdom of the dead). Hence, also, its rationale, for the sun's four moments trace in the Kongo mind a circle or a diamond about the twinned worlds of the living and the dead, the city and the cemetery" (27). However, the cemetery is not necessarily a clear demarcation between the living and the dead. Dr. Bunseki Fu-Kiau, authority on Kongo culture, reminds us that for the Kongo, "the dead are not dead: they are beings living just beyond the wall waiting for their probable return to the community . . . to the physical world" (Fu-Kiau 17).[10] This continuity between the worlds of the living and the dead is central to Kongo cosmology and to the deployment of elder, ancestor, and child figures in the works discussed here.

The relationship between these figures may be best seen by thinking of Thompson and Cornet's analysis of Kongo emblems: "Coded as a cross, a quartered circle or diamond, a seashell's spiral, or a special cross with solar emblems at each ending—the sign of the four moments of the sun is the Kongo emblem of spiritual continuity and renaissance par excellence" (28).[11] The Kongo cross with its circles at each end is an excellent rendition of the movement of people "as second suns moving through time and space, following the circle of the sun from east to north (noon) to west" (43). In fact, Thompson and Cornet assert, "In Kongo there is scarcely an initiation or ritual transformation of the person from one level of existence to another that does not take its patterning from the circle of the sun about the earth" (43). This movement is explained in great detail by Fu-Kiau in *African Cosmology of the Bântu-Kôngo* in which he explains the four life stages or four Vees: Musoni, Kala, Tukula, and Luvèmba. The Musoni stage is located in what Thompson and Cornet refer to as the midnight position because it is below the Kalûnga line, which separates terrestrial life from the spiritual world.[12] For Fu-Kiau, this is the first stage or "formation process stage of life" (137). The stages follow in a counterclockwise direction to the Kala stage or "existence stage of life" in which people "are born or rise up to the upper world" (138). I associate the Kala stage with the role of the child in the texts under discussion. The next stage is the

Tukula stage, which is an essential position of leadership and authority that allows for social and community development. Fu-Kiau says,
"[t]he tukula position occupies the center of the cone of power and leadership" (27). Because this stage represents creativity and great deeds,[13] I
link it to the elder's role. The next stage is referred to as the Luvèmba
stage, which according to Fu-Kiau is the process of dying or leaving the
physical world to re-enter the ancestors' world (141). I connect both
the Luvèmba stage and the Musoni stage with the role of the ancestor;
however, the stages reflect the different stages of personal and collective
immortality, which Mbiti distinguishes as the living-dead and spirits. This
distinction will be discussed in greater detail later; however, the essential
difference is that the living-dead are still remembered by those alive in
the physical world, whereas spirits are no longer remembered and thus
are further removed from their descendants.

   Whether we think in terms of Thompson and Cornet's "four
moments of the sun," Fu-Kiau's "Four Vees," or the elder–ancestor–
child triad, we see a continuum of different, but related life stages.
Although Thompson and Cornet begin with the position I associate with
the role of the child, dawn, and Fu-Kiau begins with Musoni, which I
connect with the role of the ancestor; I prefer to begin with the role
of the elder because the writers I discuss seem to use this position as a
way to note the disharmony in the protagonists' world. Fu-Kiau in his
discussion of Tukula notes that all individuals are not able to achieve this
stage and rather than make history these people become bad, "stunted"
ancestors because "[t]hey passed this zone of power, creativity, inven-
tions, and mastery in all aspects of life in a state of blindness" (29–30).
Perhaps it is this blindness that leads *The Salt Eaters'* Velma Henry to
try to take her own life. Surely, it is blindness that prevents *Praisesong
for the Widow*'s Avey Johnson from even recognizing her own reflection.
An elder should be a community leader, but *Beloved*'s Sethe is seen as a
pariah for murdering her child before she could be returned to slavery.
Stigmata's Sarah is stunted by her mother's abandonment and thus is
incapable of assisting her own daughter, Lizzie, when she faces years
of institutionalization after what was deemed to be a suicide attempt.
Although *Daughters of the Dust*'s Eula isn't stunted, she is certainly at
a crossroads as she carries the secret of who raped her on the eve of
the Peazant family's migration northward and must decide whether she
should also turn her back on the old ways in the face of the inability
of the bottle tree and the ancestors to keep her safe. In each of these
texts, the female protagonist is in need of ancestral cultural healing in
order to achieve well-being. This healing is achieved either through the
intersession of an elder, ancestor, or child figure; however, in each case

the figure is used to tap into ancestral knowledge and strength. Thus, I begin with a discussion of elder figures who reach out to these protagonists; however, these women are so troubled that the intercession of an elder is not sufficient—ancestors must reach beyond the grave to guide these women and in the case of the film, *Daughters of the Dust*, ancestral wisdom is solidified through the expected birth of a child.

The Elder as Culture Bearer

It is the figure of the elder or ancestor who often reminds us that the future has a past and the past must not be forgotten. The importance of elders in the African American community is evident in respect traditionally given to mothers, grandmothers, and othermothers. For example, in "Support Systems of Significant Others in Black Families," Wilhemina Manns notes the profound influence of the elder female figure on both younger relatives and community youth in reference to "validation of self and heritage-reminding" (245, 248). However, this respect for elders is not solely an African American tradition, but part of an African heritage adapted to the New World environment. According to Somé, "For most traditional African cultures, an elder is one whom the village acknowledges as having reached not only a state of old age but also a state of maturity and wisdom. Elders are repositories of tribal knowledge and life experience, essential resources for the survival of the village, anchoring it firmly to the living foundation of tradition" (*Healing* 123–24). Thus elders are a living link to a community's past, "in the absence of the elders, the container of cultural wholeness breaks and social chaos arises" (125). Elders maintain traditions and keep communities tied to their past in a way which promotes communal health.

Sophie Heywood is one such elder or culture bearer. In an interview with Robert Stepto, Toni Morrison describes the elder black woman "as parent, not as mother or father, but as a parent, a sort of umbrella figure, culture-bearer, in that community with not just her children but all children . . ." (488). This is the role that Sophie plays for *The Salt Eaters'* southern community of Claybourne—she is a community parent. Sophie has achieved elder status due in part to her role as chapter president of the Women's Auxiliary of the Sleeping Car Porters for two decades and as co-convener of The Master's Mind, a group of alternative healers. Sophie is Velma's godmother and she has been present at almost every significant event in her life from the moment she aided in her birth. Despite Sophie's guidance, Velma attempts suicide much to Sophie's disappointment and disbelief. Sophie realizes that Velma does not fully appreciate the significance of her act—the taking of her life is not a personal act, but a communal one. She wants to scold Velma, "And did you think your life is yours alone to do with as you please?" (Bambara 148), but she refuses to break her silence for that momentary satisfaction. Sophie uses her silence "To give her soul a chance to attend to its own affairs at its own level" (149). Silence also is shown to be a key component of Velma's healing as it allows her to confront her own affairs. As Velma comes through the healing process, Sophie too has strengthened herself so that she will not be caught unawares the next time Velma faces a crisis. From the moment of her birth, Sophie had sensed that Velma had special gifts and committed herself to serving as a guide or elder.

Although Velma was fortunate to have an elder committed to mentoring her from the point of her birth, others encounter elders later in life. For example, in *Daughter's of the Dust,* many members of the island community view Nana Peazant as an elder even though she may not be a blood relation. Eula married into the Peazant family, but she respects her husband's great-grandmother as her own and looks to Nana to teach her the old ways. One of these old ways is communing with the dead. She tells Yellow Mary and Trula about her mother visiting her after she wrote her a letter and placed it under the bed with a glass of water. Although this is a source of amusement for Yellow Mary, this action is reflective of Nana's beliefs regarding the importance of connections between all family members, the living and the dead. The importance of family and tradition are two of the primary lessons elders are expected to impart to the younger generation, and one of the long-standing African and African American traditions is paying respect to one's ancestors.

The Ancestor as a Beneficial Presence

In order to fully understand the role of Ancestors in African culture, one must understand that death is "a gradual process which is not completed until some years after the actual physical death" (Mbiti, *African* 154). One's physical death leads to stages of personal and collective immortality. According to Mbiti, "while the departed is remembered by name, he is not really dead: he is alive, and such a person [he] would call the *living-dead*. The living-dead is a person who is physically dead but alive in the memory of those who knew him in his life as well as being alive in the world of the spirits. So long as the living-dead is thus remembered, he is in the state of *personal immortatlity*" (25). The living-dead "are considered to be still part of their families" and thus they remain interested in their family's affairs (*Introduction*

77). The living-dead are known to visit relatives through dreams or visions in order to convey their wishes (78). Mibti asserts that the living dead "Are the guardians of family affairs, and may even warn of impending danger or rebuke those who have failed to follow their special instructions. They are the guardians of family affairs, traditions, ethics and activities. Offence in these matters is ultimately an offence against the forebearers who, in that capacity, act as the invisible police of the families and communities" (82). This investment in their family affairs passes once the living-dead transition to the realm of collective immortality. This transition generally occurs within four or five generations (125). Once they are no longer remembered by the living, the living-dead become spirits who "are no longer formal members of the human family" (*African* 25).[14] This sophisticated understanding of the roles of spirits and the living-dead does not exist in the same form within African American communities; however, scholars have discovered the existence of ancestor veneration within the slave community, which suggests that some remnant of this practice may remain within African American culture.[15]

For example, Stuckey's *Slave Culture* connects the practice of the Ring Shout with ancestor veneration.[16] Later studies by Margaret Washington Creel and Robert Farris Thompson support Stuckey's contention regarding ancestor veneration within the slave community. However, a more recent study by Nancy J. Fairley specifically addresses the role of the ancestral dream. Although her study is limited to two African American communities in eastern North Carolina, her research suggests this phenomenon exists within other African American communities. According to Fairley, "ancestors who appear in dreams are believed to communicate requests and advice to their kin." She believes that these dreams are "part of a larger system of ancestor veneration within African American culture" (Fairley 546). Fairley's research suggests:

> Among African Americans in these eastern Carolina communities, ancestral sprits are believed to be protective and supportive of the living. Most people in the region find it difficult to ignore the requests and directives given by ancestral spirits. Stories abound of individuals who incurred the ancestors' wrath because they ignored their directives and advice, especially those that fortify family relations. (551)

This view of the beneficial role of ancestors is also apparent in African American literature, which suggests that this sense of connection with one's ancestors is pervasive within African American culture.

The role of ancestors in African American literature is discussed in such books as Karla Holloway's *Moorings & Metaphors* and Farah Jasmine Griffin's *"Who set you flowin'?": The African-American Migration Narrative*, as well as, Toni Morrison's essay, "Rootedness: The Ancestor as Foundation." Holloway discusses the presence of ancestral and goddess figures in the work of black women writers and argues that, "the nearness of myth to reality in West African cultures is enabled by the realm of the ancestor. Ancestors continue to make their spiritual presence felt after their deaths" (90). Morrison describes ancestors as "timeless people whose relationships to the characters are benevolent, instructive, and protective, and they provide a certain kind of wisdom" (343). Griffin extends Morrison's definition by asserting that "[t]he ancestor is present in ritual, religion, music, food, and performance. His or her legacy is evident in discursive formations like the oral tradition" (5). Griffin's definition of ancestor is much broader in that she does not distinguish between elders, ancestors, or even rituals. Although these three notions of ancestors differ slightly, it seems as if the ancestor is seen as a beneficial presence that strengthens the African American community.[17] I build on this analysis of the ancestor by articulating a discussion of the ancestor specifically rooted within the context of Kongo cosmology. The continued traces of such specific cultural elements point to the strong bonds to African culture despite the disruption of the slave trade. Consequently, my emphasis is the continued significance of these diasporic connections as represented by the ancestor.

Thus when Avey's Aunt Cuney beckons to her in her dream, it is the ancestral call at work. Aunt Cuney inhabits the realm of the living-dead or what Fu-Kiau would call the Luvèmba stage—she is dead, but still remembered and thus has access to the living. Therefore, she is able to see that Avey has lost her way—she has moved to North White Plains and become dislocated from her Tatem island roots. The desire to save Avey from this dislocation prompts Aunt Cuney to inhabit Avey's dream and although her motivation is beneficial, the dream itself is disruptive. Aunt Cuney's initial pleading and silent exhortation eventually turn to a physical tug-of-war as Aunt Cuney's hand "with the feel of a manacle had closed around [Avey's] wrist, and she found herself being dragged forward in the direction of the Landing" (43). The dream ends with the two women brawling on the streets of North White Plains, but this will not be the end of Aunt Cuney's reaching out beyond the grave.

Although Avey's ancestral visitation is disturbing, Lizzie's communication with her ancestors might be viewed as debilitating in that it leads to an assumed suicide attempt and psychiatric institutionalization. However, one must look beyond the immediate results and take note of the benevolent motivation behind the ancestral call. In *Stigmata*, Grace and Ayo reach out to Lizzie in an attempt to heal the fractured family bonds created by Grace's abandonment of Lizzie's mother, Sarah.

The Malevolent Ancestor

Thus far I have discussed ancestors who reach out to the living to express concern and to intercede in a beneficial manner, but what do we make of the malevolent ancestor? Fu-Kiau admonishes us that everyone does not enter the Tukula stage, "a man that does not grow up, the one who deviates and is not well minded, is not in the process of making history; he enters the rank of the [n'kuyu] bad ancestors . . ." (29). What Fu-Kiau terms as bad or "stunted ancestors" are what I would call malevolent ancestors (29). Although not prevalent in the texts of African American women, these malevolent ancestors do exist. A case in point is Mudear of Ansa's *Ugly Ways*. Although Ansa depicts benevolent ancestors in *The Hand I Fan With* and *You Know Better*, Mudear is not the beneficial ancestral presence we find in her other novels. Mudear is depicted as a selfish and manipulative intrusive presence, who will not remain quietly dead. Instead, she hovers over her daughters complaining incessantly.

Although the ancestors I have discussed so far have sought to connect with their living relatives, others are not satisfied by dream communications and other such visitations. Some ancestors feel the need to actually return to the physical world. This appears to be the case in Morrison's *Beloved* in which the past seems to be reborn with the appearance of the mysterious Beloved. Although scholars disagree on exactly who or what Beloved is, many read her as the ghostly return of Sethe's murdered baby due to such clues as Sethe's urgent need to urinate upon seeing her, which seems to symbolize a mother's water breaking as well as the various things that Beloved knows about that only Sethe's child should know such as a song she used to sing and a pair of earrings Sethe used to show her baby girl. One might be tempted to classify Beloved as an example of the child figure because she was a child when she died and she returns with a child's mindset despite her young adult body; however, she is definitely not your typical child. She is also not the typical ancestral figure one might expect from Morrison considering the positive comments she makes about ancestors. Beloved often is described in negative terms, as a succubus or witch determined to punish Sethe. However, I argue that Beloved is an ogbanje or abiku, a born-to-die spirit, who did not reach ancestor status. In "Literary

Insights into the 'Ogbanje' Phenomenon," Christie C. Achebe states, "Ogbanje or abiku means, simply, a spirit child, one fated to a cycle of early death and birth to the same mother" (32). As a stunted ancestor, Beloved is not in a position to provide the beneficial guidance of an ancestor. After all, she died as a child; she did not have the opportunity to gain the wisdom of an elder let alone an ancestor.

The Child

Although I do not consider Beloved an appropriate example of the child figure, I do acknowledge a close relationship between the child and the ancestor. In fact, the close proximity of these stages as represented by Fu-Kiau is indicative of their close alignment. During the Kala or existence stage " 'things' are born, rise up to the upper world" (Fu-Kiau 138). However, it is during the Musoni stage that formation begins. In fact, Fu-Kiau compares this stage to pregnancy. This close association between the realm of the ancestor and that of the child is also reflected in the beliefs of the Dagara people as discussed by Somé: "For the Dagara, every person is an incarnation, that is, a spirit who has taken on a body. So our true nature is spiritual. The world is where one comes to carry out specific projects. A birth is therefore the arrival of someone, usually an ancestor that somebody already knows, who has important tasks to do here" (*Water* 20). Thus, the Unborn Child of the film, *Daughters of the Dust*, is an ideal example of the close relationship between the child and the ancestor.

According to Mbiti, "Children are the buds of society, and every birth is the arrival of 'spring' when life shoots out and the community thrives. The birth of a child is, therefore, the concern not only of the parents but of many relatives including the living and the departed" (*African* 107). With the character of the Unborn Child, viewers realize that even before the living, breathing life that we recognize with the birth of a child there is thought and concern for the family that one is to join. We see the Unborn Child's concern for her parents, Eula and Eli, and her desire to arrive before it is too late. She knows that Eli must see that the child that Eula carries is theirs and not the product of her rape. It is this knowledge that will calm the rage boiling inside of Eli and allay Eula's fears that Eli will do something desperate.

A Sunday in June also provides some insight into the connections between ancestors and children. The novel provides more detail about the ancestor Ayo, especially her powers of second sight, which are believed to have been inherited by her granddaughters Mary Nell and

Eva. We also see the young Grace, who cannot see into the future, but does have the ability to see her ancestor's past and in fact inhabit her ancestor's life. Although the focus of the text is on the ancestor, readers are given glimpses of the child figure, which support the depiction seen in *Daughters of the Dust*.

Conclusion

Thus, I argue in the following chapters that when the connections between ancestors and characters such as Velma, Avey, Sarah, Sethe, and Eula become frayed, their mental and emotional well-being are jeopardized. The first section of the book addresses elders and their role as culture bearers. This first chapter begins by looking at Dash's *Daughters of the Dust* and Nana Peazant in her role as elder. It continues with a discussion of Bambara's *The Salt Eaters* in which Velma Henry, a young woman who attempts suicide, engages in a journey to mental and spiritual health with the aid of an elder, who serves as a spiritual guide. In fact, much of the text is a glimpse into Velma's internal struggle and Minnie's attempt to guide Velma with the aid of her ancestor, Old Wife.

The second section, and the focal point of the book, addresses the ancestral presence. Chapter 2 discusses Marshall's Avey Johnson, a middle-aged, middle-class widow, who has forgotten her Harlem childhood and trips to Ibo Landing and become completely absorbed by white, middle-class values. However, a series of disturbing dreams, in which her deceased great-aunt Cuney beckons to her, leads her to Carriacou and the rediscovery of her African roots. Chapter 3 discusses Perry's Lizzie and her relationship with her grandmother Grace and great-great-grandmother Ayo. I argue that Grace and Ayo reach across the grave not only to give Lizzie a better understanding of her family's history, but also to help heal her mother, Sarah, who never quite recovered from Grace's abandonment of the family. Although the intercession of Grace and Ayo may initially seem unsettling and unwelcome since it leads to fourteen years of confinement in mental institutions, the story that unfolds is actually one of healing, as Lizzie reconnects to a matrilineal story of slavery and its legacy.

Chapter 4 engages Morrison's protagonist, Sethe, who also struggles with the painful legacy of slavery and the guilt of killing her own child in order to spare her from the horrors of enslavement. Sethe is only able to come to terms with her experience through the return of her "crawling-already? baby" in the form of Beloved (Morrison, *Beloved* 110). *Beloved* operates differently than the other texts discussed in that although the end result is beneficial, it is despite the presence of a malevolent ancestor. Beloved does force Sethe to come to terms with her past, but it is Ella who decides that "rescue was in order" (301). Beloved would have had her retribution without the intervention of Ella's woman-centered network and the aid of Baby Suggs' ancestral presence.

The final section of the book is a discussion of the child. Although Chapter 5 makes fleeting references to *A Sunday in June*, the focus is on Dash's *Daughters of the Dust*. Dash turns to the power of the child as Nana Peazant calls on the Unborn Child to come quickly in order to heal the breach between her parents, Eula and Eli, who are struggling with pain, shame, and helplessness associated with Eula's rape.

The conclusion points to the significance of African survivals displayed through the texts' reflection of Kongo cosmology, while also emphasizing the importance of the womb for the writers' manifestation of elders and ancestors as they revise the natal alienation implied by the practice of *partus sequitur ventrem*. However, I also look forward to the expanding genre of speculative fiction and the role African influences play in these texts. Through a discussion of Tananarive Due's *The Between* and her use of the ogbanje figure, I look back at African cosmology while looking forward with regard to the legacy of the Civil Rights Movement and the imagined future for African Americans.

Throughout this study, I use these texts as exemplars of the function, place, and status of elders and ancestors that continues even beyond the grave. These texts illustrate the power of ancestral cultural healing deployed through the intercession of elder, ancestor, or child figures that are used to tap into ancestral knowledge and strength. Although an ancestral presence may be found in many black women's texts, in the case of these texts the ancestral presence is part of a feminist response to slavery and its legacy.

I believe a discussion of these texts is particularly timely as we consider the increasing interest in DNA testing as a means of accessing one's African ancestry. As per a February 2008 *Current* article, two-dozen DNA testing companies exist and more than 260,000 Americans paid for genetic testing (Gibson 18). In 2006, Henry Louis Gates hosted and produced the PBS documentary series, *African American Lives*, which discussed African Americans' search for their roots and featured the DNA testing company, African Ancestry.[18] Writer Lydialyle Gibson remarks, "For African Americans, DNA's promise is particularly seductive" (18). "'Now for the first time in three centuries,' Gates says, 'we can begin to reverse the Middle Passage'" (qtd. in 18). In an earlier article, Gates states, "This process is so nourishing because it can enable a person to feel the inimitable sense of connection, of belonging that can only be found by unearthing the branches of your family tree, your very own roots, roots that extend back through the slave past directly into the verdant soil of Africa" (136). Thus, for Gates and the African American clients of these DNA testing companies, DNA seems to be the path to an unknown past.

But why this continued hankering after the unknown? Saidiya Hartman's *Lose Your Mother: A Journey Along the Atlantic Slave Route* may provide a bit of insight regarding both this relatively new interest in DNA testing and the continued importance of literary treatments of the slave past and its legacy. Although published in 2008, this memoir is drawn from her Fulbright year in Ghana in 1997, which makes it both a product of the 1990s and very contemporary. In her Prologue, Hartman acknowledges that she went to Ghana "in search of strangers" and "to engage the past," as she articulates the continued pull of the past:

> If slavery persists as an issue in the political life of black America, it is not because of an antiquarian obsession with bygone days or the burden of a too-long memory, but because black lives are still imperiled and devalued by a racial calculus and a political arithmetic that were entrenched centuries ago. This is the afterlife of slavery—skewed life chances, limited access to health and education, premature death, incarceration, and impoverishment. I, too, am the afterlife of slavery. (6)

Clearly, this past cannot simply be dismissed, but is DNA testing the answer? Patricia J. Williams cautions, "if we biologize our history, we will forever be less than we could be" (14). In her *Nation* article, "Emotional Truth," Williams argues "Professor Gates could not be more incautious about its [DNA testing] salutary promise for African-Americans in search of a sense of self" (14). She instead argues for an "emotional truth" which she associates with family stories. "Family stories ritualize the past. . . . It is part of what Professor Robert Pollack, head of Columbia University's Center for the Study of Science and Religion, calls the 'eschatology of repair'" (14). I argue that literature can provide the same service as these family stories. For Williams, family stories can insulate one from shame and I contend that these novels and Dash's film do the same as they revise the legacy of slavery. I also argue that this work was especially necessary during the sociohistorical moment of the texts' production. For example, Hartman comments, "Mine was an age not of dreaming but of disenchantment. I grew up in the aftermath of African independence and the civil rights and Black Power struggles, and like many of my generation I was pessimistic about my prospects at home and abroad. I came of age in the demise of liberation movements and after the visionaries had been assassinated" (38–39). In order to move beyond this pessimism, African Americans must be able to reimagine both their pasts and their futures. This is the important intervention work that literature and literary projects such as this one provide. *The Grasp That Reaches Beyond the Grave: The Ancestral Call in Black Women's Texts*, like the texts it studies, refutes the notion of kinlessness instigated by the peculiar institution of slavery.

Part I Preface

The Elder as Culture Bearer

Culture bearers transmit the culture of a people and may be male or female; however, women often are associated with this role because of the overlap between the roles of culture bearing and mothering. In *Afrikan Mothers: Bearers of Culture, Makers of Social Change*, Nah Dove asserts, "The woman is revered in her role as the mother who is the bringer of life, the conduit to the spiritual regeneration of the ancestors, the bearer of culture and the center of social organization" (4).[1] Clenora Hudson-Weems also identifies mothering and nurturing as "features of the strong Africana culture bearer" in her discussion of Africana Womanists (59). Bernice Johnson Reagon notes in "African Diaspora Women: The Making of Cultural Workers," "Among all living things in the universe, there is a nurturing process. . . . This process is called mothering. When applied to the examination and analysis of cultural data, it can reveal much within the historical picture of how a culture evolves and how and why changes occur in order to maintain the existence of a people" (272–73). Reagon also notes that for female cultural workers of the African Diaspora, the disruption and trauma of slavery meant that nurturing not only was "reconciling what was passed to them with the day-to-day reality but also sifting and transforming this experience" to fit the New World reality (273). I argue in the following chapter that the elder othermothers of *Daughters of the Dust* and *The Salt Eaters* drew on ancestral knowledge to survive the cultural trauma of slavery and its after effects.

Although the focus of this project is on women's networks in part because of the association among women, mothering, and culture bearing, this does not mean only women are capable of mothering or nurturing a culture. In fact, Dove notes that "[t]he role of motherhood

27

or mothering is not limited to mothers or women even in contemporary Afrika [*sic*]. . . . Motherhood depicts the nature of the communal responsibilities involved in the raising of children and the caring of others" (4). Thus, the observations made regarding these elder othermothers are not exclusive to female elders. For example, *Praisesong for the Widow*'s Lebert Joseph surely serves as an elder for Avey Johnson as he leads her to reconnect with her ancestors at the Big Drum; however, I argue that the gender of the elder does make a difference, which is perhaps why Lebert Joseph is presented as androgynous. As an androgynous character, he can take on characteristics typically associated with women. Malidoma Patrice Somé, author of *The Healing Wisdom of Africa: Finding Life Purpose Through Nature, Ritual, and Community*, states, "The gender of the elder is important in maintaining the stability of a social community. Female elders, though they have the same qualities as male elders, are often more in demand because of their role as containers and reconcilers" (127). Although Somé does not clarify his reference to female elders as containers, I take this as a reference to the womb. In the introduction, I refer to Toni Morrison's discussion of slave women as "natally dead" and suggest that the emphasis by black women writers on family, including elders and ancestors, might be a means of working out some unfinished business of their cultural past. Thus, in many ways, this project is in conversation with Joanne Braxton's notion of "the outraged mother." According to Braxton, "the archetypal outraged mother travels alone through the darkness to impart a sense of identity and 'belongingness' to her child. . . . Implied in all her actions and fueling her heroic ones is abuse of her people and her person" (21). The elder othermothers to whom I refer are outraged when they see their traditions and communities threatened. According to Somé, "Elders, like ancestors, are expected to identify and address what is not working in the village, not to give compliments and praise behavior" (127). He also says, "It is as if they are the ancestral ear in the village, guiding oblivious wrongdoers to act in a healing manner toward themselves and others" (129). Thus, the role of the elder is to reconcile fissures in the family and the community. They also provide guidance to youth or Kala still transitioning to elder or Tukula status. According to Fu-Kiau, "The kala, by the process of growth and maturation, becomes tukula, . . . which is the symbol of mature leadership within the community; it is also the step of the man of deeds. . . . The collective maturation, its leadership, through the process of collective growth, allows for social and community development" (27). However, in the case of *Daughters of the Dust* and *The Salt Eaters*, the maturation of the younger generation seems in jeopardy without the intervention of elder mothers, like Nana Peazant, Sophie Heywood, and Minnie Ransom. These elders take on the role of culture bearers by ensuring that the younger generation maintains some connection with their ancestral roots because they realize that ancestors are a source of strength.

1

Othermothers as Elders and Culture Bearers in *Daughters of the Dust* and *The Salt Eaters*

An elder's role is to guide his or her community and thus to lead others on the path to become elders and eventually ancestors. However, as Bunseki Fu-Kiau informs us, everyone does not achieve elder status, as this is not a natural progression like ageing, but an accomplishment dependent on drawing on the wisdom of the ancestors. In *The Way of the Elders: West African Spirituality & Tradition*, authors Adama and Naomi Doumbia observe, "We defer to those older than us to let them know that we appreciate their guidance and all they have to offer" (108). Elders are described as "those who look after us and who hold more responsibility" (108). It is clear from these comments that elders play an important role in the community; however, the respect given to elders is not merely based on their advanced age. In "Ancestors as Elders in Africa," Igor Kopytoff asserts that "the elders' authority is related to their close link to the ancestors. In some sense the elders are the representatives of the ancestors and the mediators between them and the kin-group" (412). In other words, elders serve as conduits of ancestral wisdom through their role as culture bearers because they pass down the wisdom of the ancestors. This close connection between elders and ancestors is particularly evident in Julie Dash's *Daughters of the Dust* and Toni Cade Bambara's *The Salt Eaters*.

Although everyone may not achieve this stage, I would suggest that vigilant elders such as the othermothers in *Daughters of the Dust* and *The Salt Eaters* take up their roles in earnest when they see the young people they are guiding faltering and in danger of not reaching elderhood. The Peazant family in *Daughters of the Dust* is at a crossroads with some members ready to turn their backs on tradition and migrate to the North. The tension regarding their migration plans is exacerbated by a rape, which threatens to tear a family apart. The situation in *The Salt Eaters* is so bleak that a community organizer turns from marching and signing petitions to attempting suicide. The young adults in these novels have their worldviews challenged and in turn they question their ability to go forward. Thus, the notion of their maturing and eventually becoming elders cannot be taken for granted by their elders—an intervention is necessary.

Although *Daughters of the Dust* is certainly one family's story, viewers also get the sense that their story is in many ways a microcosm of the African American experience. Bambara comments on the significance of the setting of the film at the turn of the century in 1902:

> The Peazants and guests gather on the island at Ibo Landing for a picnic at a critical juncture in history—they are one generation away from the Garvey and the New Negro movements, a decade short of the Niagra/NAACP merger. They are in the midst of rapid changes; black people are on the move North, West, and back to Africa (the Oklahoma project, for instance). Setting the story amid oak groves, salt marshes, and a glorious beach is not for the purpose of presenting a nostalgic community in a pastoral setting. They are an imperiled group. ("Reading" 122)

Bambara's choice of "imperiled" to describe the family is particularly apt, as it becomes apparent that their way of life is endangered and the Peazant family is in disarray. As the Unborn Child narrates the film, she tells viewers, "My story begins on the eve of my family's migration north. My story begins before I was born. My great-great-grandmother, Nana Peazant, saw her family coming apart. Her flowers to bloom in a distant frontier" (Dash, *Daughters: Making* 80). Nana is concerned about the impact migration will have on her family. In "Property Rights and Possession in *Daughters of the Dust*," Nancy Wright talks about this impact in terms of threats, "In the early-twentieth century, decades after the abolition of slavery, the Peazant family faces a different threat to their personhood: cultural dispossession. To leave the islands in 1902 threatens to dissociate those who migrate from their family, culture, and belief systems" (12). As an elder othermother, Nana cannot ignore this threat to the stability of the Peazant family.

Although many critics focus on Nana's status as an elder, this should not be separated from her related role as an othermother. In fact, Nana's maternal function is reflected in her name—she is known by her identity as nana or grandmother—her given name is eclipsed by her role as surrogate mother or othermother. Nana exhibits all of the trademarks of motherhood as identified by Nah Dove. Nana "is the bringer of life, the conduit to the spiritual regeneration of the ancestors, the bearer of culture and the center of social organization" (Dove 4). Nana's maternity is apparent in her role as Eli's great-grandmother, which implies her earlier roles of grandmother and mother to Eli's father and grandfather. Nana is clearly in communication with the ancestors, as indicated by her regular visits to the graveyard, but more significantly Dash uses the terminology "spiritual regeneration" in her stage directions in reference to Nana's preparation of the hand for family members to kiss (Dash, *Daughters: Making* 161). Nana's role as bearer of culture is apparent in her attitude toward tradition and her view of the land as sacred. For example, she tells Eli, "I'm trying to give you something to take North with you, along with all your great big dreams" (96). This is a cultural inheritance that Nana believes is essential for survival. As the elder or central figure of the family, Nana feels responsible for its continuity. "Nana struggles to keep intact that African-derived institution that has been relentlessly under attack through kidnap, enslavement, Christianization, peonage, forced labor gangs, smear campaigns, and mob murder—the family" (Bambara, "Reading" 125). However, keeping the Peazant family intact is a struggle that Nana cannot fight without the aid of the ancestors.

Viewers quickly realize that the family is in the midst of turmoil that Nana senses and that somehow the Unborn Child is aware of the situation. The film then cuts to an image of Eula and Eli in their bedroom. Eula turns toward Eli, but Eli keeps his back to her. The Unborn Child then provides some more information about the scene, "And then, there was my ma and daddy's problem. Nana prayed and the old souls guided me into the New World" (Dash, *Daughters: Making* 80). We then have our first indication that Nana called on the Unborn Child to heal this estrangement between her parents. The Unborn Child tells us that she is "traveling on a spiritual mission" (134). The Unborn Child's assistance is necessary to provide cultural healing to the Peazant family.

I argue that Nana Peazant's intercession to heal the rift between her great-grandson, Eli, and his wife, Eula, is an example of using ancestral cultural healing. As an elder, Nana is able to facilitate this ancestral healing by calling on the ancestors to send the Unborn Child. Significantly, many members of the island community see Nana as an elder or othermother although she may not be a blood relation. As grandmother, great-grandmother, and elder woman, Nana takes on a maternal role in relation to younger members of the island community. The first images of the film are of Nana and set the stage for all that follows. The first scene is from the 1860s and shows a young Nana with soil like dust blowing from her hands. The film then cuts to 1902 and an 88-year-old Nana rising out of the water fully dressed. According to Jacqueline Bobo, "The old woman bathing in the river symbolizes rebirth and the integral connection of the old with the new" (136). This connection between the present and past is reinforced by the opening words of the film taken from the Gnostic scriptures, "Thunder: Perfect Mind," "I am the first and the last" (Dash, *Daughters: Making* 75). This contradictory statement alerts the viewer that perhaps time is nonlinear and as the film progresses this connection between the present and the past seems to operate in a cyclical manner. In fact, this cyclical movement is indicated by the way the camera angles tap into the counter clockwise movement of the Kongo cosmogram, a quartered circle, which symbolizes the Kongo notion of the continuity of life. Bobo observes, "In *Daughters of the Dust* references to the past are usually made through scenes in which a character travels left across the screen or looks off to the left" (148). The cosmogram depicts the counterclockwise movement of people from birth, dawn; life, noon; death, sunset; and afterlife, midnight. This along with Dash's allusion to the cosmogram through the symbol painted on the turtle's back suggests her very conscious incorporation of Kongo cosmology.

In the introduction, I noted that I am not arguing that the women I am discussing have direct knowledge of Kongo cosmology, but instead that there is an uncanny reflection of Kongo cosmology in their usage of elder, ancestor, and child figures. However, such a caveat is not necessary in a discussion of *Daughters of the Dust*, which Dash researched for many years. She visited the Schomburg Center for Research in Black Culture, the National Archives in Washington, DC, the Library of Congress, the Smithsonian, and the Penn Center on St. Helena Island. She also sought the advice of Gullah expert, Dr. Margaret Washington Creel (Dash, "Making" 5–7). Yet the most explicit reference to Kongo cosmology is the use of a turtle painted with a circle and a cross in one of the picnic scenes. The stage directions and notations in the screenplay make it clear that the inclusion of the turtle is not incidental. The stage directions read: "Holding the turtle. The young boys have painted an African symbol on the back of the turtle. An encoded message, an 'S.O.S.' to relatives across the sea, markings passed down through generations who have long since forgotten their exact meaning." To the side of these directions, Dash has noted, "use Ki-Kongo symbol" (Dash, *Daughters: Making* 147). Thus, it is clear that Dash is indeed aware of some aspects of Kongo cosmology and her use of elder, ancestor, and child figures are definitely informed by these beliefs.

In a passing comment regarding *Daughters of the Dust*, educator, Annette Henry, identifies Nana Peazant as both the eldest family member and the representation of the African ancestral past (184). Nana is the glue that keeps the Peazant family connected to their ancestors. However, the nature of this connection goes beyond her role of family historian. According to cultural critic, Patricia Mellencamp, Nana Peazant is "the guardian of legend and the spirits" (151). Nana's relationship to the family's African ancestral past is revealed through her references to herself and the Unborn Child: "Nana's phrases, 'the last of the old' referring to herself, the eldest living member of the family, and 'the first of the new' referring to Eula's unborn child, define the family as a continuum maintaining the relationship of the living Gullah family to their African ancestors, African culture, and their aboriginal homeland" (Wright 21–22). Although I agree with Wright's assessment regarding the family as a continuum, it is important to note that Nana is not consistent in her use of these phrases. The first time these phrases are used, they both are directed toward herself. Early in the film as Nana watches her family prepare dinner, she reflects on the past and we hear her thoughts as a voiceover, "I'm the last of the old and the first of the new" (Dash, *Daughters: Making* 105). Then toward the end of the film, as she makes the hand to connect her migrating family to their ancestors, she says, "We are two people in one body. The last of the old, and the first of the new" (151). These statements about herself and the Unborn Child seem to reflect a belief in reincarnation as discussed by both John Mbiti and Janheinz Jahn.[1] This point is addressed further in the final chapter, but my intention here is to show the continuity of Nana as elder and ancestor in the making while also using the Unborn Child as an illustration of the close proximity between ancestors and children because children have just come from the world of the ancestors. Nana is in tune with her ancestors and is very much aware of the cyclical nature of life and she wishes to share this knowledge with her descendants so that they too will remain connected with their ancestors.

This transmission of traditions and culture is central to her role as culture bearer and elder. Although many viewers might focus on the lush imagery of the food and beach and think of the setting as merely a farewell dinner or gathering, Bambara's reference to the event as a family council seems to be more to the point: "Nana Peazant has called a family council because values are shifting. There's talk of migration.

The ancestral home is being rejected on the grounds of limited educational and job opportunities" ("Reading" 124). This is not merely a moment for leave taking, but a teaching moment. According to film critic Manthia Diawara, "As the oldest person in the Peazant family, her role is that of teacher" (17). Teaching is at the core of the elder's responsibilities. Thus even though Eula married into the Peazant family, she respects her husband's great-grandmother as her own and looks to Nana to teach her the old ways. One of these old ways is communing with the dead. Eula tells her husband's cousin, Yellow Mary, and her friend, Trula, about her mother visiting her after she wrote her a letter and placed it under the bed with a glass of water. In amusement, Yellow Mary laughs "Eula! You're a real back-water Geechee girl!" (Dash, *Daughters: Making* 120). Nana would not have laughed at Eula because she recognizes the importance of family bonds. On the eve of their migration north, Nana creates a "Hand" or charm that includes hair from her deceased mother as well as her own hair because "There must be a bond . . . a connection, between those that go up North, and those who across the sea. A connection!" (151). Nana, as an elder, realizes the importance of respecting one's ancestors.

However, although the younger island inhabitants may not fully understand Nana's ways, most hold her in high regard. This is in part out of respect for wisdom associated with a long life, but also for the elder's proximity to the ancestors. Ancestors are seen as sources of ancient wisdom, which forms the backbone of the community, as "[t]he ancestor's life crystallizes the teachings of the family, of the ethnic group and the culture" (Ela 42). Although the ancestor is the focus of the next section, this chapter's discussion of elders illustrates the overlap between these two stages. Part of Nana's wisdom as an elder is drawn from her connection to the ancestors. For example, Jahn observes in *Muntu: The New African Culture*, "the wise man is 'nearer to the dead' and has already a 'share in their nature'" (111). Thus, Nana's wisdom as an elder is akin to having the ancestor's ear. Nana recognizes the power of the ancestors and thus calls on them for aid.

Nana values the intercession of the ancestors and seeks to impart that knowledge to the young people. For example, when Eli finds Nana by her husband's grave, she tells him: "'I visit with old Peazant every day since the day he died. It's up to the living to keep in touch with the dead, Eli. Man's power doesn't end with death. We just move on to a new place, a place where we watch over our living family . . . '" (93). Nana exhorts Eli to respect his ancestors; however, she extends her point by associating the ancestors and the womb. Nana tells him, "'Those in this grave, like those who're across the sea, they're with us.

They're all the same. The ancestors and the womb are one. Call on your ancestors, Eli. Let them guide you. You need their strength'" (94–95). In Chapter 5, I note the revision of *partus sequitur ventrem* implied by Nana's association of ancestors and the womb; however, because my focus here is on Nana's role of elder rather than the relationship between the ancestors and the Unborn Child I do not elaborate on that point. With these words, Nana attempts to console Eli. However, she does this by pointing to the strength of the ancestors because she realizes that the ancestors are a source of healing powers. Both Wright and McKoy comment on the significance of the graveyard for the setting of this scene. According to Wright:

> the graveyard on Dawtaw Island [*sic*][2] is a potent symbol of the descendant family's continuing relationship to their ancestors and to the island where they survived. Dispossession from their original culture, Nana insists, did not occur when the middle passage transported ancestors to the island, and need not happen when descendants migrate from Dawtah Island [*sic*] to the North. (18)

Just as she communes with her deceased husband, Nana urges Eli to reach out to his deceased ancestors in order to retain a connection to his past. McKoy discusses Nana's respect for her ancestral past in terms of her understanding of limbo time:

> What enables Nana to embrace her culture is her understanding of limbo time; what separates Eli from his roots is his inability to understand how his ancestors' lives impact his own. Nana literally reaches across Old Eli's grave symbolically reaching across time to show Eli that his survival is dependent upon his understanding his relationship with his ancestors. Dash uses the graveyard to figure limbo time as the blending of generational narratives across time. Having never established a link with his ancestors, Eli is situated both literally and figuratively on the other side of the grave from Nana. (219–20)

Their placement on different sides of the grave is indicative of the breach in the family—both the tension in Eli and Eula's home and the strain surrounding the planned migration. Nana attempts to comfort Eli who is concerned that the child Eula is carrying is a product of rape. She wants him to understand that he "'won't ever have a baby that wasn't sent to'" him (Dash, *Daughters: Making* 94). Despite Nana's attempts to comfort him and offer him counsel, Eli is too consumed with anger to take his great-grandmother's words to heart.

Eli instead mocks his great-grandmother, when he asks "'were the old souls too deep in their graves to give a damn about my wife while some stranger was riding her?'" (95). Eula's rape has shaken Eli's belief in his grandmother and the old ways. He tells her, "When we were children, we really believed you could work the good out of evil. We believed in the newsprint on the walls. . . . Your tree of glass jars and bottles. . . . The rice you carried in your pockets. We believed in the frizzled-haired chickens. . . . The coins, the roots and the flowers. We believed they would protect us and every little thing we owned or loved" (95–96). In her interview with bell hooks, Dash observes, "The bottle trees, positioned outside of the Peazants' shanty, were for protection—protection from malevolent or evil spirits. It's my understanding that each bottle would represent a deceased family member or ancestor. The spirits would radiate good will, protection, and luck upon the family's house" (hooks and Dash 43). Eli takes his anger out on the bottle tree by shattering the bottles as he strikes the tree again and again. Between images of Eli striking the bottle tree, we see the terrified Eula covering her ears and cowering in fear.

The scene then dissolves to the Unborn Child running along the beach. In a voiceover, viewers hear: "Nana prayed for help. I got there just in time" (Dash, *Daughters: Making* 99). Nana can feel the child in the wind. In another voiceover, Nana says, "Come, child, come!" (99). Thus Nana and the Unborn Child communicate through this exchange of voiceovers, as if engaging in an ancestral call and response. The elder Nana called and the Unborn Child echoes the ancestors' response. As an elder, Nana calls on the ancestors for assistance and they respond via the Unborn Child. According to Somé, "Elders become involved with a new life practically from the moment of conception because the unborn child has just come from the place they are going to" (*Of Water* 20). Nana is not the only one to call on the ancestors. Eula reaches out to her deceased mother, ostensibly to get counsel regarding her situation with Eli. She tells Yellow Mary and Trula, "'My Ma came to me last night, you know. She took me by the hand'" (Dash, *Daughters: Making* 119). Eula's mother has been dead a long time, but as she explains: "I needed to see my Ma. I need to talk to her. So I wrote her a letter, put it beneath the bed with a glass of water, and I waited. I waited, and my Ma came to me. She came to me right away" (119). Although Eula is not an elder, she has absorbed Nana's teachings, and looks to Nana to teach her the old ways such as communicating with the dead to receive their guidance. Nana reflects on this connection, "Eula said I was the bridge that they crossed over on. I was the tie between then and now. Between the past and the story that was to come" (107). Nana's goal throughout the film seems to be getting the younger generation to recognize the power of the ancestors as a resource for survival, especially in light of the mounting lynching activity and the planned migration. Thus, Nana is not the source of cultural healing, but instead points the way to the ancestors as a source of strength and survival.

This notion of ancestors as a resource for survival is reflected in Dash's treatment of the Ibo legend. The Unborn Child leads Eli and Eula to the graveyard for a private moment to commune with the spirits. According to Foluke Ogunleye, "Eli goes into a trance-like experience in which he interacts in his spirit with his ancestors and his unborn child. Through this, he achieves an epiphanic understanding, which helps him to realize that there is a life beyond the physical. He consequently understands, in a personal way, all that his grandmother had been striving to pass across to him" (165). Nana had told Eli, " 'Call on those old Africans, Eli. They'll come to you when you least expect them. They'll hug you up quick and soft like the warm sweet wind. Let those old souls come into your heart, Eli. Let them touch you with the hands of time. Let them feed your head with wisdom that ain't from this day and time' " (97). This seems to be what both Eli and Eula do, as reflected in their acting out of the Ibo legend. Eula's reciting of the legend and Eli's mimicking of the Ibo's actions indicates their acceptance of the lessons of their ancestors—they are showing their willingness to turn to their ancestors for guidance. In "Souls at the Crossroads, Africans on the Water," Sara Clarke Kaplan notes that it is "immediately after both she and Eli have been embraced by these spirits that Eula recounts to her unborn child the first version of the legend of the Ibo: how, when brought to shore, these 'last Africans' looked around them and saw 'all that had come before and all that was yet to come' . . . and walked back over the water, home to Africa" (518). While Eula is reciting the legend to the Unborn Child, Eli is actually walking on the water, as the Ibo before him. Eli and Eula have come full circle, as their Unborn Child has led them to reconnect with their ancestors.

The film ends with Eli and Eula deciding to stay behind with Yellow Mary and Nana Peazant, rather than going north with the other members of the family. According to Joel Brouwer, "Their decision is an implicit confirmation of 'the old ways': the religion of ancestor veneration, the acute awareness of the spirits of the dead and their connection with the living and the not-yet-born, and the valuing of community above the individual" (8). Nana has successfully impressed upon Eli, Eula, and Yellow Mary the importance of honoring their ancestors. However, I would argue that Nana also makes an impression on those who still choose to leave. During the farewell ceremony in which Nana prepares a hand using her mother's hair and a bible, she imparts a message regarding the importance of their family bond with each other and with their ancestors. Wright argues that Nana "wishes to transfer this understanding of their relationship to one another and to Dawtaw Island [*sic*] as an inheritance or 'estate' to take with them when they migrate to the North" (20). Bambara has a similar reading of the gesture of kissing the hand as "a vow to struggle against amnesia, to resist the lures and bribes up North that may cause them to betray their individual and collective integrity" ("Reading" 125). Kissing the hand acts as an inoculation against cultural amnesia. This moment creates a great deal of consternation for some members of the family because they realize a clean break with the past is not possible. For example, in Bobo's reading of the film she notes how Viola begins to come undone with disheveled clothes and unruly hair as the time for departure nears and she understands that she will be leaving her grandmother and her home. However, for Bobo, Viola's discomfort is resolved when she "realizes the value of her grandmother's traditions and folk beliefs" and "kisses the 'hand' that her grandmother has fixed as a gesture of reconciliation of her past with her future" (155–56). Hagar, however, refuses to indulge in what she calls, "Hoodoo mess!" (Dash, *Daughters: Making* 161). The elder's reach is not perfect, but Nana is able to impart her message to several members of the younger generation. The Unborn Child closes the film with a voiceover, "We remained behind, growing older, wiser, stronger" (164). Surely this strength and wisdom is not possible without the guidance of elders and the intercession of ancestors.

Just as Nana is concerned about the younger generation turning their backs on the ancestors and the old ways with all of their talk of migration, the elder othermothers of Toni Cade Bambara's *The Salt Eaters* are concerned that the younger generation is ailing as a result of their disconnection from their ancestors. *The Salt Eaters* is replete with both elder and ancestral othermothers. Minnie Ransom and Sophie Heywood both serve as othermothers for Velma, while Karen Wilder was an othermother for Minnie and Sophie—thus creating concentric circles of motherly concern. Susan Willis argues that "[t]he desire to formulate a feminist perspective on history accounts for the centrality of mother figures in Bambara's writing. Her radicalism is to suggest how mothering, which in the nuclear family is necessary and acceptable to male-dominated society, might be extended into the community and transformed" (157). Yet, I would argue that this is not particularly

radical within African American circles as Patricia Hill Collins has noted
the prevalence of othermothering within African American communities
(119). Thus I would counter that the centrality of mother figures is
due to the importance of motherhood within African American culture.
In her essay, "An Angle of Seeing: Motherhood in Buchi Emecheta's
The Joys of Motherhood and Alice Walker's *Meridian*," Barbara Christian
asserts that "[t]he concept of motherhood is of central importance in
both the philosophy of African and Afro-American peoples . . ." (213).
Using the work of African philosopher Cheikh Anta Diop, African writer,
Ayi Kwei Armah, and African theologian John Mbiti, Christian illustrates
the respect given to mothers in African societies (213–24). In extending her argument to the African American community, Christian notes
the contradictions and contrasts between white and black motherhood
associated with slavery; however she suggests, "The centrality of motherhood in Afro-American culture probably has its roots in African culture"
(220). Christian also points to a recurring concern with motherhood in
African American literature from as early as *Clotel* (1850) to more recent
writers such as Sarah Wright, Toni Morrison, Toni Cade Bambara, and
Alice Walker (224–26).

Thus Bambara's othermothers are part of a larger conversation
regarding motherhood; however, I am particularly interested in the way
in which these mother figures are used to transmit culture. Yet, if we
would like to agree with Willis that Bambara is being radical in her use
of othermothers, I would say that her radicalism comes in extending
this realm beyond the grave. In discussing the pervasiveness of ghosts
in women's texts, Kathleen Brogan observes that ghosts provide "a
metaphor for how women's more restrictively defined roles as bearers of culture might be reconceived" (15). According to Brogan, "the
shift from metaphors of blood descent to ghostly inheritances reframes
cultural transmission" (15). We definitely see this at play here as Old
Wife, a non-blood relation, participates in the transmission of culture
through her role in the healing session, which ultimately leads to Velma's
acceptance of her gift, which can be read as the acceptance of her cultural inheritance.

I see this gift as an inheritance of sorts because Sophie, Velma's
godmother and the midwife who delivered her, had actually sensed
Velma's gift at the moment of her birth and had later seen the signs
of Velma's visions and rejections of her gift (Bambara, *Salt* 293–94).
Bambara's use of the word "gift" and its presence from the moment of
Velma's birth suggest that this gift is inherited or passed down to Velma
by her ancestors. I say ancestors rather than mother because Velma's
"blood mother," Mama Mae (11–12) is such a nebulous presence. The

emphasis is not on Velma's biological mother, but on the community of othermothers in her life. Thus, although Sophie is described as being at every major event in Velma's life, she is not a substitute for Mama Mae, but an additional source of maternal wisdom over the years. In *Saints, Sinners, Saviors: Strong Black Women in African American Literature*, Trudier Harris notes that Minnie "becomes 'mother' to Velma during the healing process, for Velma's godmother, M'Dear Sophie, leaves the healing room, and her biological mother, Mama Mae, is on a church retreat when Velma tries to kill herself" (80). The nurturing role that Minnie plays with regard to Velma is not unlike that played years before by Karen for Minnie and Sophie and other children of the community. This point is reiterated by Willis' assessment that "[t]he most central of the novel's mother figures is, of course, Minnie Ransom. . . . Minnie is aided in her curing by another maternal figure, one whose relationship to myth and the folk tradition are much deeper. This is 'Old Wife,'' Minnie's spirit guide . . ." (155–56). The fact that Minnie and Old Wife work together to heal Velma suggests that the healing session is a communal act. In "Mechanisms of Disease: African-American Women Writers, Social Pathologies, and the Limits of Medicine," Ann Folwell Stanford notes, "individuals are healed within community and restored to the community when well. . . ." (32). In fact, in the introduction I observe that the circular structure of the healing session is indicative of the communal nature of the healing session. However, Willis makes a related point regarding women's communities in reference to the pairing of Old Wife and Minnie. According to Willis, "In doubling the figure of the maternal healer, Bambara creates a link between present and past cultural practice and she suggests the incipient basis for sister-hood. The unity of purpose and the supportive interaction, as well as the lively banter and respectful rivalry, are all characteristics that would define a larger collectivity of women" (156). This is not to say that men are not integral to the text as represented by such characters as Obie and Serge, but there does seem to be an emphasis on maternal networks of mothers and othermothers. Old Wife or Karen Wilder is an othermother who served as an elder while living and is now in the realm of the ancestors, which illustrates my earlier point about elders being ancestors in the making.

Minnie Ransom is both healer and elder in *The Salt Eaters*, which opens and closes with a healing session for Velma, after her attempted suicide. According to literary critic, Derek Alwes, Minnie is "clearly the voice of greatest authority in the novel" (355). However, the authority Minnie has seems to be related to her own connection to her ances-tor and spiritual guide, Old Wife. When the healing session proves to be more difficult than she had anticipated, Minnie consults with Old Wife, " 'What's ailing the Henry gal so, Old Wife? Not that I'm sure I can match her frequency anyway. She's draining me' " (Bambara, *Salt* 42). Minnie doesn't understand what has happened to the young girls, " 'What is wrong, Old Wife? What is happening to the daughters of the yam? Seem like they just don't know how to draw up the powers from the deep like before. Not full sunned and sweet anymore' " (44). Old Wife responds that they are acting more like Irish potatoes than yams; in other words, these younger girls are losing touch with their culture. The potato imagery works particularly well because the notion of faded Irish potatoes versus golden yams suggests the white washing of their cultural identity while also calling attention to the possibility of drawing upon one's roots or the "powers from the deep." These women need not be like Irish potatoes, but at some point they lost their connection to their cultural roots. This conversation between Old Wife and Minnie supports David Ikard's contention:

> that the inability of blacks to usefully access or utilize their ancestral powers is inextricably linked to their acceptance of white-centered cultural values and consciousness. That is, blacks do not seek cultural-specific answers to their social and political queries because they have been conditioned to venerate the dominant culture's notions of self and reality and treat their African history and ancestry with suspicion and shame. (81)

Although Minnie understands the problem, she is not quite sure how to fix it and turns to Old Wife for advice: " 'We got a problem here. I can't quite reach this chile and you keep acting like you dumb as me stead of telling me what to do' " (Bambara, *Salt* 50). As Minnie reminiscences with Old Wife the "woman friend who'd been with her for most of her life, one way and then another," it becomes clear that for Minnie health and wholeness involve being in tune with one's elders and ancestors.

Karla Holloway observes, "In Bambara's *The Salt Eaters*, the plight of 'the daughters of the yam'—the set adrift, groundless black American women whose primal ground is Africa's is bemoaned by the ancestor who hovers over the events" (105). The ancestor, Old Wife, is disturbed that women such as Velma who should be blossoming into elders are in danger of becoming stunted ancestors. As I discussed in the introduction, everyone is not able to achieve elder status; however, the source of Old Wife, Minnie, and even Sophie's frustration seems to be Velma's willingness to turn her back on her gift and essentially her past and her potential. Yet, Minnie and Old Wife's relationship also reminds us that resistance to the unknown is not uncommon. "The women in this novel who possess the gift do so with trepidation because of the frightening and powerful images that accompany it, and the fact that it simply defies logic. Harnessing it requires years of training and discipline" (Harrison 693). Thus, Velma's fear of the unknown is understandable and to some degree resistance is to be expected, but Velma goes too far when she attempts suicide rather than accept her gift. Sophie wishes she could admonish Velma for her actions, but she has taken a vow of silence and can only criticize Velma in her thoughts, "And did you think your life is yours alone to do with as you please? That I, your folks, your family, and all who care for you have no say-so in the matter?" (Bambara, *Salt* 148). Thus, for Sophie, Velma's rejection of her gift and suicide attempt is essentially a slap in the face of her community, which is probably why she imagines slapping Velma as she thinks these thoughts. But for Velma her resistance to the visions of the mud mothers was about self-preservation.

She began seeing the images as a child and tried to avoid them as best she could:

> In the attic they came in the mirror once. Ten or more women with mud hair, storing yams in gourds and pebbles in cracked calabash. And tucking babies in hairy hides. They came like a Polaroid. Stepping out of the mouth of the cave, they tried to climb out of the speckled glass, talk to her, tell her what must be done all over again, all over again, all over again. But she hung an old velvet drape over the mirror and smothered them. They were not going to run her off her own place. Not the attic. (255)

This clearly illustrates Daryl Cumber Dance's contention that Velma is initially not "ready for the ancient wisdom born into her unconscious mind from the experiences of her foremothers, those mud mothers whose many earlier calls to her she had never heeded" (178). Velma's resistance to the ancestral call is not unlike Avey's resistance in *Praisesong*, which will be addressed in the next chapter. Both women have a similar response because they have become distanced from their cultural roots. The notion of communing with the ancestors, which Nana finds normal and comforting in *Daughters of the Dust* seems disruptive and frightening to those like Avey and Velma who are unfamiliar with the African tradition of honoring one's ancestors. Thus, Velma's visions of the mud mothers had her worried that she too would begin doing crazy things like Minnie and begin eating dirt. After all, people have already begun to whisper that Velma is a "crackpot" (Bambara 94). Harris reflects on Minnie's initial difficulties with being selected for special powers and the concern her actions generated for her family and neighbors, but notes that she is guided "through the transition of being chosen" by Karen Wilder" (*Saints* 82–83). Minnie is able to get through this difficult period in her life with the assistance of an elder.

Karen Wilder or Old Wife had been Minnie's elder before she transitioned to the realm of ancestors; however, Minnie realizes that "[n]othing much had changed since she passed" (51). Minnie and Old Wife continue to have the same type of relationship in which Old Wife provides Minnie with guidance. In fact, it was Old Wife who foretold the unfolding of Minnie's gift. The women telepathically communicate with each other as they reminisce about the past and consider the future. Minnie seems impatient to learn more from Old Wife, whom she believes must be privy to even greater knowledge now that she is deceased: " 'Seems to me Old Wife, that by now you should so well know all these things, you'd have things to tell me. You been dead long enough?' " (56). Minnie's question reveals a craving for knowledge and an expectation that as an ancestor, Old Wife is privy to privileged information. However, Old Wife's comments suggest that Minnie was not as respectful as a child. In response to Minnie's assertion, " 'When I was a young girl I thought you were the wisest,' " Old Wife counters, " 'You thought I was crazy as a loon' " (56). Minnie then acknowledges that Old Wife was "crazy as could be," but she says " 'I knew you were special' " (56). This bantering goes back and forth with Old Wife reminding Minnie that she said that she smelled and that they called her a witch, but Minnie insisting that Old Wife " 'had a way of teaching us kids things' " (57). Minnie has the last word as she reminds her about how she, Sophie, Serge, and Cleotus used to hang around her candy stand, "We used to like to hear you and Wilder talking over the old days and things like that. I know you know that or you wouldn't've been telling us kids things to do and think about and read and check out and reach for. We couldn't've grown up without you, Old Wife. None of us' " (57). This conversation is illustrative of the guiding force of elders even if the immediate effect is not apparent. However, what is particularly significant is that the other children that Minnie mentions all grow up to have some kind of special power or nontraditional knowledge. Minnie becomes a healer, while Sophie and Serge are also associated with the Southwest Community Infirmary. Sophie is described as clairvoyant, whereas Serge seems like a trickster; however, he does seem to be aware of Velma's gift as he recognizes when she is ready for training, which implies that he too may have some degree of clairvoyance. Cleotus is never actually present in the text, but is sought out as someone for others to study with, which suggests that he is seen as having some kind of specialized knowledge. Their knowledge or power seems to be related to the knowledge they gained from their elders, Karen and Wilder.

Minnie's reflections on the impact of Old Wife and Wilder are echoed by Velma's memories of her interactions with Sophie and Daddy Dolphy. For example, Velma recalls a time when a snake in the woods bit Daddy Dolphy and Sophie quickly places a salt poultice in his wound; however, Sophie's gathering basket often gets overlooked in discussions of this incident. Sophie and Daddy Dolphy had taken Velma into the woods to teach her how to gather useful plants and flowers—she was likely being indoctrinated into traditional medicinal arts. For critic Eleanor Traylor, characters such as Minnie Ransom, Old Wife, Daddy Dolphy (and I would add Sophie) represent "the ancestral best commenting on the worst values and traditions and *ethos* of the race as it evolves and meets the challenges of time, present and future" (67). Traylor asserts, "The meaning of ancestry, and consequently, the meaning of modernity is the primary focus of the Bambara narrator. . . . But ancestry . . . is no mere equivalent of the past. Rather, ancestry is the sum of the accumulated wisdom of the race through time, as it manifests itself in the living, in the *e'gungun*, and in the yet unborn" (65–66).[3] This notion of ancestry reinforces my argument regarding the triad of life stages; however, rather than looking at the living broadly I focus specifically on the elder. The *e'gungun* or ancestors occupy the next stage, while the child figure—the born and unborn—occupy the final stage. Yet, each of these stages reveal the touch of the ancestor as elders are on the way to becoming ancestors and children have just come from the realm of the ancestors. Velma's difficulty, however, is her initial resistance to the call of the ancestors, whether it comes directly from the ancestral mud mothers or is delivered via her elders.

Thus Velma, like other members of the younger generation, has resisted the lessons of her elders. Minnie complains to Old Wife that " 'the children are spoiling,' " but Old Wife reminds her that the children are still their responsibility (Alwes 359). Alwes notes that "if the children are 'spoiling,' if they are forgetting the values of the community, it is because the elders have not sufficiently indoctrinated them in the communal wisdom and values, have not kept alive the historical and cultural realities that distinguish them from other people, other races" (359). We find a similar argument coming from an unexpected source—Elizabeth Harrison, registered nurse and a professor of nursing. In her essay, "Intolerable Human Suffering and the Role of the Ancestor: Literary Criticism as a Means of Analysis," Harrison asserts, "For Velma, suffering becomes intolerable because she loses touch with the ancestor" (692). Although Harrison is using literary theory and drawing on Toni Morrison's view of the ancestor, the purpose of her essay published in the *Journal of Advanced Nursing* is to aid nurses. Harrison argues, "Nurses must learn to recognize intolerable human suffering, to identify the patient's ancestral system, and to work within that system to keep suffering patients from harm" (689). As I do in the introduction, Harrison draws on Morrison's "Rootedness: The Ancestor as Foundation," in which she describes ancestors as "timeless people whose relationships to the characters are benevolent, instructive, protective and they provide a certain kind of wisdom" (343). However, Harrison extends Morrison's notion of the ancestor to include traditions. Thus, Harrison blames Velma's pain on her violation of cultural traditions, which is essentially a rejection of her ancestral system. For instance Harrison argues, "In the process of building her career, Velma had distanced herself from a fundamental ethic (interconnectedness) of her people, and as a result, her suffering increased exponentially until her only recourse was to end her life" (693). A similar point is made by Stanford, Velma "has many friends and belongs to collectives and political organizations, but her sense of connectedness to her past and to those with whom she lives and those she seeks to serve, is weakened by her excessive reliance on herself" (33). In other words, Velma's self-reliance is not conducive to the communal perspective one might expect of an elder responsible for maintaining communal stability. In fact, if she had this communal perspective, she would realize that suicide is the ultimate selfish act. According to Willis, "Velma Henry's attempted suicide is a figural device for asking, in an agonizing way, what will be the terms of the individual's relationship to loved ones and community, to past tradition and future society. Suicide represents the individual's renunciation of any connection with society; it is the individual's ultimate statement of autonomy" (153). It is this excessive autonomy and total disregard for others that leads Sophie to consider hitting Velma in order to knock some sense into her. Velma seems to have no sense of responsibility towards her family and others who care for her, as her decision to commit suicide does not take them into account.

In fact, it is a sense of responsibility that Old Wife uses to inspire Minnie during the difficult healing session. She tells Minnie, " 'love won't let you let'm go' " (Bambara, *Salt* 61). Minnie reaffirms this by acknowledging, " 'the chirren are our glory' " (62). Prior to this,

Minnie had been stalling because the healing session had proven to be more challenging than usual. This was no routine healing session—Velma is among this generation of spoiling children and thus is in need of ancestral cultural healing. However, Minnie is only ready to proceed with this difficult healing session after she has sought guidance from her ancestor—Old Wife.

With Old Wife's assistance, Minnie finally connects with Velma. Nadeen was one of the first to notice the break through as she "saw something drop away from Mrs. Henry's face" (101). Later, as Nadeen sees Velma's wrists heal before her eyes she acknowledges that this is a real healing session, unlike the revival healings she had been to before. According to Harris, "Nadeen's function here is not simply to serve as a validating witness to the current action, but also to validate the traditions from which Minnie is drawing to heal Velma" (*Saints* 82). Gloria T. Hull asserts that "Bambara's handling of this healing stems from the fact that she believes in 'the spiritual arts'—that is, all those avenues of knowing/being which are opposed to the 'rational,' 'Western,' 'scientific' mode . . ." (220). Hull's assessment is supported by Bambara's comments in her interview with Zala Chandler, in which she notes the difficulty of validating the psychic and spiritual existence in our lives, "As a result, those of us who are adept, who have dormant powers, have to expend a great deal of time and energy denying it and suppressing it—to the detriment of the individual and the entire community" (Chandler 348). In her conversation with Chandler, Bambara repeatedly notes our preference to pretend we are not clairvoyant or telepathic and to deny one's powers. She insists, "reality is also psychic. That is to say, in addition to all the other things, for example, the political, we live in a system guided by a spiritual order" (347). For Bambara, wholeness involves the political, psychic, spiritual, cultural, intellectual, aesthetic, physical, and economic. According to Bambara, "[t]here is a responsibility to self and to history that is developed once you are 'whole,' once you are well, once you acknowledge your powers" (348). Thus, the necessity of uniting the political and the spiritual is essential for Velma's healing.

Based on her interview with Bambara, Chandler asserts that in addition to linking the political and spiritual, Bambara believes that successful movements "must rely upon the people of ancient and current yesterdays who remain spiritually in Black people's lives as they move forward" (343). Bambara's concern for the ancestral presence is reflected in her comments to Chandler regarding those Africans lost in the ocean during the Middle Passage, "All those African bones in the briny deep. All those people who said 'no' and jumped ship. All those people who tried to figure out a way to steer, to navigate amongst the sharks. We don't call upon that power. We don't call upon those spirits. We don't celebrate those ancestors" (348). Bambara's concern regarding forgotten ancestors seems to echo Holloway's observation in reference to Old Wife's worry about Velma's seeming disconnection from her roots and her ancestors—Bambara is essentially bemoaning African Americans who do not recognize the power of their ancestors. Velma is not an isolated case, but an example of the cultural disconnection within the younger generation. The fact that the novel focuses on Velma is indicative of not only her central role in the community, but of her position as the community's representative. Harris asserts, "Velma is a microcosmic representation of various ills in her community, those physical and emotional . . . as well as those spiritual and political; if she can be saved, then she in turn can save her community" (*Saints* 81). As Velma goes, so goes Claybourne. Thus, Velma's healing will effect the entire community.

Minnie eventually reaches Velma; although, it takes longer than usual. Although some of the onlookers became restless and check their watches, others realized it "[t]ook heart to flat out decide to be well and stride into the future sane and whole. And it took time. So the old-timers and the circle concentrated on their work, for of course patients argued, fought, resisted. Just as Mrs. Velma Henry was fighting still what was her birthright" (108). They, like Minnie, realize that health must be a conscious choice: Velma must choose to be well. Although before Velma can choose health, she must stop resisting her birthright—her gift. Harrison argues that in rejecting the gift, an integral part of Velma's ancestral system "was unavailable to sustain her and the result was profound alienation and suffering" (693). The exact nature of this gift is not specified, but it is connected to her visions of the mud mothers. It is this connection to her foremothers, her ancestors, which establishes Velma's gift as ancestral in nature: "The gift is part of Velma's ancestral system because it is a source of wisdom (increases self-knowledge), it is timeless (includes time-honoured practices), instructive (offers direction), and it bestows protection (re-focuses attention on tradition)" (693). However, Velma cannot benefit from this gift until she is willing to relinquish absolute self-sufficiency and accept guidance from the ancestors. It is during the healing session that "Velma comes to discover, as she embarks on a journey of memory and recollection, that those mud mothers call her to a deeper understanding of who she is within the historical and social community from which she comes" (Stanford 33). With Minnie's help, Velma can be open to the wisdom of her foremothers—wisdom she had glimpsed, but refused to absorb. For example, she remembers thinking one morning in front of the mirror that something crucial was missing "and the answer had almost come tumbling out of the mirror naked and tattooed with serrated teeth and hair alive, birds and insects peeping out at her from the mud-heavy hanks of the ancient mothers' hair. And she had fled feverish and agitated from the room . . ." (Bambara, *Salt* 259). Although Velma has been advocating for her community through a variety of organizations, it is during the healing session that it becomes clear that the spiritual is "the missing element in the progressive political movements of the 1960s. . . . [T]o achieve the goals of sixties' idealism and to respond to the new challenges of the last quarter of the twentieth century, . . . people of color need to recuperate the subjugated knowledge of their foremothers" (Wall 31). Thus Velma can only achieve health when she is willing to accept wholeness, which means accepting her ancestors.

Thus Minnie began the healing session by asking, " 'Are you sure, sweetheart, that you want to be well?' " (3). According to literary scholar, Margot Anne Kelley, "Minnie Ransom is one of the characters consistently aware that she can make choices, that she can change the trajectory of the system—and she wants to convey this power to her patients . . ." (489). Minnie not only makes Velma aware of her choices, but that her choices have consequences. So it is not just whether she wants to be well, but also " '[c]an [she] afford to be whole?' " (Bambara, *Salt* 106). Eventually, Velma answers in the affirmative by stating, " 'Health is my right' " (119). This, however, is not the end of the healing session; Velma must now decide what to do with her wholeness.

The weightiness of this decision threatens to disrupt the healing session. Velma looks out the window only to be called back by Minnie, " 'The source of health is never outside, sweetheart. What will you do when you are well?' " (220). The pressure of the choice sends Velma off as she mentally removes herself from the healing session and imagines herself running "through passageways in search of a particular chamber that might not be sealed off if she hurries and doesn't think too much on limitations" (250). The healing is then brought back on track as Velma acknowledges that she might have died. The onlookers to the healing session could see the change in Velma. Doc smiles as he watches Velma "come alive in a new way and ready for training . . ." (269). This training will be a form of enculturation and it is this enculturation, which will lead to social change.

The significance of Velma's healing is marked by an earthquake, which occurs during the session. "Velma would remember it as the moment she started back toward life, the moment when the healer's hand had touched some vital spot and she was still trying to resist . . . (278).

This is a moment of transformation for Velma and Claybourne. Harris argues, Velma:

> is intimately identified with the health of the larger community. Bambara makes clear that Velma serves a microcosmic role and that the community cannot be healthy unless she is. Several characters, therefore, experience epiphanic transformations or moments of enlightenment during the thundering interlude that presages Velma's return to complete consciousness and health. (194)

The implication is that Velma's acceptance of her ancestral gift will allow her to truly help her community and move beyond the sense of frustration that she had found so overwhelming. Velma's promise as a future leader and elder are suggested by her godmother M' Dear Sophie's reflections on the healing session, "Once Minnie brought Velma through perhaps the girl at last would be ready for training. She'd waited a long time for the godchild's gift to unfold" (293). Velma's ultimate readiness for training is apparent in the last lines of the text, "No need of Minnie's hands now so the healer withdraws them, drops them in her lap just as Velma, rising on steady legs, throws off the shawl that drops down on the stool a burst cocoon" (295). Velma has been healed through the guidance of an elder.

The image of a burst cocoon suggests a rebirth—a rewriting or revising of what has come before. This image of rebirth is linked with other birth and mothering images in the text. Alwes comments, "The cave of the 'mud mothers' operates, of course, as a symbol of the cultural or racial womb, and images of birth, of mothering (or parenting) resonate throughout the book as the characters all reflect on the responsibility of the older generation to educate and sustain the children of the community . . ." (359). In Velma's case, she has been healed with the assistance of an elder, but now it is her turn to take up the mantle of responsibility. The healing session has provided Velma with renewed strength to cope not only with her personal problems, but also with the community's problems. When Doc smiles, thinking that Velma is ready for training—it is training to be an elder—to take on a new level of responsibility.

According to Traylor it is "through Velma's negation and acceptance of the actual and her pursuit of the possible that we learn the identity and enormous re-creative powers of those who have eaten salt together and who have learned to reconcile both the brine and the savor of life" (60). Traylor is just one of many critics who have tried to make sense of Bambara's intriguing title. In her essay, "What It Is I Think I'm Doing Anyhow," Bambara explains, "Salt is a partial antidote for snakebite . . . . To struggle, to develop, one needs to master ways to neutralize poisons. 'Salt' also keeps the parable of Lot's Wife to the fore. Without a belief in the capacity for transformation, one can become ossified" (166).[4] One of the first references to salt in the text picks up on the ambiguous nature of salt. Velma has just begun the healing session as she thinks about the crowds "trying to tell her about the difference between snakes and serpents, the difference between eating salt as an antidote to snakebite and turning into salt, succumbing to the serpent" (Bambara, *Salt* 8). Thus in the words of Janelle Collins, "salt eating can have healing or poisonous results. The connotation of Lot's wife turning into a pillar of salt amplifies the meaning within the title. Velma has learned the dangers of becoming ossified by looking back to past failures, past wrongs, past sufferings" (45). The implication is that Velma has become so mired in her sorrows and sufferings that she has become dangerously inflexible. While this early reference to salt indicates the dangers of too much salt, a comment by Ahiro to Obie warns against too little salt as well: " 'A good cry, man. Good for the eyes, the sinuses, the heart. The body needs to throw off its excess salt for balance. Too little salt and wounds can't heal' " (Bambara, *Salt* 164). Philip Page seems to have this scene in mind when he argues, "they need to eat salt with each other . . . . Salt brings people together, and it helps integrate each individual by keeping the body's chemistry in harmony" (82). Willis makes a similar point when she claims, "One must eat salt to live. One must eat salt to be healed" (153). This scholarly focus on the need to eat salt together may be initiated by passages such as Sophie's thought, "You never really know a person until you've eaten salt together, she told herself. But she'd gone through many a bitter experience with Velma, and still she was baffled. What had gone wrong? What did it mean?" (Bambara, *Salt* 147). Surely lines such as these led Hull to suggest "[t]his title also calls into the subconscious images related to the folk concepts of 'swallowing a bitter pill' and 'breaking bread together' " (Hull 231). However, if one understood the role of salt in Kongo cosmology, one might have a slightly different interpretation of Bambara's title.

"In Kongo cosmology, it is believed that the ancestral dead, from whom the living derive their spiritual powers, do not eat salt. Salt repels the spirits of the dead, and thus causes weakness in the living—particularly those engaged in spiritual matters" (Bilby and Kimbwandende 43). Thus, Minnie would not be a salt eater as this would interfere with her communication with her ancestor, Old Wife. Velma, on the other hand, is a salt eater who is seeking to repel her ancestral mud mothers. However, in her attempt to protect herself from visions that she finds frightening, Velma is actually weakening herself. In fact, " 'To eat salt,' then, is to lose one's power" (44). Thus when Sophie says, "You never really know a person until you've eaten salt together," she means you do not know someone until you have been together at your weakest point. Velma's is clearly at her weakest point in that she has attempted suicide, but that Sophie is also weak is only implied. Sophie's role as elder and godmother is to guide Velma, but she "had not been attentive, gotten blocked, sidetracked. . . . Sophie vowed to concentrate more fully and stay alert and be at hand, for Velma's next trial might lead to an act far more devastating than striking out at the body or swallowing gas" (Bambara, *Salt* 294). Sophie's discipline of silence has strengthened her for the challenges ahead for she realizes that Velma's healing session is just the first of several trials ahead. Thus Velma's triumphant throwing off of her shawl like a burst cocoon at the end of the novel is not an individual triumph, but a communal triumph. Velma's healing has implications for the rest of Claybourne, but it is also indicative of the healing powers of elders and ancestors.

In both *The Salt Eaters* and *The Daughters of the Dust*, the healing powers of the ancestors are called for by elder othermothers in their role as culture bearers. Nana Peazant, Sophie Heywood, and Minnie Ransom as elders and culture bearers take it upon themselves to ensure that the younger generation maintains a connection with their ancestral roots because they recognize the strength and healing powers of the ancestors. Old Karen, when alive also played this role of elder othermother, but upon her death she transitioned to the realm of the ancestors. While elders may facilitate the healing powers of the ancestors, the actual power resides with the ancestor. In the case of *Daughters of the Dust*, this healing ancestral power is delivered indirectly to Eula and Eli via the Unborn Child, while in *The Salt Eaters*, the ancestral mud mothers directly reach out to Velma, but the elder Minnie Ransom assists Velma in accepting their message. In the next section, the ancestor will be addressed in more detail through discussions of Paule Marshall's *Praisesong to the Widow*, Phyllis Alesia Perry's *Stigmata*, and Toni Morrison's *Beloved*.

Part II Preface

The Dead Are Not Dead

The Ancestral Presence

In this study, I contend that ancestral bonds extend beyond the grave in order to maintain a sense of health and well-being in the face of a legacy of slavery and racial discrimination. Using a woman-centered network of mothers, daughters, and othermothers in the form of elders and ancestors, Paule Marshall's *Praisesong for the Widow*, Phyllis Alesia Perry's *Stigmata*, and Toni Morrison's *Beloved* are able to offer a feminist revision of a slave past by drawing on African traditions reflected in Kongo cosmology. Kongo authority, Dr. Bunseki Fu-Kiau, observes:

> When the physical body dies . . . the dual [mwèla-ngindu] of that being remains within the community or out of it. The dual of the being [Mwèla-ngîndu (*sic*)], continues to act and to talk to and among the community's members as well as to the world's community through dreams and visions, waves, radiations, and through monumental acts: the biological, material, intellectual and spiritual treasures accumulated in scrolls [ku mpèmba], the past, i.e., the perpetual bank of the generating/driving forces of life. (71, insertions in the original)

In other words, the end of the physical body does not mean the end of one's connection to the community—communication continues through such things as dreams and visions. This notion of a community of living and dead is reflected in Geoffrey Parrinder's contention, "Men belong to a community and they are related to other beings, both living and dead" (28). This conception of community is depicted in such texts as *Praisesong for the Widow, Stigmata, A Sunday in June,* and *Beloved.*

In each of these texts, the dead speak to or even visit the living. According to Sharon Holland, "speaking from . . . the place reserved for the dead, disturbs the static categories of black/white, oppressor/ oppressed, creating a plethora of tensions *within and without* existing cultures. Embracing the subjectivity of death allows marginalized peoples to speak about the unspoken— . . ." (4–5). Thus, these black women writers are able to use death via the vehicle of the ancestor to express the inexpressible. Aunt Cuney's manacle like grip, Ayo's scars embedded on Lizzie's body, and the bruises Beloved leaves on Sethe's neck can only hint at the legacy of slavery they wish to share. In reference to *Praisesong for the Widow,* Gay Wilentz observes, "It is through the acknowledgment of one's ancestors that the African American community can achieve wholeness" ("If" 28). This same point can be made regarding the other texts under discussion.

Like Wilentz, I argue that ancestors are a crucial element to communal well-being; nevertheless, the protagonists in these texts have become disconnected from their ancestors and must be reminded of the value of these relations. In fact the significance of memory is apparent in each of these texts. In *Memory and Cultural Politics: New Approaches to American Ethnic Literatures,* the editors Amritjit Singh, Joseph T. Skerrett Jr., and Robert E. Hogan argue, "As part of the ongoing argument between history and memory, marginalized groups often attempt to maintain at the center of national memory what the dominant group would often like to forget. The process results in a collective memory always in flux: not one memory but multiple memories constantly battling for attention in cultural space . . ." (6). Marshall, Perry, and Morrison are all engaging in a revisioning of slavery, which hinges in part on their treatment of memory in their novels. Whether it be the Marshall's tale of the Ibo, Perry's quilts, or Morrison's notion of rememory, it is clear that "Not only do we create and maintain the memories we need to survive and prevail, but those collective memories in turn both shape and constrain us" (8). In the case of these novels, these collective memories are closely tied to the ways of the ancestor. In *The Way of the Elders: West African Spirituality and Traditions,* Adama and Naomi Doumbia observe, "We pray for our ancestors and we perform sacrifice to honor their lives. We appreciate them for the life they gave us and the ways they continue to instruct and nurture us" (9). However, for our protagonists they have forgotten the value of their ancestors or in the case of *Beloved* are plagued by a malevolent ancestor.

I use "ancestor" to refer to the recently deceased or living-dead and thus ancestors are not necessarily forebears to the living. In *Beloved*, for example, Sethe is believed to be visited by the daughter she killed, which would make Beloved literally Sethe's descendant and not her ancestor. However, for my purposes Beloved is among the living-dead and thus might be termed an ancestor. Yet, she would not be a true ancestor due to her youth. According to Dominque Zahan, the ancestor is "distinguished from people less advanced in age and whose credulity and inexperience in life classify them with children or youths. . . ." (*Religion* 49). Like Zahan, Thomas E. Lawson in *Religions of Africa, Traditions in Transformation* argues all people who die do not become ancestors (62). As I discussed in relation to elders, this life stage must be achieved and is not a given. Fu-Kiau observes that one is prone to become "an 'n'kulu' (ancestor) or an 'n'kuyu' (ghost, bad ancestor)" (43). I contend that those living-dead who have not achieved ancestor status are liable to becoming malevolent or bad ancestors as seen in *Beloved*. Thus, in the chapters that follow, I argue that ancestors provide beneficial guidance and that when the ancestral presence appears to be malevolent it is because the living-dead is not a true ancestor, but someone who died before achieving the things that would allow this status to be granted. These malevolent or "stunted ancestors"—as Fu-Kiau refers to them—are not in a position to provide guidance because they have not matured themselves (Fu-Kiau 29). This lack of maturity is what makes Beloved a malevolent ancestor, whereas Aunt Cuney in *Praisesong for the Widow* and Ayo in *Stigmata* are beneficial despite the disruptive nature of their presence.

2

Ancestral Prodding in
Praisesong for the Widow

In "Mechanisms of Disease: African-American Women Writers, Social Pathologies, and the Limits of Medicine," Ann Folwell Stanford approaches Paule Marshall's *Praisesong for the Widow* by studying the body as an indication of social ills. According to Stanford:

> *Praisesong* chronicles Avey's experience of what might appear to be a cardiac or gastrointestinal irregularity but might also be simply dismissed as a psychosomatic complaint. In probing her illness and subsequent healing, the novel refuses to separate the community from individual bodies—or the psychosomatic from the somatic—and in so doing, foregrounds the social context of Avey's physical troubles. ("Mechanisms" 35)

In discussing Avey's visitations by her Aunt Cuney, Stanford refers to "a disturbing and recurring dream" and a "profoundly unsettling dream" along with her physical symptoms as if Aunt Cuney's visitations were merely symptoms of her illness and not a haunting (36). However, a very different perspective on this issue emerges when taking into consideration Avery F. Gordon's assertion in *Ghostly Matters: Haunting and the Sociological Imagination*: "Haunting is a constituent element of modern social life. It is neither pre-modern superstition nor individual psychosis; it is generalizable social phenomenon of great import" (7). The importance of haunting is what the ghost reflects. For Gordon, "the ghost is a crucible for political mediation and historical memory . . ."(18).

Kathleen Brogan makes a similar point in *Cultural Haunting: Ghosts and Ethnicity in Recent American Literature*. According to Brogan, "As both presence and absence, the ghost stands as an emblem of historical loss as well as a vehicle of historical recovery" (29). Thus a ghost, which in the realm of popular culture tends to have a negative connotation, may actually perform a useful service. In the case of Avey, this service is to facilitate a spiritual rebirth that allows her to reconnect with her ancestors. Therefore, I argue that *Praisesong for the Widow* is not so much a haunting, but a prodding by her ancestor, Aunt Cuney, who uses dreams and the assistance of elder culture bearers such as Lebert Joseph to remind Avey of her history and the importance of maintaining family legacies.

When her ancestor reaches out to her through her dreams, Avey's rebirth is triggered. The dream is particularly disturbing because "[a]s a rule she seldom dreamed" (Marshall 31). Avey's lack of dreams is reflected in the phenomenon discussed by G. Thomas Couser in "Oppression and Repression: Personal and Collective Memory in Paule Marshall's *Praisesong for the Widow* and Leslie Marmon Silko's *Ceremony*." Couser argues:

> rather than dwell on (and in) a painful past, minority groups may sanitize memory in order to preserve positive self-images. Reviving such memories is necessary, however, precisely because, at least for groups whose traditional culture is primarily oral, the only history *is* memory. Not to remember is to accede to the erasure or distortion of collective experience; to repress memory is to reenact and perpetuate oppression. (107)

Avey's lack of dreams is one such attempt to sanitize memory. According to the narrator, Avey stopped dreaming after experiencing nightmares during the mid-1960s in which she dreamed of images from the news: "electric cattle prods," "lunging dogs," "high-pressure hoses," and "cigarettes being ground out on the arms of those sitting in at the lunch counters" (31). She dreamed of the Birmingham bomb in 1963, but in her version she found her own daughters in the debris. It is significant that Marshall links Avey's dream of Aunt Cuney with nightmares representing the political unrest of the Civil Rights Movement. Gordon observes, "Slavery has ended, but something of it continues to live on, in the social geography of where peoples reside, in the authority of collective wisdom and shared benightedness, in the veins of the contradictory formation we call New World modernity, propelling as it always has, a something to be done. Such endings are what haunting is about" (139). Gordon's point about social geography is evident in the name of the suburb where Avey lives, North White Plains, and even the name of the cruise ship, the *Bianca Pride*. North White Plains had been a white neighborhood until blacks moved in and it underwent white flight, leaving only the Archers and Weinsteins: "The only ones for blocks around who had not sold and fled" (45). The *Bianca Pride* is described as having "dazzling white steel," but it also is full of white folks (15). In both of these locales, white had been or is the norm, and Avey had been or is the exception. The Civil Rights Movement allowed some African Americans to engage in social mobility, but the civil unrest associated with it also reflected the lingering effects of slavery. The fact that Avey stopped dreaming after the Birmingham bomb dream sug-gests a psychological withdrawal, which mirrors her assimilated exterior: mink stole, spring suit, silk blouse, and gloves. These items are meant to show that she belongs in her white upper-class neighborhood, but the flimsiness of their protective qualities is revealed in the ease with which they can be destroyed. Her great-aunt Cuney tears away these articles during the tug-of-war dream. She seems to be telling Avey that she can no longer insulate herself from the African American experience with things. These symbols of middle-class attainment will not protect her from the lingering effects of slavery. According to Couser, "Histories of oppression, such as those of Native Americans and African Americans, are especially vulnerable to suppression and repression. With regard to such groups, written history is often amnesiac or self-justifying; it tends to marginalize or exclude the 'ethnic,' other" (107). This is why Aunt Cuney prods Avey to remember the Ibos: "The story of the Ibos' resistance to oppression, once readmitted to consciousness, is seen as a kind of antidote to contemporary amnesia and alienation in the Afri-can American community" (111). Thus, Aunt Cuney returns from the grave to incite Avey to remember her ancestors and to be empowered by their story.

In the dream, Aunt Cuney beckons to Avey to join her in a walk to Ibo Landing. Avey is appalled by the suggestion: "Did she really expect her to go walking over to the Landing dressed as she was?" (40). Avey stood silently immobile in response to Aunt Cuney's beckoning; therefore, Aunt Cuney tried other tactics: coaxing, pleading, and finally dragging. The encounter develops into a full-fledged tug-of-war and finally a fistfight, as Avey continues to refuse her aunt's request. Aunt Cuney is described as furious—"fur[ious] at being defied," but Avey is surprised to find disappointment and sadness in Aunt Cuney's eyes rather than fury (44). Aunt Cuney is clearly disappointed that Avey has turned her back on her heritage. What Aunt Cuney knows and Avey is yet to realize is that Avey has given up too much in pursuit of class status. According to Gordon, "the ghost is primarily a symptom of what is missing. It gives notice not only to itself but also to what it represents. What it represents is usually a loss, sometimes of life, sometimes of a path not taken. From a certain vantage point the ghost also simultaneously represents a future possibility, a hope" (64). Aunt Cuney's presence makes visible what Avey has lost or turned her back on as she and her husband pursued economic success. For them, climbing the social ladder meant neglecting important elements of their cultural heritage, such as visiting Ibo Landing and dancing to the blues.

The unsettling dream of Aunt Cuney prompts Avey to remember things long forgotten in her past. It is almost as if the dream leads Avey to recalibrate her life by taking into account things that had been previously dismissed. Brogan notes "how stories of cultural haunting repeatedly testify to memory's instability and capriciousness. Cultural continuity is not assumed but is achieved in the course of each haunting. Memory in this literature takes the form of mourning, a way of remembering dominated by a sense of a break with the past" (28). We definitely see this at work with Avey, as her haunting stimulates memories that had been buried, while also triggering mourning once she realizes the things that she lost reflected in these buried memories.

According to Brogan:

> In commemorating the past, stories of cultural haunting are always invested in and in some cases are organized by, rituals of mourning. . . . Mourning represents a form of memory centrally marked by an awareness of a break with the past. . . . As restless or invasive spirits, the ghosts propel characters towards the completion of a mourning that if properly accomplished, allows the past to be in some sense revised and incorporated into the present. (134)

For Avey, the break with the past is represented by her failure to keep alive the story of Ibo Landing. Avey's failure to keep the story alive is particularly significant because she appears to have been sent by the ancestors to do just that. Her great-aunt Cuney "sent word months before her birth that it would be a girl and she was to be called after her grandmother who had come to her in a dream with the news" (Marshall 42). Aunt Cuney believed her gran, Avatara, had sent Avey. In fact, John Pobee notes in "Aspects of African Traditional Religions," "The ancestors are believed to give children to the living for the continuance of the family, clan and tribe in which alone is found self-fulfillment"

(9). For Aunt Cuney and her grandmother, it has been predestined that Avey will carry on the family tradition of remembering the Ibos. She has been selected to join the matrilineal line of culture bearers. Consequently, Kimberly Rae Connor in *Conversions and Visions: In the Writings of African-American Women* asserts, "she is chosen by Avatara to carry on the legacy Aunt Cuney was guarding, and she must answer the call" (237). Avey is expected to carry on the tradition of remembering the Ibos. According to Dominique Zahan, author of *The Religion, Spirituality, and Thought of Traditional Africa*, "Tradition for Africans is, then, a communication between the dead and the living, as it represents the 'word' of the ancestors" (48). Thus from age seven on, Avey was inducted into this tradition as she spent every August in Tatem with her Aunt Cuney, who shared with her the story of Ibo Landing; however, Avey did not fully appreciate the significance of the tale. Avey recalls, "in instilling the story of the Ibos in her child's mind, the old woman had entrusted her with a mission she couldn't even name yet had felt duty-bound to fulfill. It had taken her years to rid herself of the notion" (Marshall 42). It may have taken time, but Avey eventually disassociates herself from the tale of Ibo Landing because she never truly valued it. Ibo Landing is part of the cultural baggage that she discards on her path to success. Toni Cade Bambara observes:

> Avey and Jay have been in flight; the fear of poverty and humiliation drove them to jettison cultural 'baggage' for a fleeter, unencumbered, foot up the ladder. Avey receives visitations from her dead elder, Great Aunt Cuney, who directs her to *remember*. Avey's journey to wholeness begins with remembering the story of the Ibos as handed down through generations in the Carolina Sea Islands where she spent her girlhood summers. In short, in order to move forward, Avey has to first go backwards. ("Reading" 131)

In the dream, Avey sees Aunt Cuney's disappointment and sadness, which leads her to remember not only the tale of Ibo Landing, but also Aunt Cuney's earlier disappointment.

Aunt Cuney's disappointment and sadness in the dream is paralleled with the time that Avey questioned the marvelous story of Ibo Landing:

> "It was here that they brought 'em. [. . .] And the minute those Ibos was brought on shore they just stopped, my gran' said, and taken a look around. A good long look. Not saying

a word. Just studying the place real good. Just taking their time and studying on it.

And they seen things that day you and me don't have the power to see. 'Cause those pure-born Africans was peoples my gran' said could see in more ways than one. The kind can tell you 'bout things happened long before they was born and things to come long after they's dead. [. . .] And when they got through sizing up the place real good and seen what was to come, they turned, my gran' said, and looked at the white folks what brought 'em here. [. . .] And when they got through studying 'em, when they *knew* just from looking at 'em how those folks was gonna do, do you know what the Ibos did? Do you . . . ?"

[. . .] ". . . They just turned, my gran' said, all of 'em—" [. . .] "and walked on back down to the edge of the river here. [. . .] They just kept walking right on out over the river. Now you wouldna thought they'd of got very far seeing as it was water they was walking on. Besides they had all that iron on 'em. Iron on they ankles and they wrists and fastened 'round they necks like a dog collar. 'Nuff iron to sink an army. And chains hooking up the iron. But chains didn't stop those Ibos none." (37–39)

Avey was so mesmerized by the story that she committed it to memory and "recounted the whole thing almost word for word to her three brothers, complete with the old woman's inflections and gestures" (38). However, the summer she was ten after having heard the story for four summers it occurred to her to ask her great-aunt why they had not drowned. Aunt Cuney looked at her in silence and with such disappointment and sadness that Avey wished "she could have reached up that day and snatched her question like a fly out of the air and swallowed it whole" (40). When Aunt Cuney finally responded it was with a "quietly dangerous note" to her voice:

"Did it say Jesus drowned when he went walking on the water in that Sunday School book your momma always sends with you?"

"No ma'am."

"I din' think so. You got any more questions?"

[Avey] had shaken her head "no." (40)

Aunt Cuney's response illustrates the sacred nature of the story for her. In fact, "[p]eople in Tatem said she had made the Landing her religion . . ." (34). The way in which Aunt Cuney cherishes her grandmother's rendition of the story and seeks to pass it down through the family seems very much like ancestor worship. Zahan, however, describes the relationship between the living and the dead as reciprocal in nature: "By conforming to the legacy of the dead, the living in turn recognize their authority and avoid 'dangerous' undertakings. Presence on the one hand and submission on the other, this is the very object of the exchanges between two worlds whose reciprocal permeability is never contested by any African" (*Religion* 48). However, it is clear from Avey's response to her dream of Aunt Cuney that she has not established this reciprocal relationship with her deceased ancestors.

Although these characters are not Africans, Jane Olmsted notes in "The Pull to Memory and the Language of Place in Paule Marshall's *The Chosen Place, The Timeless People* and *Praisesong for the Widow*" that Marshall "has admitted to being an unabashed ancestor worshipper and has emphasized on numerous occasions the importance of historical roots in Africa" (249). As the novel unfolds, it becomes clear that the physical and mental discomfort plaguing Avey is in direct response to her turning her back on Aunt Cuney and the voice of the ancestors. Her life in White Plains, New York, has dislodged her from her roots and it is only her trip to Carriacou, a sort of reverse Middle Passage, which brings her back to her roots and the story of Ibo Landing. Connor asserts:

> When Avey undertakes her journey it is a symbolic reversal of
> the journey that the slaves took to America and a refiguration
> of the journey the Ibos took back to Africa. In this sense the
> meaning of slavery is overturned and by reversal becomes a
> metaphor for the articulation individuals achieve for naming their newly acquired racial consciousness and liberation.
> Moreover, Avey's own suffering is diminished, its meaning
> modified by the knowledge of her heritage. (235–36)

Thus, although *Praisesong for the Widow* is not directly about slavery, it is very much about its legacy and in fact, an attempt to rewrite this legacy.

In an interview with Alexis De Veaux, Marshall speaks to her desire to address the effect of history:

"I'm trying to trace history. First of all to make some sense of my own history and also to make some sense of the history of Black people. To take, for example, the infamous triangular route of slavery and to reverse it so that we make the journey back from America to the West Indies, to Africa. Because I am convinced that, as a people, we have not as yet really engaged our past. . . . I'm really convinced one *has to* engage the past if you are going to shape a future that reflects you. You have to deal with it rather than accept the kind of past that has been fostered upon us by white historians." (De Veaux 128)

De Veaux concludes, "Paule Marshall is not a safe writer. . . . Paule Marshall is painfully aware of the importance and power of history creatively written" (128). Lene Brøndum echoes this point:

In much the same way that storytelling serves to disrupt the representation of history by revising it, so mythmaking emphasizes a reworking of tradition. . . . In actuality, African American women's use of myth is another disruption of dominant discourse: first by valuing myth in contrast to 'history' and, second, by the writer's sense of agency and subjectivity in the discussion of a communal historic past. (156)

Thus the story of Ibo Landing is so much more than a quaint story—it is a response to hegemony. Wilentz argues in her discussion of Marshall's use of the legend of flying Africans that, "Flight, in this case, functions not merely as an individual or 'universal' symbol of transcendence, but as a collective symbol of resistance by a specific group within a socio-historical context" ("If You Surrender" 21). It is this notion of resistance that is meant to empower those who may not have flown, but who can cling to the possibility, and thus not be encumbered by mental shackles.

However, it is only years later that Avey comes to understand Ibo Landing's significance. This ancestral story is meant to be shared as a source of strength, but Avey's question at ten years of age reveals that she did not yet comprehend the full import of the tale. Her question demonstrates that Avey did not learn the lesson regarding self-determination that the tale seeks to impart. In her essay, " 'One of Dese Mornings, Bright and Fair/Take My Wings and Cleave De Air': The Legend of the Flying Africans and Diasporic Consciousness," Wendy W. Walters argues that Marshall's "transformation of the legend of the fly-

ing Africans, articulate[s] a counterdiscursive historiography of slavery"
(4). Walters argues, "Although the 'Ibo Landing' story does not contain
flying, it is similar in many respects to several versions of the flying
African legend. Both stories contain specifically-empowered slaves who
leave slavery and travel back to Africa by 'super human' means" (19).
Undoubtedly, the reference to super human methods made this story
very attractive to both an enslaved and formerly enslaved population. In
fact, in her interview with bell hooks, Julie Dash comments on the fact
that while conducting research for *Daughters of the Dust*, she discovered
that almost every Sea Island claimed to have an Ibo Landing:

> And so, why is it that on every little island—and there are so
> many places—people say, "This is actually Ibo Landing"? It's
> because that message is so strong, so powerful, so sustaining
> to the tradition of resistance, by any means possible, that
> every Gullah community embraces this myth. So I learned
> that myth is very important in the struggle to maintain a
> sense of self and to move forward into the future." (hooks
> and Dash 30)

It is this lesson about the importance of myth that Avey must
relearn from her Aunt Cuney. Aunt Cuney tried to teach it to the young
Avey during her visits to Tatem, but she must return from the grave
to reteach the lesson of self-determination imbedded in the actions of
the Ibo. For Barbara Christian, it is the emphasis on self-determination
in the tale that stands out:

> This story of Africans who were forced to come across the
> sea—but through their own power, a power which seems
> irrational, were able to return to Africa—is a touchstone of
> New World black folklore. Through this story, peoples of
> African descent emphasized their own power to determine
> their freedom, though their bodies might be enslaved. They
> recalled Africa as the source of their being. ("Ritualistic" 76)

However, this is not the case for Avey, who has clearly lost sight of
Africa as the source of her being.

Unfortunately, Avey is just one of many who don't know their
nation, who have become removed from their heritage. In fact, according to Abena P. A. Busia, "Marshall articulates the scattering of the
African peoples as a trauma—a trauma that is constantly repeated anew
in the lives of her lost children" (197). However, for Avey the effects of

this trauma are ameliorated by the intercession of her ancestor. According to Joyce Pettis, ancestors

> bridge history, melding present strategies with those of the past as they assume responsibility for instructing new generations in survival techniques. This cultural role is a part of the heritage of West Africa, where the elderly are revered. The ancestral presence, visible in nonfiction as well as fiction, is thus heavily valued as a factor in cultural continuity. Ancestors function as mentors, sustaining the moorings of fragile spirits. (*Toward Wholeness* 117)

Pettis and I agree that Aunt Cuney's visitation, although disruptive, is ultimately healing. Pettis says of Aunt Cuney, "As Avey's ancestor, she becomes the catalyst in resurrecting Avey's memories of the past" (121). She argues, "The ancestral interference precipitates dreams, flashbacks, and journeys that cumulatively bring Avey to realize her fractured psyche. More important, though, the ancestors direct Avey through a process of spiritual regeneration" (121). Thus, the ancestor is presented by Marshall as a means of responding to the cultural trauma of slavery and its aftermath.

For Brogan, "Avey's great-aunt Cuney, functions as the return of the culturally repressed, recalling Avey through reawakened memories to a past denied in the quest for middle-class economic security and (white-bestowed) respectability" (145). In Avey's case, she was not unaware of the rituals associated with her heritage, but she failed to realize their significance and thus inadvertently left behind key elements of her identity. In fact, it gets to the point that Avey actually fails to recognize her own reflection on occasion. Although Avey describes this stranger in the mirror as "a black woman of average height with a full-figured yet compact body," her clothes and bearing seem to deracinate her. She is described as wearing "carefully coordinated accessories. The muted colors. Everything in good taste and appropriate to her age" (Marshall 48). However, what is more telling is the description of her "composed face with its folded-in lip and carefully barred gaze. She was clearly someone who kept her thoughts and feelings to herself" (48). It is almost as if Avey is wearing a mask to protect her inner thoughts from outsiders. Yet the most revealing comment is about her bearing: "her Marian Anderson poise and reserve. The look of acceptability about her. She would never be sent to eat in the kitchen when company came!—" (49). This reference to Langston Hughes' poem, "I, Too," along with the dream tug-of-war over her mink stole suggest that the look of acceptability Avey has crafted, much like the trappings of middle-class status, are meant to gain white-bestowed respectability, which entails muting her ethnic identity.

However, Aunt Cuney's visitations prompt Avey to reconnect with her ethnic identity: "It is not simply in embodying memory or 'bringing the past to life' that the ghosts in *Praisesong* become vehicles of ethnicity; they propel the protagonist toward rituals of mourning or commemoration through which she 'performs' a newly redefined ethnic identity" (Brogan 146). Like Brogan, Geraldine Smith-Wright in "In Spite of the Klan: Ghosts in the Fiction of Black Women Writers" places Avey's husband Jerome and Aunt Cuney on similar ghostly planes. According to Smith-Wright, "When Cuney, in the dream, and later Avey's husband, Jerome, return as ghosts, each parallels an aspect of her divided self" (Smith-Wright 161). However, I would argue that there is a significant difference between these figures—Jerome haunts Avey, whereas Cuney visits to provide guidance. I argue that this difference is connected to ancestor status—ancestors, such as Aunt Cuney, are beneficial, whereas ghosts, like Jerome, may cause harm. The deceased, or the living dead, may become ancestors who continue to provide guidance to the living or they may become bad ancestors or ghosts. Because the role of ancestors is to provide guidance and protection their actions by definition are benevolent. However, John Mbiti has noted that ghosts sometimes "act in unpleasant ways towards people, and sometimes in beneficial ways" (*Intro* 77). More is discussed about this in Chapter 4 in relation to the malevolent ancestor, but one must remember that death does not ensure ancestor status. Zahan notes, "Not just anyone can become an ancestor. The society of the living 'directs' towards this 'paradise' only those dead who satisfy certain well-defined conditions" (*Religion* 49). For Zahan, these conditions include such things as "longevity [and] a profound experience of people and things" (49). I contend that Jerome did not satisfy these conditions. In fact, one might argue that his pursuit of wealth at any cost led Jerome to an early grave. Thus not having lived a life of distinction that would qualify him for ancestor status, Jerome is in a position to haunt rather than aid Avey. However, even this haunting moves Avey to mourn the loss of Jay—the man she married before he hardened into the cold, unfeeling Jerome Johnson who seems to have forgotten his roots.

The significance of mourning in the novel is suggested by the title of the second section, "Sleeper's Wake," which implies both an awakening and a wake. Aunt Cuney's visitation calls attention to all that Avey has lost, thus triggering sincere mourning for her husband and their former way of life. Aunt Cuney reminds Avey of a past rich with cultural nuances that had been gradually shed in the pursuit of things. As Avey and her husband progressed economically they removed themselves physically and mentally from the African American community by discarding the rituals that kept them connected to their heritage. "The problem is to reach and maintain a compromise between material excess and spiritual propriety," argues Angelita Reyes in "Politics and Metaphors of Materialism in Paule Marshall's *Praisesong for the Widow* and Toni Morrison's *Tar Baby*" (181). It is not that economic success is not to be valued, but that it should not be unmoored from one's cultural heritage. Avey had not realized that in pursuing class status, she and Jay had exchanged Euro-American values for "those modalities of the African-American connected consciousness. A knowledge of history and mythic heritage allows African-Americans to grapple with the politics of day-to-day living, survival, and collective inspiration without indiscriminately succumbing to another group's value system" (183). Thus, she and Jay inadvertently gave up the very things that were essential to their survival.

Avey first comes to this recognition by acknowledging the transformation of her husband Jay into Jerome Johnson with the "sealed face" (Marshall 133). Jerome would say things that were not like the Jay of old: " 'The trouble with half these Negroes out here is that they spend all their time blaming the white man for everything. . . . If they'd just cut out all the good-timing and get down to some hard work, put their minds to something, they'd get somewhere' " (134–35). He seems to have forgotten his own struggles and all the jobs refused him despite his education. Christian observes, "Jay knows poverty and its possible attendants of dehumanization and spiritual death. Ironically, in trying to avoid such a fate, he and Avey commit a kind of spiritual suicide, for they give up their music, heritage, sensuality, their expression of themselves . . ." ("Ritualistic" 77). The experience of struggling to succeed has deadened Jay to the circumstances of other African Americans, as he seeks to separate himself from the poverty that they share. In order to be successful, he must not be like them and in not being like them he denies his racial heritage. Now, years after Jerome's death, Avey is able to really mourn him, not the Jerome Johnson that she buried but rather the Jay who had "simply ceased to be" (Marshall 136). She is finally able to recognize her loss.

It is these reflections that lead Avey to mourn the rituals she had enjoyed with Jay: "They were things which would have counted for little in the world's eye. To an outsider, some of them would even appear ridiculous, childish, *cullud*" (136). With this last descriptor—cullud— Avey makes the connection between her family rituals and her African

American heritage. The dancing to blues in the living room, listening to gospels, reciting Langston Hughes poems, and summer visits to Ibo Landing were things that kept Avey and Jay connected to their culture: "something in those small rites, an ethos they held in common, had reached back beyond her life and beyond Jay's to join them to the vast unknown lineage that had made their being possible" (137). These rituals could be referred to as *lieux de mémoire* or sites of memory as defined by Pierre Nora. It is in these rituals "where memory crystallizes and secretes itself" (Nora 7). However, Avey did not initially realize the importance of these rites. In discussing the difference between memory and history, Nora observes, "The remnants of experience still lived in the warmth of tradition, in the silence of custom, in the repetition of the ancestral, have been displaced under the pressure of a fundamentally historical sensibility. . . . We speak so much of memory because there is so little of it left" (7). Thus in mourning Jay and their lost rituals, Avey begins to realize that in abandoning the rituals they abandoned a part of themselves.

This then is the point where Avey begins to dimly perceive her own transformation from Avey or Avatara to Avey Johnson: "The names 'Avey' and 'Avatara' were those of someone who was no longer present, and she had become Avey Johnson even in her thoughts, a woman whose face, reflected in a window or mirror, she sometimes failed to recognize" (Marshall 141). Smith-Wright observes that this shift in names is a reflection of Avey's failure to live up to the expectations of her namesake: "It is apparent that Avey is not Avatara, as Cuney had insisted she be called out of respect for Cuney's grandmother, who named the child to be born several generations later. The shortened form of her name is appropriate since she is a lesser incarnation of her namesake" (161). With the recognition of her own shift from Avatara to Avey, Avey realizes that she and Jay gave up too much in pursuit of success and wealth. This then brings to a close Section II, Sleeper's Wake, as Avey both awakes from her illusions and experiences "a wake of memories for her dead husband—her beloved Jay, not the man he became" (Olmsted 259). This double-edged meaning of wake picks up on Gordon's observation that ghosts simultaneously represent loss and hope. Thus, Avey mourns the loss of her husband, but her awakening signals hope for the future.

Thus, Aunt Cuney's visits are not just about loss, but also about hope. The novel opens with Avey running away from the cruise, which is a fitting beginning for the section entitled, "Runagate," for Robert Hayden's poem about runaway slaves. Christian observes, "Like that archetypal slave figure, Avey stumbles from darkness to darkness.

Ironically, her unconscious run for freedom takes her South, physically South to the Caribbean, psychically south to Tatem, South Carolina, while consciously she believes her promised land to be North, her safe, comfortable home in North White Plains" ("Ritualistic" 75). Thus, when Avey is initially prompted by the dream of Aunt Cuney to flee the cruise, she really does not know what she is running to, but she does not feel that she can stay. Eventually, Avey will find herself on the island of Carriacou and her trip there on the *Emmanuel C* is frequently likened to a reverse Middle Passage. However, this symbolic return to Africa actually begins on the *Bianca Pride*. Couser observes "her involuntarily initiated ·quest has led her metaphorically back to Africa. . . . In travelling there 'on water,' she has reenacted, remembered, and memorialized the miraculous mythic flight of the Ibos" (111). Like the Ibos, Avey flees the evil she senses and is ultimately led to a symbolic return home. Thus, her flight, although instigated by a disturbance, is prompted by her ancestor's desire to reconnect her to her history.

Avey had only recently embarked on the Caribbean cruise when she had the disturbing dream. The dream along with her strange sensation of repulsion when she tried to eat the parfait dessert and the strange hallucinations she experiences lead Avey to pack her bags, abandon the cruise, and attempt to return home. Avey does indeed need to experience the healing atmosphere of home, but it is not the White Plains, New York, home to which she must return, but her African home. Busia observes:

> Before Avey can return home she is taken to the farthest reaches of her physical journey, off course, as she sees it, to the island of Carriacou, even called the "outisland" by the people of Grenada, which is one of the most easterly of the Caribbean Islands. That is, it is closest, physically, to the home continent of Africa. This physical closeness is simply a physical representation of the spiritual proximity that the widow is to see manifest. (201)

Dorothy Hamer Denniston makes a similar point in noting that Grenada and Carriacou "are geographically and culturally closer to Africa. It is especially in Carriacou that Avey connects with African rituals that have lain dormant in her consciousness" (132). Olmsted also comments on the significance of Carriacou, noting that "[a]lthough it seems inexplicable to her at the time, [Avey's] unease is deep-rooted and directly caused by her proximity to Carriacou, a tiny island where an annual celebration to honor the Old People is underway" (259). In fact, Olmsted argues that the dream of Aunt Cuney is actually "triggered by the sound of the islanders speaking the Patois that her old Aunt Cuney used to speak" (259). According to Olmsted, "what pulls Avey off the cruise and out of her lethargy is a spiritual and historical force resonating from the place itself, Carriacou" (260). Although this is a plausible explanation, I prefer to see Aunt Cuney rather than the island as the source of this force. I believe Aunt Cuney chose the island as the setting for her message because it allows her to connect the story of Ibo Landing and their family's history with a larger cultural memory. The Caribbean island of Carriacou provides an ideal location for a reverse Middle Passage, which takes Avey from the United States back metaphorically to Africa and reminds her of the importance of Ibo Landing.

What better time and place for a connection with one's ancestor than during the celebration to honor the Old Parents[1]? Clearly, Aunt Cuney's beckoning of Avey to join her in a pilgrimage to Ibo Landing is a means of asking her to honor the Old Parents as Aunt Cuney's grandmother had done and as Aunt Cuney had taught Avey to do. However, rather than honor the Old Parents by taking on the role of griot and passing along the story of Ibo Landing, Avey had turned her back on the lessons of her childhood and disappeared in White Plains, New York. Nevertheless, Avey's disappearance in White Plains is not as much about Avey's physical removal from Tatem as it is a symbol for Avey's complete immersion in white society. Yet according to Wilentz, "By affirming the values and traditions, passed on to her by her great aunt in childhood, Avey comes to accept her African heritage, hidden for years by the hegemony of mainstream cultural values and the ironic pressure to assimilate into a restrictive society" ("If You Surrender" 29). This affirmation of values and traditions, however, hinges on Avey's recognition of what she has lost and renewed determination to honor her ancestors. Brogan claims, "Only by participating in a ritual of mourning in which she incorporates the spirits of the dead does Avey recuperate a denied past and redefine her own ethnic identity" (151). However, this incorporation of her ancestors does not happen immediately following Aunt Cuney's visitation, rather the visitation is preparation for the next stage of Avey's spiritual journey.

This next stage, reflected in Section III of the novel, Lavé Tête, illustrates the combined efforts of ancestral and elder intervention as indicated in the process of culture bearing. Lavé Tête, according to Christian "refers to the Haitian voodoo ceremony in which one is washed clean" ("Ritualistic" 79). In this section of the book, Avey is purged through nausea and excretion in order to prepare her to participate in the Beg Pardon, which will ultimately reconnect Avey to her African past. However, this purging is made possible through the intercession of various elder figures who also serve as culture bearers, those who help to maintain and pass on the culture. At the same time, this role of culture bearer is not limited to living elders. For Reyes, "Marshall clearly indicates, the sustaining values come from the kin who still walk and breathe as well as from the ancestors who have passed on. Furthermore, these values are primarily sustained through the culture-bearer of the community . . ." ("Politics" 182). Reyes identifies Aunt Cuney as "the culture-bearer who reestablishes Avey's spiritual relationship to family, community, and history" (182). Like Reyes, Connor finds a significant role for women culture bearers in Marshall's text. Connor argues, "Paule Marshall demonstrates in her novels how characters and culture transform each other and how black women, as bearers of ancestral wisdom, can witness and give voice to this transformation" (216). As a culture bearer, Aunt Cuney tries to prod Avey to follow in her ancestors' footsteps, but she requires the assistance of living elder culture bearers to fully make her point.

These elder culture bearers include Rosalie Parvay and the women on the *Emmanuel C.* Yet the most interesting elder culture bearer of the text is Lebert Joseph. As I commented earlier, women are often associated with culture bearing. In "Civilizations Underneath: African Heritage as Cultural Discourse in Toni Morrison's *Song of Solomon*," Wilentz notes "the importance of women in transmitting the stories of the past to maintain the culture within an Afrocentric world view . . ." (66). According to Wilentz, "Within an African context, the role of the woman has been that of educator of the children into the culture" (64). This point is confirmed by Filomena Steady, who contends that the African woman "is of intrinsic value in the ideology of many African societies and represents the ultimate value in life, namely the continuation of the group" (32). Although culture bearers are typically depicted as women, Lebert Joseph is a man with androgynous characteristics who seems to change shapes, much like Morrison's character Pilate from *Song of Solomon*. In "The Gospel According to Pilate," Brenda Marshall asserts, "Pilate is outside society, often outside the laws of man, and seemingly outside the laws of nature, and yet she is the most reliable commentator on society, man, and nature. Because she is outside the norm she must at times take on roles to conform to society's expectations, and she is so easily protean because of her total alienation from any of these recognizable roles or identities" (486). These comments are made in reference to the "Aunt Jemima act" Pilate performs to ensure Guitar and Milkman's release from jail. According to Brenda Marshall, "Pilate slips into the shapes and forms that society recognizes when it suits her purpose, as an actress slips into a role" (487). I argue that Lebert Joseph engages in a similar type of shape shifting in order to persuade Avey to participate in the Carriacou excursion. Thus he plays on her sympathies by highlighting his old age and need of a walking stick, whereas at other times he appears to be strong and virile.

Although Pettis describes Lebert Joseph and Aunt Cuney as "Marshall's most elaborately characterized ancestors" (*Toward Wholeness* 118), I classify him as an elder as he is still among the living. However, the fact that Pettis and others have referred to Lebert Joseph as an ancestor is a testament to his importance in Marshall's text as well as an acknowledgment of the fluidity between the roles of elder and ancestor. In Chapter 1, I noted that elders often were thought about as ancestors in the making. In order to achieve ancestor status, one must live a good life, which would entail achieving elder status. Nevertheless, Lebert Joseph's significance is not just about his status as an elder and ancestor in the making, but also about his relationship to culture. His concern about preserving traditions reveals his desire to pass on the wisdom of the ancestors and thus serve as a culture bearer. According to Reyes, "As culture-bearers, women are primary transmitters of the culture and its traditions" ("Politics" 182). However, with Lebert Joseph's concern about those like Avey who can't call their nation, it is clear that he is just as concerned with maintaining culture and tradition. He tells Avey, "People who can't call their nation. For one reason or another they just don' know. Is a hard thing. I don' even like to think about it" (Marshall 175). It is Lebert Joseph who convinces Avey to travel to Carriacou for the Big Drum; however, I believe he is only able to do this because of his own mythical qualities.

Pettis describes him as a "mythical, timeless, sage, androgynous, and futuristic visionar[y]" (*Toward Wholeness* 118). Even Avey's initial meeting with Lebert Joseph is presented in a mystical manner as if she was meant to meet him. She is wandering on the beach and becomes overcome by the heat when she feels drawn into his bar despite the closed sign on the door:

> All she was conscious of as she finally dragged herself to the entrance was that the door stood slightly ajar, and that through the opening there came a cool dark current of air like a hand extended in welcome. And without her having anything to do with it, it seemed, before she could even knock or find the voice to ask if anyone was there, the hand reached out and drew her in. (Marshall 157)

Was this perhaps the influence of Aunt Cuney at work? One might recall that Nana, the elder figure in Julie Dash's *Daughters of the Dust* called on the ancestors for assistance—in this instance perhaps the ancestor is turning to the elder for assistance. Although Lebert Joseph tells Avey that he is closed for the excursion, he does not put her out of the bar but instead explains that he has never missed an excursion because the Long-time People expect him to go and give his remembrance, " 'I tell you, you best remember them!' he cried, fixing Avey Johnson with a gaze that was slowly turning inward. 'If not they'll vex and cause you nothing but trouble. They can turn your life around in a minute, you know. All of a sudden everything start gon' wrong and you don' know the reason' " (165). Here Avey receives the first indication of what has happened to her. She has not remembered her ancestors—the Long-time People or Old Parents as Lebert Joseph calls them—and now everything is going wrong.

In an unusual move for Avey, she finds herself telling Lebert Joseph about her dream and the strange experiences on the cruise ship that led her to get off at Carriacou. Although she tells him that she does not put much store in dreams, she also admits that she wishes she had her mother's dream book to explain her dream with Aunt Cuney. Interestingly, Avey is astonished to find herself speaking so freely to Lebert Joseph. But as Christian notes, "Elders in Africa and the New World Black communities are known for their ability to interpret dreams. It is no wonder Lebert Joseph is able to perform this function" ("Ritualistic" 79). Although Lebert Joseph does not tell Avey what her dream and visions mean, she has a sense that he understands: "He saw how far she had come since leaving the ship and the distance she had yet to go . . ." (Marshall 172). Lebert Joseph's sense of understanding seems to be connected to his association with Papa Legba[2] of Haitian Vodun.

The third section of the novel opens with two epigraphs—one a choral response from Haitian Vodun, "Papa Legba, ouvri barrier pou' mwè"—Papa Legba, open the barrier for me—and the second from Randall Jarrell's poem, "The Woman at the Washington Zoo," "Oh, Bars of my . . . body, open, open!" (148). Critics such as Renu Juneja and James Kingsland contend Lebert Joseph "is very evocatively connected by Marshall to Papa Legba of Vodun, the Ewe god of thresholds and the Yoruba god of crossroads, a messenger of gods to earth, one who links the earthly and the spiritual realms together" (64). Eugenia Collier also links Lebert Joseph with Legba, "guardian of the crossroads where all ways meet. . . . Legba is the liason between man and the gods. . . . Thus Lebert, in his implied role of Legba, contains many linkages: Africa and the Diaspora, the carnate and the spirit worlds; the present generation, the ancestors, and the yet unborn" (312). These linkages also include male and female as Pettis describes Lebert Joseph as androgynous while Henry Louis Gates Jr. observes that "Esu [another name for Papa Legba] is also genderless, or of dual gender, as recorded Yoruba and Fon myths suggest . . ." (29). This notion of Lebert Joseph being of dual gender is particularly apparent when he demonstrates the Juba, a dance typically performed by pairs of women, to Avey. He is described as singing and dancing like someone half his age: "his voice also sounded more youthful. Moreover, it had taken on a noticeably feminine tone. The same was true of his gestures. The hand snapping the invisible skirt back and forth, the thrusting shoulders, the elbow flicking out—all were the movements of a woman" (Marshall 179). In noting Lebert Joseph's transformation into a woman, Missy Dehn Kubitschek asserts, "Even Lebert becomes female during the dance. Clearly, female forces serve as midwives for Avey's rebirth into her true self, Avatara" ("Paule" 52). This emphasis on female forces seems to align with women's association with the role of culture bearers, but also seems to point to the possibility of a more expansive notion of culture bearing.

Although Marshall seems to suggest that men have a role in culture bearing, the significance of women culture bearers in the novel is apparent in Kubitschek's observation that "Although Lebert/Legba secures Avey's presence on Carriacou, the characters who enable her to retain her sense of worth through her purging ordeal, and to participate in the fete, are women" (51). The first of these are the unnamed women on the *Emanuel C.* When Lebert Joseph led Avey to sit with the women, "she experienced a shock of recognition that for a moment made her forget her desire to bolt" (Marshall 193–94). The women reminded her of the presiding mothers of her mother's church, Mount Olivet Baptist, who were responsible for "steady[ing] those taken too violently with the spirit" (194). These women perform a similar service for Avey during the voyage. They are described as speaking to her with "soothing, lilting words full of maternal solicitude" (197). And their voices put her at ease, as "their murmurous voices now set about divesting her of the troubling thoughts, quietly and deftly stripping her of them as if they were so many layers of winter clothing . . ." (197). Her mind is described as unburdened, but physically her stomach and bowels become unburdened as she becomes violently ill during the passage. The women quickly realize that Avey is about to vomit and turn her so that she can retch over the railing of the boat. In response to her retching, they whisper "Bon," or good. In essence, they are encouraging this release. Avey is described as having "some mass of overly rich, undigestible food" and "all of her body's fury was suddenly concentrated there" (207). Then the vomiting shifts to diarrhea, but even to this the women's response is the same: " 'Bon, li bon.' Saying it as if even this final ignominy was a good thing in their eyes" (208–09). In "Embodying Cultural Memory in Paule Marshall's *Praisesong for the Widow*," Susan Rogers claims "Avey's extreme affliction is clearly a purging of the intense bloatedness she has been suffering, brought about by her swallowing of false values" (86). The sight of the *Peach Parfait à la Versailles* initially triggered Avey's sense of indigestion. Her response to this decadent dessert is indicative of a physical aversion to the opulence it represents. For Avey the dessert and her dream of Aunt Cuney "were linked, she sensed, in some obscure but profound way, with her decision to leave" (Marshall 31). These events propel her toward a personal quest, a reverse Middle Passage that allows her to rediscover "what it means to bond with people and with the spirit, and not with *things*" (Reyes, "Politics" 186). Thus, the violent purging during the course of her voyage on the *Emanuel C* is a necessary rite of passage.

After the purging of vomit and diarrhea, Avey has the sensation of other bodies packed around her as if on the Middle Passage. This reverse Middle Passage experience is transformative for Avey because it allows her to see herself as part of a larger history and community rather than the rugged individuals she and Jay became in pursuing economic success. Pettis states, "this experience reestablishes her severed union to her African ancestors and reestablishes her inseparableness from the inarticulate pain of that act" ("Self" 98). As I noted earlier, the tale of the Ibos was meant to maintain this connection, but Avey stopped reciting the tale and appears to have forgotten its significance. Hence, her ancestor, Aunt Cuney, intercedes to forge a renewed connection between Avey and her ancestors. This connection is initially experienced through her body. According to Rogers:

> The first "memory" that surfaces is the earliest possible memory relating to the experience of African Americans. It is a collective rather than individual memory that Avey experiences, initiated by physical experience, and itself a memory of the body. Avey's profoundly disturbing illness conveys the extent of the damage resulting from cultural dislocation created by the forced transition of Africans to America. (86)

While Rogers approaches *Praisesong* via her concern with the problematic depiction of Avey's "body as a repository of memory, as a place where physical sensation echoes emotional feeling" which in turn suggests that her memories of Africa are an essential part of her being while her American identity is merely a social construction, I am concerned with the way in which Avey's ancestor uses the body to remind Avey of her duty to her ancestors. There are moments in the text in which Avey's body appears to remember before her mind can fully process the moment. For example, at the Big Drum when Avey dances the Carriacou Tramp it is as if her body has a mind of its own: "she had slipped without being conscious of it into a step that was something more than just walking" (Marshall 248). Although she is in Carriacou, her mind has actually travelled back in time to Tatem and the Ring Shout. Although this is an instance of embodied memory, this memory was not accessible to Avey before the intercession of her ancestor. It is the disturbing dream with Aunt Cuney that positions Avey to tap into these bodily memories associated with her African heritage.

However, Avey is not able to move beyond her distressing dreams and hallucinations and tap into these ancestral memories until she undergoes this purging that is central to the Lavé Tête section of the novel. Christian notes, "In 'Lavé Tête,' the bars of Avey's body do begin to open, as her mind wipes itself clean" ("Ritualistic" 78). Thus she is prepared for the final section of the book, "The Beg Pardon," in which the ancestors are asked for forgiveness. It is Rosalie Parvay, another female culture bearer, who makes the final preparations for Avey's participation in the Beg Pardon. After her illness on the boat, Avey was brought to Lebert Joseph's daughter's home where Rosalie washed her up and put her to bed. Upon awakening, Rosalie announces that it is time for "a proper wash—down"; however, Avey experiences it as "A laying on of hands" (Marshall 217). In "A Laying On of Hands: Black Women Writers Exploring the Roots of their Folk and Cultural Tradition," Joanne V. Gabbin states:

> The term signifies an ancient practice of using hands in a symbolical act of blessing, healing, and ordination. By its very act it appears to bestow some gift. Some identify the practice with one of the gifts of the Spirit that Paul speaks of in Corinthians. Thus it is associated with the healing power of Christ as he lays his hands on sufferers and they are cured. Others see the practices as central to the African concept that the body and spirit are one. (247)

During the course of the bath, Rosalie is described as washing Avey's body "as if she were a new-born, stretching her limbs the way she did those of her own children so that their limbs would grow straight"

(Christian, "Ritualistic" 81). Rogers comments on this ceremonial cleansing process, noting, "Avey is being attended to as though she is a helpless newborn, perpetuating the idea of rebirth, of beginning again" (88). I would contend that this image of rebirth operates not only as a rite of passage for Avey, but also, like Velma's burst cocoon, is a moment of revision or rethinking regarding what has gone before. For example, Pettis claims, "Spiritual rebirth has empowered her to perpetuate tradition and, perhaps, will invest her with the foresight to reclaim the spiritually bereft" (*Toward Wholeness* 134). The stage has been set for Avey to transform herself and her community. With her rebirth, she is positioned to claim true elder status and serve as a guide and role model for others.

According to Christian, "The bathing ritual also takes Avey through childhood to womanhood" ("Ritualistic" 81). Christian continues, "That Avey is now ready to assume her adult role is emphasized by Rosalie's utterance, 'Bon' (Good), the same word that the presiding mothers had uttered over the sick widow on the *Emanuel C*" (81). However, I contend that Rosalie's "Bon" is not just in response to Avey's arrival at womanhood, but also in response to her flesh awakening to the sensation of her kneading. Rosalie had left Avey's upper legs for last and at that point was confronted with flesh "which had grown thick and inert from years of the long-line girdle" (Marshall 223). The girdle, like the mink stole, suit, and gloves, was meant to restrain Avatara—it was part of the mask that made her Avey Johnson, deracinated and respectable. Rosalie's kneading stimulates Avey's body and her memory as she recalls love making with her husband, Jerome. Avey's recollection, "Just take it from me! Jerome Johnson used to say" (224) also suggests their past tradition of dancing in the living room, which was one of the things that had helped them stay rooted in their African American heritage. Thus, when Rosalie says, "Bon," I argue it is not about Avey's womanhood, but about Avey's preparation to beg pardon from the ancestors and reconnect. At this point, Avey has dropped the various props she has used to distance herself from her ancestors and is thus ready to reconnect with her ancestors and her African heritage.

Avey's spiritual rebirth is reflected in her changed outlook towards the lit candle and plate with roasted corn, placed in the main room of the house as a remembrance to the ancestors. "She had grown uneasy yesterday when he had started talking of such things. Senile, she had thought to herself, or even slightly demented. . . . Today, presented with the candle and the innocent ear of corn on the buffet in the main room . . . she found nothing odd or disconcerting about them" (224–25). In fact, rather than distance herself from the traditions of

Carriacou, Avey begins to see connections to her own traditions: "They were no more strange than the plate of food that used to be placed beside the coffin at funerals in Tatem" (225). It seems as if Avey is no longer invested in distinguishing herself as a tourist, but is instead open to seeing the ties that bind her to these people and to her ancestors.

During the Big Drum ceremony Avey is able to make connections between the Ring Shout of Tatem and the Big Drum of Carriacou. The ceremony, however, did not just remind Avey of Tatem, but also gave her a sense of connection to the people around her that she hadn't experienced since childhood: "she felt the threads, that myriad of shiny, silken, brightly colored threads [. . .] which were thin to the point of invisibility yet as strong as the ropes at Coney Island" (249). This seems to be the message that Aunt Cuney has sought to deliver—the powerful influence of heritage, of ancestors. Avey is also experiencing the power of memory. According to Nora, "Memory is blind to all but the group it binds . . . that memory is by nature multiple and yet specific; collective, plural, and yet individual" (9). The sensation of threads linking her to those around her suggests the power of collective memory. This ancestral influence may not be readily visible, but it is powerful just the same and on deeper reflection it may be seen in practices one engages in without fully recognizing its significance, such as the Ring Shout.

In her essay, "In the Spirit: Dance as Healing Ritual in Paule Marshall's *Praisesong for the Widow*," Paulette Brown-Hinds explores the important role of the Ring Shout:

> These dance rituals, derivatives of the sacred West African Circle Dance, function not only as healing rites but as unique spiritual ties which bind blacks together throughout the diaspora. The circle dance, allegorically employed by Marshall to illustrate a conjunctive diasporic experience, is presumably the central element of West African-based spiritual rituals. The symbolic circle shapes the text, from its use as central metaphor to Marshall's circular narrative structure. (107)

As I noted in the introduction, the circle is the key component of both the Ring Shout and the Kongo cosmogram. Sterling Stuckey argues, "The circle is linked to the most important of all African ceremonies, the burial ceremony" (11). Robert Farris Thompson and Joseph Cornet describe a Bakongo burial ceremony: "A pair of long, narrow *ndungu* drums provide percussion for the mourners, who dance in a broken counter clockwise circle" around the deceased who "lies in state on a textile-decorated bier" (54). Stuckey notes, "Wherever in Africa the counterclockwise dance ceremony was performed—it is called the ring shout in North America—the dancing and singing were directed to the ancestors and gods, the tempo and revolution of the circle quickening during the course of movement" (12). In fact, La Vinia Delois Jennings refers to the Ring Shout as a physical manifestation of the Kongo cosmogram because the "shuffling counterclockwise sacred dance" is "performed to remember familial ancestors . . ." (20). We see this manifested in the Big Drum ceremony as participants dance nation dances as a tribute to their ancestors.

It is clear that Marshall links the Ring Shout of Tatem with the Big Drum of Carriacou, with both rituals sharing the counter clockwise circular movement and implying a Diasporic connection. Brown-Hinds explains:

> The Big Drum ritual, initially performed by Blacks prior to emancipation, like the Ring Shout, was developed from common African traditions. Not much scholarship has been done on the Big Drum ceremony, but what is written does link it to the West African Circle Dance. During slavery, both in the United States and the Caribbean, dance and music become a unifying element for the transported Africans. (113)

In their essay, "The Caribbean-American Connection: A Paradox of Success and Subversion," Juneja and Kingsland address some of the Diasporic issues at play in the novel. In exploring the question, "Why should Marshall come at the recovery of the African past and an alternative system of values through the Caribbean experience," Juneja and Kingsland argue that "There are some cultural and historical reasons which favor the Caribbean as being more connected with the African past" (64). Because the Caribbean continued to bring captives directly from Africa until nearly the end of the slave trade and these enslaved people tended to live in close proximity, Africanisms had a greater chance for survival in the Caribbean than in the United States. Thus, for Juneja and Kingsland the Caribbean setting is an ideal locale for Avey to "relive the Middle Passage, and to reverse it in a fashion" (64). As she crossed the waters from Grenada to Carriacou, Avey's body was purged in preparation for the rituals that would allow her to reconnect with her ancestors—the Beg Pardon and the Big Drum.

According to Brown-Hinds, "During the Beg Pardon, the obligatory introduction held in most Big Drum rites, the household head circles around the ring on his knees, ritually asking the ancestors for forgiveness. During this 'free ring,' no humans are allowed to dance in the ring because it is reserved for the ancestors" (113). The Beg Pardon and Big Drum ceremonies reveal a different conception of life and death. "Contrary to the Western notion of death as the termination of life, death becomes for the people of Carriacou a celebration of the continuity of life . . ." (Connor 232). From the Beg Pardon to the nation dances, the ancestors were called on. During the course of the Big Drum, Avey began to notice a pattern, "Saluting their nations. Summoning the Old Parents. Inviting them to join them in the circle. And invariably they came. A small land crab might suddenly scuttle past the feet of one of the dancers. . . . Sometimes it was nothing more than a moth, a fly, a mosquito. In whimsical disguise they made their presence known" (Marshall 238–39). Marshall describes the Big Drum as "[k]in, visible, metamorphosed and invisible" circling the clearing together (239). In other words, the living and the dead move side by side.

According to Brown-Hinds, "participation in the circle dance is an important step for Avey because it allows her to petition her ancestors, among them Aunt Cuney, for forgiveness from her spiritual and cultural transgressions" (113). I agree that participation in the Beg Pardon and Big Drum are turning points for Avey, but it is not just joining in the celebration that makes the difference, but seeing the tenacity with which they cling to their rituals that affect Avey. Upon seeing how little there was to the Big Drum—what she describes as "the bare bones of a fete"—Avey should have been disappointed by the remnants of the rituals: "All that was left were a few names of what they called nations which they could no longer even pronounce properly, the fragments of a dozen or so songs, the shadowy forms of long-ago dances and rum kegs for drums. The bare bones. The burnt-out ends. And they clung to them with a tenacity she suddenly loved in them and longed for in herself" (Marshall 240).

The Big Drum as performed on Carriacou appears to be a shadow of its earlier grandeur. Wilentz observes, "The festival itself, honoring the dead ancestors and the African nations from whence the slaves came, is a New World ritual based on West African traditions and festivals that exist now only in memory" ("Towards" 15). This notion of a festival exist-ing only in memory and being described as "burnt-out ends" initially seems rather bleak. However, it is the very defense of the remainder of this celebration that is remarkable. Nora asserts,

> The defense by certain minorities, of a privileged memory that has retreated to jealously protected enclaves in this sense intensely illuminates the truth of *lieux de mémoire*—that without commemorative vigilance, history would soon sweep

them away. We buttress our identities upon such bastions, but if what they defended were not threatened there would be no need to build them. (12)

Thus, the Big Drum serves as a *lieux de mémoire*. In "Universalization and its Discontents: Morrison's *Song of Solomon*—A (W)hol(e)y Black Text," Richard Heyman argues, "Only by anchoring his newly found 'memory' on the *lieux de mémoire* of Solomon's Leap can Milkman achieve the synthesis of the past ('where he had been') and the present to create a future ('where he was going')" (385). This same phenomenon is seen in Avey's approach to the Big Drum.

Marshall seems to emphasize the importance of knowing one's past in order to move forward. In her interview with De Veaux, Marshall talks about the importance of going back to Africa: "I'm talking about a psychological and spiritual journey back in order to move forward. You have to psychologically go through the chaos in order to move forward" (128). This is exactly what happens with Avey—she psychologically experiences the Middle Passage and spiritually connects with her ancestors and is now rejuvenated. This sense of rejuvenation is suggested by Kubitschek's reading of the Carriacou rituals, "Rituals reenacting past events with necessarily contemporaneous actors emphasize the characters' awareness of their heritages and their own importance. Myth thus becomes not the distorted history of a dead past but a living embodiment of lasting forces" ("Paule" 45). Avey initially longs for the tenacity of the out-islanders who put so much stock in the Carriacou excursion and Big Drum celebration that they drop what they are doing each year to cling to the "burnt-out ends" of this ritual. However, by the end of the Big Drum, Avey herself is transformed and can now claim this tenacity for herself. Brown-Hinds asserts, "the Big Drum functions as a celebration of renewal and rebirth, or as the death of Avey's old life" (114). Upon feeling those threads of connection between the other dancers and herself, Avey began to really dance. She is described as moving "with a vigor and passion she hadn't felt in years, and with something of the stylishness and sass she had once been known for" (Marshall 249). However, the clearest indication of Avey's rebirth is her reclaiming of her full name, Avatara.

Toward the end of the Big Drum an elderly woman introduces herself to Avey and upon giving her own name, Avey remembers Aunt Cuney's admonition, "whenever anyone in Tatem, even another child, asked her her name she was not to say simply 'Avey,' or even 'Avey Williams.' But always 'Avey, short for Avatara'" (251). Christian maintains, "That Avey now recognizes herself as Avatara, is also essential to the ritual, for in African cosmology it is through *nommo*, through the correct naming of a thing, that it comes into existence. By knowing her proper name, Avey becomes herself" ("Ritualistic" 83). Rogers makes a similar observation in noting the difference between Avey's use of her full name and the shorter nickname: "Avey's full name suggests the idea of an avatar, meaning the manifestation of a deity or the embodiment of a concept. With her name shortened its signification was obscured, its power abbreviated. Her acknowledgment of her name returns the power to connect with the past" (90). In other words, Avey has claimed the fullness of her being by claiming her full name—the name given to her by her ancestor.

She has now reconnected with her ancestors and her heritage. It is this reconnection that allows her to fulfill her great-aunt Cuney's wish that she serve as a griot and pass on the story of Ibo Landing. As she returned home from her unexpected excursion to Carriacou, Avey made plans to sell the house in North White Plains and to set up a summer camp in Tatem and share the story of Ibo Landing with grandchildren and visitors. Olmsted reads Avey's actions as her acknowledgment "that she must take her place as the 'culture-bearer' who will pass on Aunt Cuney's ritual storytelling and keep alive the ancestors memories" (261–62). Just as Lebert Joseph tenaciously holds onto the tradition of the Big Drum ceremony, Avey must hold onto the story of Ibo Landing. These memories of slavery, which the tale of Ibo Landing represents, are now recognized by Avey as an essential component of her history. According to Connor, "Marshall suggests by weaving antebellum legends into her contemporary tale, slavery must be confronted and retrieved for individuals to affirm their selves . . ." (235). Surely, Avey would not now ask why the Ibos did not drown. Her experience in Carriacou allows her to recognize the story of Ibo Landing "as the representation of spiritual understanding and the will to survive and triumph" (Busia 199). Avey can now appreciate why her Aunt Cuney's grandmother, Avatara, would say that her mind would be with the Ibos. Avey's ancestor understood the importance of looking beyond physical restraints and with the assistance of Aunt Cuney's rousing dream, Avey has come to realize that "Reclaiming one's sacred stories is a form of self-recognition and spiritual healing" (Connor 236–37). Avey has undergone a rite of passage and is now willing and able to accept her role as family griot and culture bearer. However, she will be taking on the role of family griot in a different manner than her namesake Avatara or her Aunt Cuney. These foremothers sought to pass on the story of Ibo Landing to the women in the family. Thus Aunt Cuney summoned Avey to Tatem every summer, but not her three brothers.

Avey will not be making this distinction as she plans on summoning her grandsons to Tatem each summer as well as inviting children from Marion's school. This break from a matrilineal form of culture bearing along with Lebert Joseph's depiction as a male culture bearer suggests that Marshall intends for both women and men to take on the role of culture bearing to ensure the health of future generations.

By the end of the novel, Avey's focus is no longer on herself, but on future generations. For Christian, this is in part what makes the novel a praisesong: "it is an African ritual that shows the relationship between the individual and the community by recounting the essence of a life so that future generations may flourish" ("Ritualistic" 83). However, Wilentz takes a slightly different approach to the novel, by calling it "a praisesong to this widow: Avey not only learns to sing the praises of the ancestors but she too, is remembered" ("Towards" 4). Yet, Busia's focus on social transitions and praisesongs seems to best capture the title's allusion:

> For Africans, a praisesong is a particular kind of traditional heroic poem. . . . praisesongs embrace all manner of elaborate poetic form, but are always specifically ceremonial social poems, intended to be sung in public at anniversaries and other celebrations, including the funerals of the great. . . . they can also be sung to mark social transition. Sung as a part of rites of passage, they mark the upward movement of a person from one group to the next. (198)

By assuming the griot's mantle, Avey is showing her desire to guide the younger generations. In other words, she has assumed the elder's responsibility. The novel's plot seems to replicate the concepts described by Fu-Kiau's theory of the Four Vees discussed in the introduction. At the beginning of the text, Avey although she has lived a number of years has not achieved the Tukula or elder stage. Rather than provide guidance to her children, she is a source of frustration to her youngest daughter, Marion, who can't understand why her mother would "go on some meaningless cruise with a bunch of white folks anyway" (Marshall 13). Marion's accusation that Avey does not even like one of her companions suggests that Avey may not even be in touch with her own feelings. Thus, Avey seems to be mired in the Kala or first stage of life and unable to transition fully to the next stage, which Fu-Kiau describes as "the center of the cone of power and leadership" (27). We also see elements of the Luvèmba stage, which refers to dying and re-entering the ancestors' world. Aunt Cuney is in the Luvèmba stage as she has joined the realm of the ancestors and unlike those in the Musoni stage, she is still remembered. The Ring Shout in Tatem and the Big Drum of Carriacou also reflect a belief in these stages of life rather than a sharp distinction between the living and the dead. Marshall's novel demonstrates Fu-Kiau's contention that "Man is a second sun rising and setting around the earth" (25). The various characters in the text illustrate points on the Kongo cosmogram indicating a life cycle that might be depicted as a counterclockwise circular movement beginning with dawn and moving toward midnight. In asking Avey to honor the Old Parents, the Long-time People, the ancestors, Aunt Cuney is demonstrating that the dead are not dead and indeed have a role to play in this world.

In the next two chapters, "Ancestral Disturbances in *Stigmata*" and "*Beloved*—A Ghost Story with an Ogbanje Twist," I will continue this discussion of ancestors, arguing that the ancestral presence is generally beneficial unless the ancestor is not truly an ancestor but a stunted ancestor who has not achieved true ancestor status. Although these next novels take a different approach to the ancestor, like *Praisesong*, slavery's lingering effects concern them. In fact, as contemporary novels of slavery *Stigmata* and *Beloved* are even more directly concerned with slavery's legacy than *Praisesong* which relies on slavery for its subtext, but is not as directly addressed as these novels which depict direct descendants of former slaves and former slaves. Despite the different degree with which slavery is referenced by these novels, each of the authors seems to agree that one cannot turn one's back on this history and in fact it is the role of the ancestor to ensure one's history is not forgotten.

3

Ancestral Disturbances in *Stigmata*

Alesia Perry's *Stigmata* opens in Atlanta in 1994 with Lizzie having been in her latest mental institution for the previous two years. She finds it funny that the doctor thinks he has cured her madness because she knows there is no cure for her condition. After fourteen years "and some well-acted moments of sanity," she is headed home to Tuskegee (Perry 6). It is clear from the outset that Lizzie is playing the role of the cured patient. However, what becomes increasingly clear is that her diagnosis of insanity may have been a misreading of slavery's scars.

The story unfolds in a nonlinear format of multilayered flashbacks, present tense, and excerpts from her great-great-grandmother's journal. A sense of circularity is introduced by the first entry from Ayo's diary, dated December 26, 1898, in which Ayo explains to Lizzie's great-grandmother, Joy, why she wants her to record her history. Ayo's insistence in documenting her story is her first attempt to rewrite the legacy of slavery. With enslavement, Ayo was expected to forget her African past, but the first thing Ayo does with her journal is to deny her slave name and claim her African name: "'Bessie ain't my name. . . . My name Ayo'" (7). Bessie, we assume is the name Ayo was given by her owners, but this is her story, not theirs. After stating that her true name is Ayo, not Bessie, Ayo notes the importance of remembering who one is and what one means to the world: "'I come from a long line of forever people. We are forever. Here at the bottom of heaven we live in the circle. We back and gone and back again'" (7). African religion authority, John Mbiti notes in *Introduction to African Religion* that Africans view the universe as eternal, which is symbolized through the use of circles (37). The circle illustrates the African concept of time, which is synchronic or cyclical in nature. This cyclical sense of time is also apparent in African religious beliefs "that human life does not terminate at the death of the individual, but continues beyond death" (75). Ayo uses this continuity to tell a story that can't be sufficiently told by entries in a diary. As the novel progresses, we find Perry appearing to draw on African notions of reincarnation as Ayo must reach out from the grave in order to tell her story. She reaches out to her granddaughter and great-great-granddaughter who must pick up the thread and help their foremother tell this unspeakable tale. The integrative nature of this process is explained by Kathleen Brogran, "In tale after tale of cultural haunting, mourning is an essentially incorporative process through which the living struggle to integrate the dead in the new reality (and the new identities) they construct. These stories work to reconnect experience to memory by redefining the legacy bequeathed by earlier generations" (171). Thus, Lizzie finds herself inhabiting the lives of her foremothers as a means of accessing their memories as Ayo and Grace attempt to rewrite the legacy of slavery.

In *Ghostly Matters: Haunting and the Sociological Imagination*, Avery Gordon asserts, "To write stories concerning exclusions and invisibilities is to write ghost stories. To write ghost stories implies that ghosts are real, that is to say that they produce material effects" (17). *Stigmata* is a ghost story prompted by the erasures of slavery. The plot of the novel focuses on the enslavement of Ayo and the ripple effects of this traumatic event on ensuing generations: her daughter Joy, her granddaughter Grace, her great-granddaughter Sarah, and great-great-granddaughter Lizzie. This notion of slavery as trauma is reflected in Abena P. A. Busia's contention that Paule Marshall's *Praisesong for the Widow* approaches the dispersal of African peoples as trauma "repeated anew in the lives of her lost children" (197). In *Cultural Trauma: Slavery and the Formation of African American Identity*, Ron Eyerman explores slavery as a cultural trauma, which he defines as "a collective memory, a form of remembrance that grounded the identity-formation of a people" (1). Thus like *Praisesong for the Widow*, *Stigmata* is motivated by an ancestral concern with memory. This ancestral concern is not surprising considering the fact that ancestors only remain among the living dead while they are remembered. In fact, Pierre Nora's research on sites of memory asserts that "the most fundamental purpose of the *lieux de mémoire* is to stop time, to block the work of forgetting, to establish a state of things, to immortalize death, to materialize the immaterial" (19). *Stigmata*'s ancestor, Ayo, disturbs her descendants with her memories to ensure that she and her story of enslavement are not forgotten and that she is the one who determines the meaning of her experience.

The fact that the deceased Ayo cannot simply rest in peace but instead must interact with her descendants is indicative of literary critic Ashraf Rushdy's contention that "historical events have enduring afterlives" (6). I argue that Ayo's afterlife cannot be peaceful until she is able to correct the exclusions and invisibilities surrounding her life as a result of her enslavement. Thus, I would situate Ayo in the Luvèmba stage as described by Bunseki Fu-Kiau because although she has departed this world, she is still remembered by her descendants and is actively involved in their lives. In his introduction to *Africanisms in American Cultures*, Joseph E. Holloway observes that "death was not considered an end of life but the beginning of a new life as an ancestor. In other words, death did not signal a break with the community of the living; it represented a continuity between the communities of the living and the dead" (10). Ayo remains an active member of her extended family. Although Ayo is deceased, she is not forgotten.

However, the way in which Ayo's descendants remember her is not one's typical understanding of remembrance, but more in line with Toni Morrison's notion of "rememory." Rushdy defines rememory as "a mental-spatial structure where what happened in one place at one time to one person becomes experientially available at another time for another person" (6). This is what occurs when Ayo reaches across the grave to her descendants—they do not merely remember their foremother; Grace and Lizzie literally relive moments of Ayo's life. Thus, I argue that *Stigmata* conforms to Rushdy's definition of a palimpsest narrative in that it "represents the effects of a slave past on a personal present by showing how ancestors' lives act as a palimpsest on the lives of their contemporary progeny" (9). Thus, despite her death, Ayo continues to impact the lives of her descendants, particularly her granddaughter, Grace, and her great-great-granddaughter, Lizzie. And as noted by Gordon, Ayo's presence produces material effects, the most apparent being the stigmata or scars that cover Lizzie's body. These scars serve as testimony regarding Ayo's experiences in slavery. Although she sought to pass on her story through a diary that she narrates to her daughter, Joy, the diary cannot fully capture her harrowing tale. In her essay, "Witnessing to Heal the Self in Gayle Jones's *Corregidora* and Phyllis Alesia Perry's *Stigmata*," Camille Passalacqua argues that "familial memories of slavery come through the injured bodies, which consequently access a past that often exceeds language's ability to articulate such experiences of severe violation" (140). Thus Ayo crosses the Kalûnga line separating the living and the dead in order to share her story in a visceral way as words cannot explain the depth of her experiences and she wants to ensure that her story is shared and understood.

According to Adama and Naomi Doumbia, authors of *The Way of the Elders: West African Spirituality & Tradition*, "Our ancestors maintain their role in our families and lives, more significantly than when they were physically present" (9). Thus the notion of spirit visitation is welcomed; however, Perry's depiction of the ancestral presence moves beyond mere visitation as Ayo seems to pass on pieces of herself to her descendants. In *Religion in Africa*, Geoffrey Parrinder comments on the seemingly contradictory nature of African conceptions of reincarnation:

> Ancestors are reincarnated yet offerings are still made to them at their graves; they are in heaven, yet back on earth, and they may enter not only one body but perhaps several. . . . So it is not the single "soul" of the ancestor that passes from one embodiment to another in an endless round or chain of existence. Rather it is the "ontological influence," as Tempels calls it, which a forefather exerts on his grandson or grandsons, it is the immortal vitality that continues to reinforce and uplift. (85)

This is exactly what we see at work in *Stigmata*, as it becomes increasingly clear that Ayo's descendants are not only being visited by Ayo but inhabiting her life. Ayo, Grace, and Lizzie share a matrilineal line of descent that allows them to essentially inherit their foremothers' lives, particularly their painful memories. In fact, I believe it is the emphasis on painful memories which overshadows Ayo's role as an ancestral presence. For instance, Doumbia and Doumbia state ancestors "are always available to us, offering their guidance and protection" (9). This conception of guidance and protection implies a beneficial ancestral presence; however, Ayo's visits to her descendants are clearly disruptive, which makes the protective nature of her visit less apparent.

Unlike the prodding that Avey receives from her Aunt Cuney in *Praisesong for the Widow*, which seems like good intentioned ancestral intercession, the ancestral disturbances depicted in *Stigmata* may initially seem like unwarranted haunting, which leave the characters debilitated—Grace fears going insane in response to her foremother Ayo's visitations and Lizzie is institutionalized after visions and visitations by Grace and Ayo appear to drive her to a suicide attempt. However, I assert that Perry, like other authors of contemporary novels of slavery such as Toni Morrison (*Beloved*), Octavia Butler (*Kindred*), and Gayle Jones (*Corregidora*), does not return to the site of slavery in order to emphasize its devastating effects, but instead uses her writing as a means to heal the wounds of slavery. Thus, the ancestral disturbances experienced by

Grace and Lizzie serve as a means to rewrite the legacy of slavery. The condition of slavery is often seen as one that eradicated ties to African homelands and traditions and left a broken or damaged person; however, we see in *Stigmata* an insistence on remembering not just the harm inflicted by slavery, but a determination to cling to scraps of African heritage as well. As with other contemporary novels of slavery, *Stigmata* is concerned with the role of memory. At different points in the narrative, Ayo assures her daughter Joy that she remembers. Author of *Black Time: Fiction of Africa, the Caribbean, and the United States,* Bonnie J. Barthold argues, "Memory serves not only the continuity of personal experience but the continuity of the culture. Implicit in this conjunction of the personal and the cultural is an affirmation of community, at least a tentative echo of a traditional Africa in which temporal continuity signaled well-being for the community as well as the individual" (94). Thus Ayo's determination to remember and to pass on her experiences to her descendants is a testament to the will to survive. Ayo may be physically damaged, but she refuses to be mentally broken. Slavery then becomes a legacy of survival, not defeat. Gordon notes that "ghost stories . . . not only repair representational mistakes, but also strive to understand the conditions under which a memory was produced in the first place, toward a countermemory, for the future" (22). Thus Ayo returns from the grave in order to bring her descendants back to the original site of her trauma as a first step toward understanding and then rewriting the story of her enslavement from her perspective, not from that of the slave owner. As a slave, Ayo was rendered completely dependent on her master. She could claim nothing herself, not her name, not her issue, but with freedom Ayo has the ability to set the record straight, even from the grave. Ayo's rewriting of her enslavement will also allow her family to heal from generational wounds related to her initial abduction.

A number of critics have approached *Stigmata* via the lens of trauma theory because slavery can be seen as what Dominick LaCapra refers to as a founding trauma, which becomes the basis for individual or group identity (23). For example, in "A Relative Pain: The Rape of History in Octavia Butler's *Kindred* and Phyllis Alesia Perry's *Stigmata*, Lisa Long draws on trauma theorist Cathy Caruth to argue that the authors utilize "the intimacy and immediacy of their protagonists' pain as strategies to obscure the distance of a traumatic history" (462). In "Trauma Narrative, Memorialization, and Mourning in Phyllis Alesia Perry's *Stigmata*," Corinne Duboin uses such trauma specialists as Caruth, LaCapra, and Judith Lewis Herman to assert that self-writing and storytelling become "liberating space[s] of resistance, reclamation,

and rehabilitation" in the face of "the transgenerational traumatic memory of slavery and the Middle Passage" (284). Drawing on the work of
Caruth, Herman, and Dori Laub, Camille Passalacqua focuses instead on
the black female body's role in the "integrative process of recuperation
and healing from trauma" of "a familial past rooted in slavery" (139).
However, Lisa Woolfork's *Embodying American Slavery in Contemporary
Culture* attempts to use "a distinctly African American trauma theory"
due to its equal interest in the mind and the body (8). According to
Woolfork, "bodily epistemology is a representational strategy that uses
the body of a present-day protagonist to register the traumatic slave
past" (2). Although my particular concern is with the ancestor and her
desire to connect with her descendants in order to rewrite her legacy
of slavery, I incorporate trauma theory in my discussion because it is
such a salient aspect of current discussions of *Stigmata*.

"According to the *Comprehensive Textbook of Psychiatry*, the common denominator of psychological trauma is a feeling of 'intense fear,
helplessness, loss of control, and the threat of annihilation'" (qtd. in
Herman 33). This definition of trauma certainly encapsulates Ayo's experiences of kidnapping and enslavement. However, Perry does not focus
on Ayo's trauma as much as her recovery. Herman, a psychiatrist, notes,
"The fundamental stages of recovery are establishing safety, reconstructing the trauma story, and restoring the connection between survivors
and their community" (3). The narrative of *Stigmata* addresses these
latter two components. However, they are achieved via the intercession
of the ancestor. Ayo reaches out from the dead in order to have her story
heard, but one of the most significant components to telling her story
is the promotion of familial healing, as Sarah comes to terms with her
mother's abandonment, which was part of the family's legacy of slavery.

The lives of Ayo, Grace, and Lizzie become intertwined in a matri-
lineal legacy of slavery as Ayo and her descendants attempt to deal
with Ayo's traumatic enslavement and its aftermath. Herman observes,
"Sharing the traumatic experience with others is a precondition for the
restitution of a sense of a meaningful world" (70). As previously noted,
Ayo begins to do this by dictating her diary to Joy; however, as I explain
later this process is not completely satisfying and thus after her death
Ayo tries to share her story with her granddaughter, Grace.[1] Grace, in
turn, passes on the story after her death to her granddaughter, Lizzie and
thus begins a tradition of quilting as a form of storytelling and testifying.

At the age of fourteen, Lizzie inherited her grandmother's quilt
and her great-great-grandmother's papers. Grace left instructions to give
her trunk not to one of her daughters, but to a granddaughter who had
not even been born. Lizzie's father says, "I think your Grandma Grace
must have had some kind of premonition about you" (Perry, *Stigmata*

23). This ability to know the future seems to be an inherited trait, as Ayo also predicted the birth of Joy's long-awaited first child. Not only does she predict Grace's birth, but she also foretells her ability to see into the future. In the March 22, 1899 diary entry, Ayo says of the yet unborn Grace, "She cant get here cause Im in the way she say. But when Im gone she come to take my place. She gon know things the one that's comin" (34). Ayo's prediction of Grace's birth and Grace's injunction to leave her trunk to a granddaughter who had not yet been born echo Aunt Cuney's anticipation of Avey's birth in *Praisesong for the Widow*. Like Avey, Grace and Lizzie are expected to join a matri-lineal line of culture bearers. They are meant to pass on Ayo's story. Ayo dies the same year Grace is born, which suggests that Grace does indeed come to take Ayo's place and with it she inherits Ayo's slavery experience.

Long, notes that "It is significant that in *Stigmata* the 'possession' skips generations from grandmother to granddaughter, so that the woman who suffers the Middle Passage and slavery never visits that experience on her own daughter. Still, the further from slavery one moves, the more pain those granddaughters must bear" (473). I do not believe this skipping of generations is incidental, but is in fact a rewriting of *partus sequitur ventrem*—the U.S. legal doctrine that proscribed that a child follows the condition of the mother. Within the bounds of slavery, the mother essentially passed on the condition of slavery to her child. However, the foremothers' refusal to visit or haunt their own daughters may be read as a condemnation of a practice intended to undermine maternity. For example, in his discussion of slavery as social death, Orlando Patterson contends, "The incapacity to make any claims of birth or to pass on such claims is considered a natural injustice among all peoples, so that those who are obliged to suffer it had to be regarded as somehow socially dead" (8). However, just as enslaved Africans disputed this disruption of kin networks by creating their own, Ayo and her descendants talk back to the notion of *partus sequitur ventrem* by instituting the skipping of generations with the possession. While enslaved, Ayo might have bequeathed her slave status, but as a free woman she can determine who will inherit her memories of slavery. Thus while Lizzie must attend to both her great-great-grandmother Ayo and her grandmother Grace's experiences, Grace only had to contend with her grandmother Ayo's and her daughter Sarah is spared any visions or visitations. Although *partus sequitur ventrem* essentially denied the slave mother's ability to save her child, by skipping generations with the possession, these women are able to spare their daughters pain. Hence, Ayo, Grace, and Lizzie form a matri-lineal line of descent in which every other generation is bestowed with the gift of second sight, which allows them to see and experience the lives of their foremothers.

Lizzie's visions of her foremothers seem to be the triggered by Grace's quilt. Although, Lizzie does not at first understand the dreams she begins to have while sleeping under her inherited quilt, she instinctively recognizes the connection between her life and the pictures on the quilt. However, her mother, Sarah, quickly dismisses the significance of the quilt, " 'Just some pictures stuck to a background. No rhyme or reason" (Perry, *Stigmata* 22). Yet, Lizzie has a visceral response to the quilt, as she realizes the pictures have meaning, "It's a story. My skin tingles just below the surface" (23). Lizzie recognizes the pictures as her story because she describes herself sleeping under the quilt as sleeping "underneath the story of my life" (24). She dreams of Ayo's life in Africa, going to market with her mother, but she has called this her life. Lizzie's acceptance of Ayo's life as her own is reflective of Mbiti's contention "[i]n some societies it is believed that the living-dead are reincarnated in part . . ." (*African* 130). However, this is no ordinary dream, as she wakes up with dust on her feet. The dust, like the searing pain and bleeding sores which will come later, is a tangible indication that Lizzie's dreams or visions are real events. According to Gordon, "The ghost makes itself known to us through haunting and pulls us affectively into a structure of feeling of a reality we came to experience as a recognition. Haunting recognition is a special way of knowing what has happened or is happening" (63). Although Lizzie's therapists will eventually dismiss dreams such as these as merely a result of Lizzie's active imagination, Lizzie is actually recognizing an aspect of her foremother's history. As these visions intensify, Lizzie comes to experience the horrors of her foremother's enslavement despite the fact that slavery has been over for generations. "The presence of the ghost informs us that the over and done with 'extremity' of a domestic and international slavery has not entirely gone away, even if it seems to have passed into the register of history and symbol" (168). Thus, Perry uses Lizzie to illustrate the continuing legacy of slavery even for those who were never enslaved. Lizzie is able to experience Ayo's enslavement as well as its effect on Grace, Ayo's granddaughter and Lizzie's grandmother.

Lizzie and Grace both see visions of their ancestors and experience what Long describes as possession. Although possession seems like a one-way process in which the ancestor controls her descendant; Mbiti includes it among the practices used by people to recognize the presence of the departed. "Thus in African life, the departed are not readily forgotten. . . . Through rituals, dreams, visions, possessions and names they are recalled and respected. . . . The departed are considered to be still alive, and people show by these practices that they recognize their presence" (Mbiti, *Introduction* 130). This recognition of her ancestors seems indicative of Lizzie's curiosity about her ancestors despite the unsettling nature of the visitations. However, the ability to crisscross space and time to inhabit the past and present is generally not seen as a gift but as a form of madness. In fact, it is the fear of being put in an asylum that leads Grace to abandon her husband and children. Ayo's memories invade Grace and she believes she has lost her mind because she knows things she should not know and feels excruciating pain for no apparent reason. Grace realizes that if she stays, her husband will be forced to commit her, and her mother and sisters will not be able to help her. Although Grace ran away to avoid an insane asylum, Lizzie is institutionalized for fourteen years before faking her recovery. Upon her release, however, she picks up where Grace left off. Just as Grace was compelled to record her Grandmother Ayo's life story through a quilt, Lizzie must tell Grace's story through a new quilt. This passing on of her foremother's story will not end with Lizzie, as she realizes the quilt's fabric has to last long enough for the next storyteller. Lizzie has joined a long line of women who refuse to let the painful history of slavery be forgotten. Thus, the rewriting of her enslavement begins with Ayo's diary and continues with the story quilts of her descendants, Grace and Lizzie. Through these quilts, Lizzie and Grace serve as culture bearers by passing on the familial history. It is significant that like Ayo's diary these quilts are tangible objects. Nora contends, "Modern memory is, above all, archival. It relies entirely on the materiality of the trace, the immediacy of the recording, the visibility of the image" (13). The granddaughter and the great-great-granddaughter are driven to quilting in order to document and make sense of their visions and scars.

Thus, the marks Lizzie bears on her arms and legs are not only symbolic of the manacles worn by Ayo, but also serve as a testament to the will to remember. Interestingly, *Praisesong for the Widow*'s Avey describes Aunt Cuney's grasp as being like a manacle. Critic Susan Rogers, observes, "The image of the manacle here implies Avey's feeling that her aunt wants to chain her to the past, to prevent her breaking free from memory. . . . The manacle also clearly signifies the memory of slavery which she is trying to ignore" (81). Whereas Avey tries to hide from the past, Ayo insists that her descendants remember the past by inscribing their bodies with her memories. The scars Ayo transfers to her granddaughters testify to Ayo's experience. The scars Lizzie bears, like the quilts and diary, are *lieux de mémoire* or sites of memory. "*Lieux de mémoire* are created by a play of memory and history, an interaction of two factors that results in their reciprocal overdetermination. To begin with, there must be a will to remember. If we abandon this criterion, we would quickly drift into admitting virtually everything as worthy of remembrance" (Nora 19). Through the scars or stigmata, Ayo is ensuring that her progeny remember her enslavement. Just as Ayo before her chose to remember, Lizzie's very body demands that the horrors of slavery never be forgotten. When Father Tom asks Lizzie how she got the scars around her wrists, she responds, " 'A legacy. Two lifetimes ago. I was a slave then' " (Perry, *Stigmata* 212). Earlier in their conversation, she explained, " 'My trouble is, Father, that I'm an old soul in a young body' " (211). She has tried to explain her visions to many doctors only to have them dismissed as fantasies brought on by the reading of her great-great-grandmother's diary. Yet she has no way of explaining how she knows things about the past that she could not possibly know without having been there herself.

Yet, her Aunt Eva considers Lizzie lucky because she has been here before. Eva sees her sister Grace in Lizzie and knows about her visions of Ayo, but for Eva reincarnation is a given, as she believes "all of us have been around once or twice" (117). Ayo seems to share this sentiment, as she recounts a memory of her mother, "*This is the hand of my mother*, she says. *And of my grandmother. Petals of the flower. Your life is many lives*" (176). The multiplicity of Lizzie's life is reflected by the scars on her wrists, ankles, and back, as these scars speak of the horrors endured not by Lizzie, but by her foremother. Although Lizzie's therapists dismiss the possibility of reincarnation, reincarnation is central to African belief systems. Historian, Margaret Washington argues, "All African ethnic groups believed in life beyond physical death" (168). For example, "Using the sun through its course around the earth, the BaKongo pointed out the four stages that make up one's life cycle: rising (birth, beginning or regrowth), ascendancy (maturity and responsibility), setting (death and transformation), and midnight (existence in the other world and eventual rebirth)" (166). Yet, Lizzie's doctors have told her that reincarnation is not real, and so she has pretended that she cut her own wrists and ankles, but for Lizzie, reincarnation is real and her scars are stigmata, a physical trauma to remind her of a past not to be forgotten. Woolfork observes:

> Ayo's wounds do not correspond to those of Christ's cru-
> cifixion but are instead marks of her capture, Middle Pas-
> sage, and enslavement: circular raised scars on her wrists and
> ankles, a maze of whip scars on her back. This substitution
> suggests new conceptions of the black female body, trauma,
> and history. Perry's revision of the stigmatic concept explores
> one way to redeem the black female body and its historical

experience. . . . [T]his sanctification of the black body is part
of a broader effort to remember slavery and its legacy. (47)

It is via these scars that Lizzie is meant to understand her foremother's
traumatic experience with slavery—an experience so profound that it
cannot be captured by the written word.

Initially, Lizzie does not have a word to describe the connection
she experiences with her ancestor, Ayo. In a moment of frustrated sar-
casm, she displays her scarred back to her psychiatrist, Dr. Brun, and
tells her, " 'what you're looking at was rather commonplace back then.
Scars like these. That's the thing, Doctor, I'm just a typical nineteenth-
century nigger with an extraordinary gift. The gift of memory' " (204).
This reference again highlights the significance of memory for *Stigmata*
and other contemporary novels of slavery. In "Memory Work in Octavia
Butler's *Kindred* and Women's Neo-slave Narratives," Guiliano Bettanin
addresses the complex relationship between memory and history. He
notes that neo-slave narratives:[2]

> mean to be innovative as they seek to rediscover and rewrite
> a significant part of history that was deliberately forgotten and
> denied. . . . Yet, we must remember that while the original
> slave narratives aimed to recover history, neo-slave narratives
> are based on a re-invention of history, a re-invention which is
> conscious of the principle that every narration of history, be
> it a chronicle or a piece of fiction, was born from a process
> of interpretation from which it cannot be separated. (96)

Drawing on Aleida Assmann's work on functional memory and archival
memory, Bettanin suggests:

> we can interpret the history of African American people under
> slavery as a part of archival memory that was not included,
> for political, prejudicial, racist reasons, into the functional
> memory that constituted the basis of the individuality of the
> American nation. Yet that history that was denied an active
> function in shaping the nation's identity and future persisted
> in the archival memory and was documented in the historical
> reports constituted by the original slave narratives. What the
> revisionist historiography and the fictional recovery of the
> slave narratives do is to use a particular form of functional
> memory, consisting of *delegitimation*. Through this form a

> social (or political) force of resistance conserves a memory different from official history and keeps it until this same force manages to express that memory freely and change, or even subvert, official history. (97)

Thus, Ayo's diary and Grace and Lizzie's quilts are examples of archival memory that seek to intercede on functional memory. Yet it is Ayo's scars that she transmits across generations, that have the greatest affect. Earlier, I noted Parrinder's explanation of African reincarnation that allowed for the transmission of immortal vitality; however, Mbiti points out that some societies believe "physical characteristics are 're-born' in their descendants" (*African* 130). Although we typically think of fore-bears passing on such physical traits as height, hair color, and dimples, Ayo transmits hideous scars from her enslavement. The wounds on Lizzie literally scream for attention, but they are inexplicable to most who attempt to read them. Just as Sarah had dismissed Grace's story quilt as lacking meaning because she could not see Ayo's life story depicted on it, Lizzie's scars are misread. They are not seen as sores from manacles or whips because that time is supposedly past. They only become legible when one recognizes the presence of the ancestor and the enduring effects of history.

It is not until a discussion with a Catholic priest that Lizzie learns about stigmata and realizes that there is a precedent for what she is experiencing. Father Tom tells Lizzie about a monk wounded like Christ's crucifixion, "It's called stigmata, child. That's what you have" (Perry, *Stigmata* 213). Although Perry does not name the monk, this appears to be a reference to Saint Francis of Assisi.[3] St. Bonaventure, one of St. Francis' early biographers read his stigmata "as an indicator of an inner condition" (Kiely 32). I believe this is how Perry intends for her readers to read the scars on Lizzie's body—they are representative of her inner turmoil. Robert Kiely observes, "For Christians, the wounds of the crucified Christ are the paradigm of transformative stigmata, marks of punishment and pain reread as signs of healing and salvation" (21). It is this type of rereading that Lizzie is able to do once she has a word for what is happening to her body. Rather than merely thinking of herself as crazy, Lizzie can learn from her body and her ancestor. Although Father Tom is not sure if Lizzie is experiencing reincarnation, he does not think she is crazy, but is in fact in the presence of her ancestor. He tells her, " 'this ancestor, is with you in some way, just as Christ was with the monk. The merging of spirits and all that' " (Perry, *Stigmata* 213). Father Tom suggests, " 'Maybe you're marked so you won't forget this time, so you will remember and move on' " (213). Father Tom's remarks imply that the stigmata is not just about remembering, but working through these memories. It is almost as if Ayo has had three chances to contend with these memories: first as Ayo, then as Grace, and now as Lizzie. In fact, recognizing the importance of remembering seems to be what leads Lizzie from apparent mental illness to healing and wholeness. It is almost as if the repression of memory or its denial is the cause of Lizzie's anguish, but once she is willing to remember she is in a position to heal.

However, this movement from illness to healing is not easy. Lizzie spends fourteen years in mental institutions contending with a trauma she and her doctors cannot comprehend. Psychotherapist Laura S. Brown, notes that a key aspect to the definition of a traumatic event according to the *Diagnostic and Statistical Manual Third Edition-Revised* (DSM III-R) is that " 'The person has experienced an event that is outside the range of human experience' " (qtd. in Brown 100). Clearly what Lizzie is experiencing as she flashes back in time to the lives of her foremothers is beyond the pale of human experience, as was the initial experience of slavery by Ayo which triggers these episodes for her descendants, Grace and Lizzie. "The trauma is a repeated suffering of the event, but it is also a continual leaving of its site" (Caruth, "Introduction" 10). Part of the trauma for both Lizzie and Grace is that they are yanked back and forth between their worlds and the world(s) of their ancestor(s). Grace and Lizzie have no control over when they will be snatched from their lives into the past and Lizzie may be thrown into either Grace or Ayo's experiences. And unlike Ayo who accepts reincarnation and conceives of herself as "from a long line of forever people," Grace and Lizzie seem to have no knowledge regarding African beliefs about reincarnation (Perry, *Stigmata* 7). Thus, these moments are quite disconcerting to say the least. Passalacqua observes, "The past and present occur simultaneously, which suggests that Lizzie cannot escape the past. . . ." (145). Nor does inhabiting these moments of their ancestor's life mean that Lizzie and Grace fully understand their foremother. They are just as perplexed by Ayo's predicament as Ayo must have been. Psychiatrist Dori Laub and psychologist Nanette Auerhahn have argued that "since neither culture nor experience provide structures for formulating acts of massive aggression, survivors cannot articulate trauma, even to themselves. . . . Close to the experience, survivors are captive observers who can only repeat it. They cannot make sense of it; they cannot know it cognitively" (288). Thus even though Grace and Lizzie relive Ayo's experiences, they cannot protect Ayo; they can merely share her pain and confusion, but at a distance. These visions or memories are confused in their minds. Thus reflecting Cathy Caruth's observation, "The traumatized, we might say, carry an impossible history within them, or they become themselves the symptom of a history that they cannot entirely possess" ("Introduction" 5). Thus, Grace and Lizzie also display the symptoms of Ayo who endured the horrors of the Middle Passage, but they cannot fully grasp what is happening to them.

Ayo's painful history begins this matrilineal legacy of cultural trauma. Interestingly, Laub and Auerhahn note a connection between trauma and familial dysfunction, "as trauma disrupts the link between self and empathic other, a link first established by the expectation of mutual responsiveness in the mother–child bond and 'objectified' in the maternal introject" (287).[4] For Laub and Auerhahn, trauma is the "absence of a mothering function" (287) to prevent trauma, which is akin to what is experienced by Ayo and her descendants. Ayo's mother could not prevent her abduction and Ayo and Grace cannot shield their granddaughter(s) from Ayo's painful memories. In *Scarring the Black Body: Race and Representation in African American Literature*, Carol E. Henderson argues if one is to understand "the generational 'begetting' of cultural wounds, one must return to the figure of the black mother" (14). This brings one back to Laura Doyle's point of the precarious position of the black mother as "maker and marker of boundaries" (27). This role places her in the unenviable position of being "the instrument and embodiment of their oppression" (33). This is why the skipping of generations for the possession is so significant. I read this skipping of generations as an attempt to respond to this problematic positioning of the black mother. Although the sharing of her story of enslavement necessitates the "'begetting' of cultural wounds," as Henderson puts it, at least these foremothers can avoid wounding their own daughters. However, Ayo must not only contend with her transition from Ayo to Bessie, she must also confront the legacy she has bequeathed to her descendants. Grace has a similar dilemma as she contends with her guilt for abandoning her daughter Sarah when she feared her husband would be forced to commit her to an insane asylum due to the visions she was experiencing. Grace grapples with abandoning her daughter, explaining her actions, and making amends. However, Grace's sorrows begin with Ayo's initial traumatic transformation from Ayo to Bessie.

Just as Grace cannot escape her guilt for abandoning Sarah, neither can Ayo absolve her guilt for wandering away from her mother and being caught by slave catchers. According to Sidney S. Furst, author of "Psychic Trauma and Its Reconstruction with Particular Reference to Post Childhood Trauma," "Adults are less vulnerable to trauma than children because they have a longer path to regress before reaching a state of helplessness. . . . In more severe, trauma, the greatest danger is the separation from or loss of parents which of course, stems from the child's dependence" (36–37). Thus, Ayo's youth at the time of her capture and enslavement made the terrifying ordeal even more traumatic. Unfortunately, the separation of families was a common feature of slavery, which operated as though enslaved Africans were commodities rather than sensate beings. In fact, Patterson describes the situation of slavery as, "natal alienation" because the slave is denied all claims of birth (5). However, Patterson also is quick to note that, "When we say that the slave was natally alienated and ceased to belong independently to any formally recognized community, this does not mean that he or she did not experience or share informal social relations. . . . The important point, however, is that these relationships were never recognized as legitimate or binding" (6). This lack of recognition of her relationship with her mother is part of Ayo's trauma, and thus part of the rewriting of slavery's legacy for Ayo is an attempt to reconnect with her mother via her memories. Joy writes in the diary, "*She once told me that Ayo got los when she crossed the water. Bessie kinda took over. She had to think like her not like Ayo from Afraca*" (Perry, *Stigmata* 50). This notion that Ayo got lost touches on Herman's contention that "[l]ong after the event, many traumatized people feel that a part of themselves has died" (49). In sharing her story with her daughter; however, Ayo is able to remember and reclaim her lost identity. By telling her story, she can begin to think like Ayo from Africa again, and not be constrained by the New World identity of Bessie.

When telling Joy about her capture, Ayo explains the pain that her wanderlust created because it led to her enslavement. However, when Ayo recounts this pain, it is not her pain alone, but also her mother's pain that she remembers. Ayo has not only lost her mother and homeland, but her mother has lost a daughter. This was the moment that engendered psychic trauma for generations of women, but in order to move beyond Ayo's pain Lizzie must figure out how to face her foremother's painful past. Henderson believes that "for African Americans to reconstitute their humanity, they must return to the site of that violence—their own captive bodies" (38). The stigmata that Lizzie experiences seems to be a means of drawing her back to her body and her foremothers' bodies. Her body is demanding that she remember her cultural past.

Lizzie begins by seeing visions, but they quickly become more intense and physically painful. Lizzie's response is similar to her grandmother Grace's—she resists the memories and tries to avoid them. Lizzie believes she has "to get out of the past or perish" (Perry, *Stigmata* 120). However, on the evening her parents believe she has attempted suicide, Lizzie has no choice but to confront what is happening to her. She has been experiencing Ayo's terrifying Middle Passage ordeal only to discover that "All the aches and mysterious stabs of pain now have their corresponding wounds. Raggedy, ugly, familiar skin openings and welted patterns" (146). Ana Nunes observes that in "African American literature, the disfigurement of the body constitutes a central vehicle of both personal and collective history. Lizzie's stigmata work as a physical manifestation of Morrison's concept of rememory, the never-ending resurfacing of a traumatic and partially lost history" (230). However, this physical manifestation of trauma is not limited to African American contexts. Caruth asserts that trauma "is always the story of a wound that cries out" (*Unclaimed* 4). Laurie Vickroy shares this assessment, as she notes in *Trauma and Survival in Contemporary Fiction*, "Survivors' painful connection to past trauma is also displayed and replayed through the body, even branded into their flesh" (32). Vickroy goes on to observe that "[t]rauma writers make the suffering body the small, focused universe of the tormented and a vehicle for rendering unimaginable experience tangible to readers" (33). Although Perry is not one of the writers included in Vickroy's study, it is clear that she would fit within this category of trauma writers. According to Vickroy, "serious trauma writers attempt to guide readers through a re-created process of traumatic memory in order that this experience be understood more widely. . . ." (8). This is exactly what Long argues Perry does by using physical pain as a means to authenticate her historical renderings: "The protagonists believe that history really happened because it hurts them. Without the bodily transubstantiation of distant suffering, there is no apprehension of the past" (461). Thus for Perry, the wound and associated pain are essential aspects of her story. After all, Lizzie can pass off her visions as dreams, but there is no denying the bloody wounds that cover her body.

Yet Lizzie's parents are horrified when they see their wounded and bloodied daughter and can only read the scene as one of self-mutilation; however, one must remember "the dual functionality of scars as simultaneously signs of wounding and signs of healing" (Henderson 7). Lizzie's parents see her bloody bedroom as symbolic of her downward spiral to insanity, but this is actually a step toward healing. One can read this scene as a transitional moment for Lizzie. The wounds are not simply marks of pain, but also symbols of "connection between the ancestors and Lizzie, the past and present" (Nunes 230). Dennis Slattery asserts that "[t]he wounded body is sacred in some deep level of its existence; it is a body specialized and formed by experience; in its new way of being present to the world, the wounded body gains something not possessed before" (7). Slattery elaborates on this point by noting "that a richer experience of being open to the world occurs through wounding" (13). He believes "[o]ur wounds have the capacity to advance our consciousness to new levels of awareness" (16). Lizzie seems to move toward this new level of awareness through her two years of silence. Silence often is associated with contemplation and this seems to be the case for Lizzie. Although nothing appears to be happening with regard to her therapy due to her silence, much is transpiring in her thoughts as she tries to understand her situation.

According to Vickroy: "Silence has multivalent meanings when considering trauma and narrating specific elements and processes of that experience. . . . Silence can represent a traumatic gap, a withholding of words because of terror, guilt, or coercion; it characterizes traumatic memory as wordless, visual, and reenactive rather than cognitive/verbal when facing the unspeakable" (187). Lizzie tries to explain her silence by saying, "if they knew, if they heard and smelled and saw all, they'd understand how speech, for me, has become inadequate" (Perry 157). Bessel Van der Kolk and Onno Van der Hart note that trauma "cannot be easily translated into the symbolic language necessary for linguistic retrieval" because this "speechless terror" is experienced on a "somato-sensory or iconic level: as somatic sensations, behavioral reenactments, nightmares and flashbacks" (443, 442–43). At this point, Lizzie cannot form the words to make her experience understandable to others because she is not yet in a position to fully process what is happening to her.

"During the two years of silence, I dream memories of Africa every night and wake to mornings of fiery pain. My scars burn at the edges" (Perry, *Stigmata* 157). Since Lizzie has never been to Africa, these must be Ayo's memories. Ayo is determined to cling to whatever pieces of her heritage she can hold onto despite the horrors of slavery. Yes, she remembers the pain inflicted, but she refuses to allow this to eradicate her memory of home. The burning sensation Lizzie experiences also seems to be an indication that something is going on below the surface of the scars just as something is going on beneath the façade of her silence. According to Stefanie Sievers, "despite the overall negative connotations of this long period of external stasis and lack of genuine communication, the novel also suggests that a necessary development is happening within Lizzie during that time" (135). For example, it is during this time that she meets Mrs. Corday, another patient who confirms for Lizzie and the reader that Lizzie is not imagining what is happening to her because Mrs. Corday actually sees Lizzie as Grace. On another occasion Mrs. Corday sees Lizzie as a young Ayo. At this point, Lizzie would like to speak, but instead she begins to bleed from her wounds. Mrs. Corday stares in awe and fusses over Lizzie, while asking her to teach her how to do that. These two episodes with Mrs. Corday precede the healing of Lizzie's wounds, which suggests that she needed some indication that what she was experiencing was real before she could move forward in the healing process. Lizzie notes that the scars have healed, but they leave ugly marks. Dr. Cremrick puzzles over the fact that the scars look a few years old despite the fact that she was bleeding only the week before. This odd timetable for the healing of her wounds suggests that the healing process was more than a physical endeavor. A few months after her wounds have healed, Lizzie begins speaking again. Passalacqua observes, "By the time of her departure from the mental institutions, the physical marks no longer sear with pain and exude blood, which reflects the larger reality that she now possesses the knowledge of her family's history in a way that no longer hounds and hurts her" (153). Thus, Lizzie has achieved something during her institutionalization that Grace could not achieve by running away. Grace runs away from Alabama, hoping to leave her visions of Ayo behind, but even in Detroit her ankles bleed, which suggests there is no running from the past. Although Lizzie recognizes that her many therapists have not cured her, she does admit that her institutionalization cured her of something. Lizzie reflects, "Cured me of fear. Made me live with every part of myself every day. Cured me of the certainty that I was lost" (Perry, *Stigmata* 47). Unlike, Grace, Lizzie is finally able to integrate the memories of Ayo and Grace with her own life. Passalacqua concurs, ". . . Lizzie discovers that facing the fear and horrors of the past is psychologically and physically liberating. Rather than escaping from her familial legacy of slavery, Lizzie creates a way to merge and integrate this history with her present self" (153). For example, readers see this integration develop as Lizzie is able to speak from the perspective of Grace without being violently thrust into one of Grace's memories. I would contend that the significant difference between Lizzie and Grace is that ultimately Lizzie comes to accept the presence of her ancestors. Although she does not accept the diagnosis of her therapists, she uses her time in therapy as an opportunity to accept, as Father Tom noted, that her ancestor is with her.

However, this integration takes place only after a two-year period of silence. Lizzie's decision to speak suggests that she is moving forward in her recovery, while her conversation with her cousin Ruth calls into question the original determination of attempted suicide. During their conversation, Ruth observes, "'Sanity . . . is a mutual agreement between folks trying to control their world. . . . The definitions of sanity change every day'" (Perry, *Stigmata* 192). This acknowledgment by Ruth leads Lizzie to explain that she did not try to commit suicide. Although Ruth does not say she believes Lizzie, her response implies her belief, "'I'm sorry they hurt you. . . . I don't know why they have to do that'" (193). Ruth may not understand the reason why, but Lizzie has come to understand the importance of remembering. She tells Ruth, it is to keep her from forgetting again. Lizzie realizes that she cannot run away from the past. Henderson argues, "writing becomes an antidote to pain, a way to reinterpret the language of the body and heal the wounds of the psyche" (58). Ayo chose writing in the form of the diary she narrated to her daughter Joy. She tells her daughter, "*I am Ayo. I remember. This is for those whose bones lay sleepin in the heart of mother ocean for those who tomorrows I never knew who groaned and died in that dark damp aside a me. You rite this daughter for me and for them*" (Perry, *Stigmata* 7). Interestingly, Perry records a similar statement from Ayo, but with a significant difference in the opening lines, "*I am Ayo. Joy. I choose to remember*" (17). In the first account Ayo is described as merely remembering, but in the second account she reports her decision to remember. Thus, memory is linked to will. In fact, Ayo's determination to remember is apparent in the naming of her daughter, Joy. When she tells Joy that her name is Ayo, not Bessie, she also explains its meaning, "*My name mean happiness she say. Joy. That why I name you that so I don't forget who I am what I mean to this world*" (7). Joy is Ayo's first child born after emancipation and she names her in a manner that reminds her of her African heritage.[5]

Despite the pain associated with her memories, Ayo consciously decides to remember and she induces her descendants to keep her memories alive. Nora asserts, "*Lieux de mémoire* originate with the sense that there is no spontaneous memory, that we must deliberately create archives . . ." (12). Ayo's visitation of her descendants is prompted by this desire to create archives—to have something tangible to represent her story of enslavement. Remembering is important not only for her but for those who did not live to tell their stories. She and her descendants must serve as witnesses to what was done to them. Her first act as a witness is to recite her diary to Joy. According to Duboin, "as a storyteller, she has gained vision. She can now testify and become an agent who takes possession of her own past through words that denounce the evils she has survived" (Duboin, "Trauma" 291). This is why it is so important for Ayo to begin by claiming her rightful name—this is not Bessie's story, for that would be someone else's view of her life. "Ayo tells her haunting story more than three decades after her emancipation. Speaking out is a way for her to exorcize her demons and feel free at last" (291). Ayo is speaking for herself and for those who did not make it, and she insists on speaking in her own words.

Vickroy believes that "for healing to take place, survivors must find ways to tell their stories and to receive some social acknowledgement if not acceptance" (19). Ayo began seeking this acknowledgment through her diary, but as a dialogic text it is not a fully satisfying approach to telling her story. Duboin notes that the diary "interweaves the mother's effort to articulate her pain . . . with the daughter's difficulty in writing it down, her unwillingness to listen to a story she cannot fully comprehend" ("Trauma" 290). Joy tells her mother that she's tired talking about stuff that isn't real because she "is unprepared to face the reality of hard facts, and the unconceivable yet real atrocities of slavery" (290). In reciting her story to Joy, Ayo is asking her daughter to bear witness to her trauma. However, Laub notes, "The listener to the narrative of extreme human pain, of massive psychic trauma faces a unique situation. . . . The testimony to the trauma thus includes its hearer, who is, so to speak, the blank screen on which the event comes to be inscribed for the first time" (57). Laub goes on to argue that the listener partially experiences trauma by feeling "the bewilderment, injury, confusion, dread and conflicts that the trauma victim feels" (58). Joy vacillates between denying the reality of her mother's memories and being fearful of her mother's nightmares. Perhaps it is Joy's inability to be an empathic listener that leads Ayo to reach out across generations to her descendants in order to have her story really heard and accepted. According to Laub, "The absence of an empathic listener, or more radically, the absence of an *addressable other*, an other who can hear the anguish of one's memories and thus affirm and recognize their realness, annihilates the story" (68). Perhaps this also is how the practice of the possession skipping generations begins. It is as if speaking directly to one's daughter is too painful because the bond is too close, but with the distance of a granddaughter one is better able to communicate. Thus, Ayo turns to Grace after encountering Joy's resistance and Grace turns to Lizzie rather than burdening her daughter Sarah.

However, Grace, like her mother Joy, initially resists Ayo's story by trying to run away from the scenes in her head. "Erecting barriers against knowing is often the first response to such trauma" (Laub and Auerhahn 290). Grace flees Alabama for Detroit, thinking that she can leave Ayo behind. She has no visions or voices while on the train, but shortly after settling into the Detroit roominghouse her ankles begin to bleed. Grace becomes hysterical once she realizes that Ayo is still with her and not back in Alabama. Laub and Auerhahn describe the traumatic experience as "being caught between the compulsion to complete the process of knowing and the inability or fear of doing so" (288). Grace's initial reaction is fear and avoidance, but she eventually comes to accept the importance of remembering and documenting Ayo's experience. Rather than a diary, she chooses to use a quilt as her vehicle to record her grandmother's story of being stolen from Africa and forced into slavery. Before leaving her family, Grace begins a story quilt based on the visions from Ayo's life.

According to Duboin, Perry uses the appliqué quilt:

> as an overarching metaphor for the legacy of the past, the permanence of rich traditions, and the construction of self within a matrilineage. The quilts crafted or inherited by her female characters are to be seen as narratives that relate individual and collective experiences. They are the gendered expression of a shared cultural memory, the re-writing of American and African American history. ("Trauma" 293)

As an artifact of shared cultural memory, the quilt has a communal nature, which seems to differentiate it from the dialogic text of the diary. Ayo does not have to prove her experiences to Grace, as she did with Joy, because Grace shares her experiences by inhabiting key moments of Ayo's life. However, for Grace, "Quilting serves the same purposes as writing. . . . Sewing allows Grace to complete the healing process. . . . It is an outlet . . . to memorialize the dead, as well as a historical testimony to be passed on" (294). Thus Grace uses the quilt as a means to gain some understanding of her visions, but also as a means of telling Ayo's story. The appliqué quilt is a particularly apt design to depict Ayo's tale because of the similarity between the raised scars and the texture of the quilt:

> Unlike the geometric symmetry and squares of patchwork quilts, appliqué relies on a less structured visual field, telling a story through slightly raised figures on a smooth terrain. Likewise, Lizzie's scars—raised circular areas of flesh around her wrists and ankles and a textured smattering of lash marks on her back—signify on her otherwise whole body, bearing witness to the trauma of her captive and enslaved foremother. (Woolfork 13)

Woolfork notes the scars alone do not tell Ayo's story, "Because scars reference Ayo's pain but do not transmit the narrative behind it, Grace and Lizzie use appliquéd quilts to tell Ayo's wounded (and wounding) story in a material way" (48). The material and symbolic aspects of the appliqué quilts allow them to function as *lieux de mémoire*. Nora argues that sites of memory are simultaneously "material, symbolic, and functional" (19). The quilts fulfill each of these roles while also pointing to their African American heritage.

Duboin observes, "Quilting is a family tradition that has roots in African history and culture; it ties up the past with the present, the old with the new. It also facilitates female bonding and bridging across generations and continents" ("Trauma" 294). However, it is important to note that Grace and Lizzie's quilts are hybrid artifacts, representing their African American identities. According to Houston Baker and Charlotte Pierce-Baker, "The transmutation of quilting, a European, feminine tradition, into a black women's folk art, represents an innovative fusion of African cloth manufacture, piecing, and appliqué with awesome New World experiences—and expediencies" (156). This fusion of European and African traditions is particularly apparent in the appliquéd narrative quilts created by Grace and Lizzie. Their technique "in the making of the quilt is similar to that used in the tapestries of West Africa, while the narrative structure roots it in an American tradition, evoking the geographical and cultural journey of black people from the African continent to the New World" (Nunes 237). Thus, the appliqué style creates a link to their African heritage, much like Ayo's insistence on using her African name. The story that they are telling is necessarily rooted in their African heritage.

Although she feels better with the completion of the quilt and sends it home to her sister Mary Nell, Grace writes strict instructions not to show the quilt to her daughter Sarah in hopes that she will *"not curse her with these things that are happening to me. I thought getting all that down on the quilt in front of me out of me would get rid of it somehow"* (Perry, *Stigmata* 15). Through the quilt, Grace also has sought to rewrite Ayo's legacy of slavery, but just as the diary was not sufficient to tell the tale, neither is the quilt. Neither words, nor images can fully capture Ayo's story. This seems to be the motivation for Ayo to pass down "that knowin . . . a gift from me her family that's lost" (34). Ayo wants to share her story with her descendants, but must turn to extraordinary methods to tell a story beyond the realm of the human imagination. The difficult nature of Ayo's story is implied by the recipients' response. Both Grace and Lizzie initially resist the images that they see and try to escape Ayo's memories. In fact, Grace continues to struggle with Ayo's memories throughout her life. Herman notes the importance of striking the right balance in approaching traumatic memories. "Avoiding the traumatic memories leads to stagnation in the recovery process, while approaching them too precipitately leads to a fruitless and damaging reliving of the trauma" (Herman 176). Grace never achieves the appropriate balance and eventually dies from cancer without fully coming to terms with her visions or her decision to abandon her family.

Grace's failure to work through her traumatic memories is certainly linked to her decision to flee Alabama and abandon her family. Herman asserts, "Traumatic events destroy the sustaining bonds between individual and community. . . . The solidarity of a group provides the strongest protection against terror and despair, and the strongest antidote to traumatic experience. Trauma isolates; the group re-creates a sense of belonging" (214). Without her familial group, Grace lessens her chances of finding empathic listeners. Based on Eva's interactions with and apparent understanding of Lizzie, one may assume that she would have been a likely confidant who might have eased Grace's suffering. Yet Grace's refusal to heed the ancestral call of Ayo is ultimately to blame for her failure to cope with Ayo's painful memories. I would argue that if Grace had stopped trying to run from Ayo, she could have deciphered Ayo's message.

Surely, part of Lizzie's success in heeding the ancestor's call is having empathic listeners. These listeners allow Lizzie to work through her conflicted feelings regarding the intrusion of her ancestors in her life. Her cousin Ruth not only listens to her story, but also can actually feel her pain. "She turns my hands over, sliding her fingers over the scars on my wrists. At first it's an examination, then a communication between us. Her hands are very warm. A spasm of pain crosses her face, then it's calm again" (Perry, *Stigmata* 192–93). It is significant that this moment is described as communication—they are exchanging information here and thus Lizzie feels a sense of understanding. Ruth feels the pain and acknowledges it when she says she's sorry they hurt her. Even Mrs. Corday can in part recognize the veracity of Lizzie's experience because she can see Grace and Ayo. However, the most intriguing of Lizzie's empathic listeners is Anthony Paul.

Lizzie meets Anthony Paul a little over a year after her release from her last mental institution, but it becomes increasingly clear that they have met before—in a previous life, which creates a bond that enhances his ability to serve as an empathic listener. The role that Anthony Paul will play is foreshadowed in one of their first meetings when he refers to Lizzie's illness. Lizzie responds, " 'That's a nice sympathetic word for it' " (79), which suggests that she finds his attitude receptive. The relationship progresses to the point of lovemaking for the first time when Lizzie is startled by Anthony Paul's comment, " 'I already know you, old woman'" (131). This might seem like an odd thing to say to a 35-year-old woman, but Lizzie takes it as a sign of understanding. Recall that she describes herself to Father Tom as "'an old soul in a young body'" (211). Thus when she hears Anthony Paul's comment she is momentarily confused: "I haven't told him a thing about my past lives and yet here he is looking in my eyes with a knowledge so deep" (131). Their lovemaking convinces Lizzie that she has loved Anthony Paul before and his comment, "'Don't ever leave me again'" (132) suggests that he too recognizes their previous connection.

However, it is Anthony Paul's response to Lizzie's scarred back that clarifies their connection. "'There's something so beautiful about it,' Anthony Paul says, following the raised pattern on my back with his fingertips like a blind man trying to read a horror story. 'Gut-wrenching to look at. But so beautiful it's hard to stop looking'" (147). Anthony Paul's re-reading of the horror story on Lizzie's back is certainly a revisionary reading of that tale. Passalacqua argues,

> The verbal and physical exchange between Lizzie and Anthony Paul counters the spectacle from more than a century earlier when Ayo's mistress savagely whipped her as others watched. Anthony Paul sees them (Lizzie and Ayo) as fully human in their nakedness, and Lizzie's body becomes a physical space for the translation of the black female body as deserving of dignity and love. (155)

Although I concur with Passalcqua's reading of Anthony Paul's reaction to Lizzie's scars, Duboin has a very different interpretation. While likening his response to Paul D caressing Sethe's back in *Beloved*, Duboin asserts, "Anthony Paul's sensory emotions, his scopic urge, his unhealthy fascination for scars all emphasize the eroticization of unbearable pain inscribed onto the black female body" ("Trauma" 288). Yet I would argue that this response does not take into account the context of their relationship. When Anthony Paul sees Lizzie's scars for the first time, he is not really surprised because years before meeting Lizzie he had painted her picture, including her scarred back. When Lizzie uncovers a large painting in his bedroom, she sees a picture of a woman with her face and her scarred back in the midst of a storm with a ship in the background. It turns out that Anthony Paul did not know Lizzie from school, but from a painting he completed in 1982, thirteen years before they met. He thinks the image came from a dream—I suspect a dream similar to the dreams Lizzie used to have of Ayo.

Almost a year into their relationship Lizzie risks telling Anthony Paul about her past lives, " 'I'm taking a chance by telling you this. The doctor—my father—is still legally my guardian. You could go tell what I told you—that would be the end of me. I'd probably never see the outside again. I'm trusting you with my life' " (Perry, *Stigmata* 182). Lizzie tells Anthony Paul about her belief in reincarnation—Ayo returned as Grace and Grace as her. She tells him that the picture he painted is her, but really Ayo because her scars came from Ayo. She assures him that they have met before. Although Anthony Paul is not sure about reincarnation and all that Lizzie tells him, he assures her that he would never let her go back to the mental institution. Perry leaves the future of their relationship unresolved as Lizzie intends to leave Tuskegee and it is unclear whether they will continue their relationship despite Lizzie's assertions to Anthony Paul that she doesn't want to lose him. Although readers are not told what ultimately happens between Lizzie and Anthony Paul, the fact that Lizzie had painted a similar picture to his in 1988 suggests that they will remain connected. In the words of Lizzie, " 'this ain't going nowhere. It ain't the beginning or the end' " (183). Thus, although Anthony Paul cannot fully understand Lizzie's experience, he can help her cope with it. I should note that Anthony Paul is an important intervention in a matri-lineal story, which suggests that although the women of Lizzie's family have unfinished business to attend to which seems very focused on recuperating the products of their wombs, it does not mean that there is no space for men in their lives. Perry's focus is on responding to the effects of slavery on mothers and daughters, but the inclusion of Anthony Paul reminds the reader that men were not untouched by the painful sundering of families during slavery. According to Passalacqua, "Anthony Paul helps to bridge the gap between the unspeakable nature of Lizzie's family trauma and the expression of it. The visual image of Lizzie's humanity bound to Ayo's humanity involves a delicate process of reinscription and translation of bodies into the narrative frame of *Stigmata* and into other narrative forms such as quilting and painting" (155). While in therapy, Lizzie paints scenes from Ayo's life and Anthony Paul's painting of Ayo/Lizzie also is inspired by a dream; however, Lizzie eventually turns to quilting as her preferred method of exploring and documenting her memories.

Yet Lizzie's drive to tell Grace's story through the quilt is not only to document the pain of slavery across generations, it is also an attempt by Grace to reach out through Lizzie to the daughter she abandoned. For Lizzie's mother Sarah, all that matters about Grace is that "[s]he left. She died" (Perry, *Stigmata* 70). But it is clear that Sarah has never gotten over returning from her grandmother's house only to find her mother gone. Sarah needs resolution regarding her mother's abandonment as much as Grace needs to make amends for leaving her daughter. Because of her unresolved pain regarding her mother's abandonment, Sarah cannot be a strong mother for her own daughter. Sarah is supposed to be the elder, providing guidance for her daughter, but in many ways it is the daughter who nurtures the mother. In fact, Long goes so far as to describe Lizzie as a slave mother, "nurturing and protecting [her] older kin and ancestors" (473). In an interview with Duboin, Perry comments on Sarah's relationship with her mother, "There are losses there. There was a treasure that Sarah had not allowed herself to be privy to" ("Confronting" 640). Sarah does not know her mother and resists knowing her because of the pain surrounding her abandonment. Even Grace's decision to leave her trunk to an unknown granddaughter rather than to Sarah is taken as another sign of rejection. Sarah returns the favor by rejecting her own mother, thus she cannot see her mother's story in the quilt Lizzie is sewing. Sarah's inability to see Grace's story in the quilt is linked to a preference for linear narratives. Woolfork notes, "Whereas Sarah would prefer to make a pieced quilt, Lizzie insists on appliqué. Each woman's choice of quilt modality reflects the way they conceptualize time and history" (51–52). Sarah is at first uncomfortable with Lizzie's circular design and thus cannot see/read her mother's story of Ayo. With the denial of her mother, Sarah is essentially shutting the door on her past and her slave past as represented by Ayo. Thus although Sarah is spared the visions that tormented her mother, Long suggests, "Sarah is perhaps the most damaged character in *Stigmata*, stifled by her inability or unwillingness to see the history her daughter embodies for her" (473). Lizzie gradually unfolds Grace's story to Sarah through the quilt, but Sarah initially refuses to accept that Lizzie is her mother, great-grandmother, and daughter in one body.[6]

As much as Sarah tries to deny what Lizzie tries to explain about her reincarnation, she also cannot deny that Lizzie knows things that only her mother could know. Sarah's acceptance of the truth comes only after Lizzie adds the last piece to the quilt—a blue scrap from the dress Ayo wore on the day she was kidnapped and enslaved. Nunes refers to this blue scrap as a "fragment of cultural memory," which "functions in the narrative as a link to Africa, but it also symbolizes the passing on of the historical testimony along the generational line" (236). With this last piece, Ayo's descendants have come full circle—Grace's story is only complete once the symbol of Ayo's capture and enslavement has been added to the quilt. As she adds the piece, Lizzie explains, " 'That's what this quilt is about. The past. And putting the past aside when we're through'" (Perry 228). The pain of the past can only be healed after it's confronted.

According to Long's reading of *Stigmata*, Perry challenges "readers to conceive of remembering as a palpable, physical experience" (460). Thus it is not enough for Lizzie to merely remember her foremother's experience, she must relive it and bear the scars. Her body can then "attest to the reality of slavery" (460). Long asserts in her discussion of *Stigmata* and Butler's *Kindred* that "the suffering that ordinarily cannot be conveyed is invoked in these novels as metonymic proof of a knowable past" (461). Sarah has escaped this traumatic embodiment of slavery's pain since the matrilineal line of reincarnation skips every other generation. Grace thinks that her daughter will be safe because she cannot relive these painful memories, but ultimately Sarah is the most damaged. Thus, in order for Sarah to be healed, her mother, Grace, must return in the figure of Lizzie to reconnect her with her familial history of slavery. Only after Sarah confronts the past can she come to terms with it.

Sarah is able to finally come to terms with the past and her mother's abandonment through the assistance of her ancestors—Grace and Ayo—as embodied in Lizzie, thus suggesting, "one's access to the past is determined by the intensity of one's connection to ancestors" (462). Sarah accesses the past only with the return of her mother from the dead. Towards the end of the novel Grace through Lizzie observes, "The circle is complete and my daughter sits across from me with the gap finally closed" (Perry, *Stigmata* 230). Although Sarah used to pray for God to send her mother back to her, Grace could only return through her granddaughter, Lizzie.

This reunion of mother and daughter is followed by an excerpt from Ayo's journal in which Joy records Ayo's death and the passing down of the scrap of blue cloth from the dress she wore when she was captured in Africa, *"Take care of that little girl she say and she smiled and say I meant to put this in but I never did and she gave me a piece of blue cloth she had balled up in her hand"* (230). The scene is more than a parallel scene of mother–daughter affection; it is a fitting example of the way in which Lizzie has managed to merge the lives of Ayo and Grace with her own. Sievers observes:

> Following her release in 1994, Lizzie then consciously integrates Ayo's and Grace's lives into her own. . . . This intersection of identities is supported structurally by having all chapters in this narrative strand conclude with entries from Ayo's diary. To have Ayo's words accompany the time period

in Lizzie's life when she is supposedly cured is an indication that she is, in fact, able to integrate the life stories of her foremothers into her own without being overwhelmed by them. (136)

This point is supported by Van der Kolk and Van der Hart's assertion that, "In the case of complete recovery, the person does not suffer anymore from the reappearance of traumatic memories in the form of flashbacks, behavioral re-enactments, etc. Instead the story can be told, the person can look back at what happened; he has given it a place in his life history . . . and thereby in the whole of his personality" (447–48). Thus despite Lizzie's claim that there is no cure for her condition, she has successfully merged her life with that of her foremother's and like the scars on her body, she is proof of the intersection of the past and present (Perry, *Stigmata* 204). The scars serve as both a reminder of the past and as a legacy connecting Ayo's descendants across generations.

This matri-lineal legacy of Ayo's descendants is just one thread of a larger cultural trauma. A distinguishing component of cultural trauma is that one need not directly experience an event that induces trauma. "It is through time-delayed and negotiated recollection that cultural trauma is experienced, a process which places representation in a key role" (Eyerman 12). Thus, although Ayo may have experienced trauma, her descendants experienced cultural trauma. However, in reaching across the grave and contacting her descendants Ayo does not merely transmit cultural trauma, but also begins the healing process. The disruption of slavery begun with Ayo's kidnapping in Africa engenders generations of trauma as her descendants seek to cope with their foremother's experience, yet it is the process of remembering and working through the trauma over generations and across the terrain of the living and the dead that finally brings some measure of closure for Ayo's descendants. Although Long contends that the cycle of possession depicted in *Stigmata* "does not bode well for Lizzie's future granddaughter, who, we presume, will endure the weight of Lizzie's fourteen-year institutionalization" (473), I am not so convinced that the cycle will continue in its current pattern.[7] For example, in her reading of *Praisesong for the Widow*, Missy Dehn Kubitschek takes issue with Avey's decision to retell the story of the Ibo "word-for-word as she received it from her Great-Aunt Cuney. . . . Disturbingly, she plans the same exact experience for her grandsons that she has had with her great-aunt. This re-creation suggests that the story's message is finished, complete; the griot's tale need not incorporate Avey's experience" (*Claiming* 88). Although I disagree with Kubitschek's interpretation of the story's potential impact without rephrasing, I do understand her concern about the potential lack of involvement of the griot. However, we see Avey's incorporation of her experience in what she does with the story of the Ibos—her summer camp is not what her foremothers did with the story. A similar process happens with Lizzie in response to her experience with Ayo and Grace. She, like Grace, uses a story quilt to tell the stories of Ayo and Grace, yet, unlike Grace, she does not shut Sarah out of the story. In her desire to protect her daughter, Grace tells Sarah nothing regarding her experiences. This is not what Ayo did, who recited her story to Joy, so that she would write it down for her, nor is this what Lizzie does, who slowly uses the quilt to present Sarah with the truth of her identity. However, in each of these instances Ayo's story remains the same. The story that engendered the trauma has not changed, but how Grace and Lizzie navigate the story and work through the trauma does change, which suggests that perhaps the completed circle of mothers and daughters around the quilt as Sarah acknowledges that Lizzie is both her daughter and her mother is truly a sign of closure and not just a stop on an unending cycle of trauma.

According to Herman, "Survivors challenge us to reconnect fragments, to reconstruct history, to make meaning of their present symptoms in light of past events" (3). By the end of *Stigmata*, these things have been done due to the intercession of ancestors. Lizzie and Sarah sit before a quilt which literally reconnects the fragments of Ayo and Grace's lives. Sarah's initial response to Lizzie's semi-circular depiction of Grace's life on the quilt is that it is hopelessly jumbled; however, by the time the quilt is complete she can recognize her mother's story and appreciate it. One of the components of recovery is the restored connection between survivors and their community. With the breach between Sarah and Grace healed, Grace, Ayo, Lizzie, and Sarah have found a peace they did not have before. Ayo lost her mother when she was enslaved and Grace lost her daughter while besieged with Ayo's memories, but Lizzie has allowed her ancestors to rewrite the legacy of slavery and begin to heal its wounds. I contend that this re-visioning of slavery is reliant on ancestral interventions and that Perry's text is reflective of Kongo cosmology. I cannot say that Perry has any knowledge of African spirituality; she does not indicate this in her interview with Duboin. However, she does indicate a tolerance for "people who do subscribe to belief systems outside the mainstream. A lot of those beliefs are based on African American spirituality that's inherited from African ancestors and from other traditions . . ." (Duboin, "Confronting" 643). Perry goes on to note that within African American culture various "beliefs exist side by side. You would go to a root doctor, an herbalist, you might get a charm, you would go to church on Sunday, and you would believe that spirits were talking to you" (643).[8] I assert that the persistence of elements of Kongo cosmology in the work of African American artists like Perry is indicative of the continuing effect of Africanisms within the African American community. Thus, I argue that the traumatic legacy of slavery reflected in *Stigmata* cannot be fully understood without some knowledge of Kongo cosmology and the role of the ancestor.

While *Stigmata* depicts the return of a mother in the guise of a daughter to heal the generational wounds of slavery, a very different mother–daughter relationship is depicted in Morrison's *Beloved*. In *Beloved,* a murdered daughter returns to confront her mother. This is a different scenario than what I have discussed in both *Stigmata* and *Praisesong for the Widow,* which feature returning elders as the ancestral figures. In "Ancestors as Elders in Africa," Igor Kopytoff notes "Every junior owes buzitu ('honour,' 'respect') to his seniors, be they 'elders' or 'ancestors' in Western terminology" (416). However, in *Beloved* we see this expectation of respect become disrupted when the child returns from the afterlife. Although I have referred to deceased characters such as Ayo, Grace, and Aunt Cuney as ancestors, I cannot designate Beloved as such. In the chapter that follows I discuss Beloved as an exemplar of the malevolent ancestor or stunted ancestor—the person who does not achieve ancestor status.

4

Beloved

A Ghost Story With an Ogbanje Twist

One might describe Toni Morrison's *Beloved* as a ghost story. Literary critic, Trudier Harris observes, "Certainly in the black folk tradition, a ghost might occasionally appear among the living—to indicate all is well, to teach a lesson, or to guide the living to some good fortune, including buried treasure" (*Fiction* 156). According to Geraldine Smith-Wright, "While the ghost tale in recent African-American literature has its deepest roots in West African culture, the genre's more immediate development is traceable to the era of slavery in the American South" (142). In her essay, "In Spite of the Klan: Ghosts in the Fiction of Black Women Writers," Smith-Wright traces the use of ghosts by twentieth-century women writers to folktales, which reconciled African supernatural beliefs with the experience of slavery. Smith-Wright argues, "The survival of African beliefs about the spirit world in the African-American oral and literary traditions is paradigmatic of Blacks' survival in the diaspora" (145). Although slave owners sought to use ghost stories as a means to instill fear and maintain order, enslaved Africans believed that "the living and the dead are intimately connected" (164). For example, scholars John S. Mbiti and John Pobee both articulate the notion of the continued involvement of the dead in familial affairs. Thus Pobee defines the family as consisting "of the living, the dead and the still unborn. It is not only the living. Consequently, these ancestors, though dead are still believed to be concerned with and involved in the affairs of the living" (8). While Mbiti asserts, "African peoples believe that death is not the end of human life. A person continues to exist in the hereafter. This continuation of life beyond death is recognized through a very widespread practice of remembering the departed, which is found throughout Africa" (*Intro* 128). Just as the living continue to remember the departed, the deceased remember the living: "the dead do not just fall into oblivion because they continue to be involved in the affairs of the living. They may from time to time appear in the world of the living as ghosts or in dreams" (Pobee 8). Thus, there is a sense of continuity between the world of the living and the dead.

However, as Smith-Wright notes, because slave owners did not understand Africans' view of the relationship between the living and the dead, they could not fully terrorize them through ghost stories. According to Mbiti, "While surviving relatives remember the departed, the spirit more or less leads a personal continuation of life. It has become what we have called the living dead" (*Intro* 125). Smith-Wright observes, "It is the inclusive definition of being that ultimately confounded whites' efforts to use bastardized forms of African traditions to control the slaves but which bound together enslaved African peoples in a common heritage" (145). Although folktales featuring ghosts were told by black storytellers in such a way as to emphasize the prowess of the slave victim rather than the threatening aspect of the ghosts, ghosts in twentieth-century narratives suggest that "African Americans can achieve justice, autonomy, and racial pride in an environment that from the era of slavery exacted their submission and fear" (164). Representation of the supernatural in these twentieth-century texts suggest "that empowerment for African Americans depends on the sense of connection with their rich African past. The ghost tale is both narrative strategy and theme" (164). This is certainly what we see in Paule Marshall's *Praisesong for the Widow* and Phyllis Alesis Perry's *Stigmata*. Although the characters are haunted, this haunting is a means of empowerment through reconnection with their ancestors. However, one must wonder if the same scenario holds in Morrison's *Beloved* in which the ghost is depicted as strangling her mother and essentially draining her of life.

In her 1984 essay, "Rootedness: The Ancestor as Foundation," Morrison describes ancestors as "benevolent, instructive, and protective" (343). The importance of ancestors for Morrison is reconfirmed ten years later in her interview with Angels Carabi when she states, "They [ancestors] are just waiting there for you to ask them to do something, but if you don't know them, don't honor them, don't think of them, mourn them or praise them, then you are like a cripple" (87). *Beloved*, published in 1987, appears between these articulations of Morrison's views regarding ancestors, so what is one to make of a ghost story that is not peopled by benevolent, instructive, protective ancestors such as Marshall's Aunt Cuney, but instead haunted by some sort of demon?

Harris suggests, "We can describe the title character as a witch, a ghost, a devil, or a succubus; in her manipulation of those around her, she exerts a power not of this world" (*Fiction* 153). Although previous chapters have focused on the benevolent effects of the ancestral presence, the benevolent presence of Baby Suggs, who is deceased for the majority of the novel, is overshadowed by the malevolent ancestor, Beloved, who is in fact an ogbanje set on claiming retribution from Sethe for her murder; however, in the process of tormenting Sethe, Beloved forces Sethe to come to terms with her past, and hopefully this will allow her to move on with her life.

According to Christopher N. Okonkwo, author of "A Critical Divination: Reading Sula as Ogbanje-Abiku," " 'ogbanje' and 'abiku' are Igbo and Yoruba names respectively for a spirit-child or spirit-children who are said to die early only to be reborn again and again to the same mother" (653). Although this may sound like reincarnation, Christie C. Achebe warns of the importance of distinguishing between reincarnation and ogbanje in her study of the ogbanje phenomenon:

> In Igbo world view, reincarnation "inyọ uwa," or "ibia uwa," symbolizes a rebirth after a full life cycle. A man or woman who lives to a ripe old age can be reincarnated in one of his or her grandchildren, in which case, he or she dies and returns to the same family. For the Igbos, therefore, and this is also true of the many ethnic groups in Nigeria, reincarnation is a common, desirable and understood phenomenon. (33)

However, it is the disruption of the life cycle that separates ogbanje from ancestors. In the words of Bunseki Fu-Kiau, they are stunted ancestors—they do not reach ancestor status because their lives are cut short. Misty L. Bastian remarks on the lack of ancestor status for ogbanje in her essay, "Married in the Water: Spirit Kin and Other Afflictions of Modernity in Southeastern Nigeria." According to Bastian, "this is a spirit that has never been ancestral . . ." (120). Bastian's analysis aptly pertains to Beloved in Morrison's novel; thus one should not expect Beloved to be benevolent, instructive, or protective, as these qualities have not had time to develop.

However, Beloved is not the only ghost to populate 124 Bluestone Road. Baby Suggs dies shortly after the narrative begins; yet, while living she commented to Sethe, " 'Not a house in the country ain't packed to its rafters with some dead Negro's grief' " (Morrison, *Beloved* 6). This comment was meant to dismiss Sethe's notion of moving from their haunted house by suggesting there is no escape from such haunting. This association between "Negro grief" and haunting is tied to the history of slavery. Ashraf H.A. Rushdy makes this connection in *Remembering Generations: Race and Family in Contemporary African American Fiction*:

> Two metaphors that resonate effectively in the current dialogue draw on haunted imagery: the American slave past is "that ghost which we have not entirely faced," and the memory of that institution is "a haunted house" we fear to inhabit. These are telling figures. A domestic space haunted by a liminal apparition beyond the grave indicates the ways the past is not dead, but likewise not seen or acknowledged by all. (2–3)

Beloved uses ghosts to illustrate the continued effect of our slave past on our contemporary present; however, our attention is generally consumed by Beloved—the ghost who died a horrific death rather than Baby Suggs—who went to bed to contemplate color. Although my focus is on Beloved, I also draw attention to Baby Suggs whose quiet ancestral presence proves to be beneficial, instructive, and protective.

For much of the novel, Baby Suggs' quiet ancestral presence seems dominated by the noisy baby ghost. "124 was spiteful. Full of a baby's venom" (Morrison, *Beloved* 3). This reference to the haunting of 124 is exemplary of a larger cultural haunting. According to Avery Gordon, "Haunting is a part of our social world, and understanding it is essential to grasping the nature of our society and for changing it" (27). For Rushdy, haunting points to family secrets—"Slavery, in American intellectual discourse, is not only or merely a metaphor, a sin, a cancer, a crime, or a shame, although it is also all of those things. Slavery is the family secret of America" (*Remembering* 2). Rushdy continues, "Slavery, in other words, functions in American thinking as the partially hidden phantom of a past that needs to be revised in order to be revered" (2). This correlation between haunting and slavery reveals our discomfort with this aspect of our national history. Kathleen Brogan makes a similar point with her contention, "Haunting in *Beloved* signals the return of a past that can neither be properly remembered nor entirely forgotten" (63). Yet with *Beloved*, Morrison provides readers with the opportunity to grapple with this troublesome past and, like Sethe, find some measure of healing. In her interview with Carabi, Morrison states:

> With *Beloved*, I am trying to insert this memory that was unbearable and unspeakable into the literature. Not only to write about a woman who did what Sethe did, but to have

the ghost of the daughter return as a remnant of a period that was unspoken. It was a silence within the race. So it's a kind of healing experience. There are certain things that are repressed because they are unthinkable, and the only way to come free of that is to go back and deal with them. (38)

At the opening of the narrative, Sethe is stymied by her inability to cope with her past, particularly her decision to kill her daughter before she could be remanded to slavery; however, by the end of the novel Sethe seems to be on the verge of moving forward in her life after battling her daughter's ghost and receiving the healing guidance of elders and ancestors.

It is clear from the opening pages of the text that *Beloved* will ask its readers to confront the past before moving forward. In a 1981 interview with Thomas LeClair, Morrison says of her writing, "My work bears witness . . ." (26). In the case of *Beloved*, Morrison is bearing witness not only to the pain and injustice of slavery, but also to the disappeared and unaccounted for victims of the Middle Passage referenced in her dedication: "Sixty Million and more." The dedication is followed by an epigraph from Romans 9:25: "I will call them my people,/which were not my people; and her beloved,/which was not beloved." According to literary critic, Mae Henderson, "By citing a New Testament passage that echoes a passage from the Old Testament, the author not only problematizes the nature of the relation between the past and present but also thematizes the importance of historical reclamation and repossession" (82). Picking up on the significance of historical reclamation, Caroline Rody argues for the memorial aspect of *Beloved* in "Toni Morrison's *Beloved*: History, 'Rememory,' and a 'Clamor for a Kiss'": "Reconceiving the historical novel as a memorial, Morrison illuminates the psychological structure of ethnic historical fiction. Like all memorials, *Beloved* is not a 'place' of the dead but a place where survivors can go to 'summon' and 'recollect,' to look upon the sculpted shape of their own sorrow" (98). However, *Beloved* is not merely a memorial, but a revisioning of our slave past. In other words, Morrison is not only paying tribute to the victims of the Middle Passage, but also asking readers to rethink our understanding of slavery and particularly its impact on mothers.

In her essay, "The Site of Memory," Morrison describes her work as "literary archeology: On the basis of some information and a little bit of guesswork you journey to a site to see what remains were left behind and to reconstruct the world that these remains imply" (92). Brogan likens Morrison's literary archeology to a reburial process, "The search for 'remains' leads to a revivification of the dead, often described by Morrison as a summoning of dead predecessors, an imaginative process that gives birth to the ghost as a partly invented, embodied memory" (64). According to Brogan, "The exorcism of deadly forms of haunting in *Beloved* requires a ritual burial of the unmourned dead—or more accurately, reburial, since the task of laying the dead to rest begins with an exhumation" (64). Surely it is this process of reburial that led Barbara Christian to refer to *Beloved* as ancestral worship (Christian, "Fixing" 8).

In *Beloved*, Morrison gives honor to ancestors, particularly the unnamed victims of the Middle Passage. In her interview with Carabi, Morrison shares her concern regarding the disremembered Middle Passage:

> All those people who threw themselves into the sea had been violently ignored; no one praised them, nobody knows their names, nobody can remember them, not in the United States nor in Africa. Millions of people disappeared without a trace, and there is not one monument anywhere to pay homage to them, because they never arrived safely on shore. So it's like a whole nation that is under the sea. A nameless, violent extermination. (38)

In response to Morrison's concerns, Christian understands *Beloved* to be a prayer, memorial, or fixing ceremony recognizing these disremembered ancestors.

> Morrison has in *Beloved*, not just written a powerful novel, she has designed a fixing ceremony. . . . In a process that is central to African spirituality, her fixing ceremony is not merely that of remembrance as the only way to begin the process of healing that psychic wound, which continues to have grave effects on the present. Those whose names we can no longer specifically call know that we have not forgotten them, that they are our "Beloveds," and that unless they release us from the wrath of the past, the future will be tormented and fractured. ("Fixing" 14)

According to Mbiti, the departed who are still remembered are among the living dead and are still considered to be part of their families.[1] Thus, the inability to name the departed—one's ancestors—has a profound effect on those still living. Christian notes that in not being able to remember or name "those who passed on in the Middle Passage, those who survived *had* to abandon their living dead to the worst possible fate that could befall a West African: complete annihilation" (13). Christian goes so far as to refer to this as "the psychic horror of those who can no longer call their ancestors' names" in her discussion of "the dilemma of the mother who knows her children will be born into and live in the realm of those who *cannot* call their ancestors' names" (14). The significance of names, particularly disremembered names, highlights the important role of memory in Morrison's text.

In *Raising the Dead: Readings of Death and (Black) Subjectivity*, Sharon Holland argues, "Morrison wields memory so that it circumvents traditional ideas of past, present, and future. . . . Beloved/*Beloved* is about remembering, slowly, easily, and painfully" (50). The pain associated with memory is apparent in the baby's haunting of 124. When Paul D arrives and sees the red undulating light, he wants to know what kind of evil is in the house. However, Sethe claims, " 'It's not evil, just sad' " (Morrison, *Beloved* 10). Yet, Denver contends that the ghost is not evil or sad, but " 'Rebuked. Lonely and rebuked' " (16). Marilyn Sanders Mobley argues in "A Different Remembering: Memory, History and Meaning in Toni Morrison's *Beloved*" that "[t]he obsolete meaning of rebuked—repressed—not only suggests that the ghost represents repressed memory, but that, as with anything that is repressed, it eventually resurfaces or returns in one form or another" (23). Thus, Denver's comment about the rebuked ghost may be seen as a foreshadowing of Beloved's incarnation. Sethe has been repressing the memories of her enslavement, especially slitting the throat of her own child to prevent the Fugitive Slave Law from returning her daughter to slavery, but she can only hold back the past for so long.

Initially it seems as if Paul D will rescue Sethe from her memories as he drives off the ghost. The pulse of red light has disappeared and the house has stopped rocking. However, Harris warns: "In this seeming rite of exorcism, it is not Beloved who is removed but Paul D who is lulled into a false sense of victory" (*Fiction* 131). Although it appears that the ghost is gone, Beloved is merely changing form. Critics J. Brooks Bouson and Paula Gallant Eckard both comment on the red pool as a rememory or incarnation of the baby's spilt blood; however, Eckard takes the point further by noting, "It also represents the primordial mass of blood and menstrual fluids waiting to form into life again, which it does when the fully grown Beloved emerges out of the stream" (Bouson 149; Eckard 69). Although Sethe and Denver welcome Beloved's return, it also is fraught with pain. As Denver's namesake, Amy Denver commented years before, " 'Anything dead coming back to life hurts' " (Morrison, *Beloved* 42). In fact it is the pain associated with the cycle of death and return which makes the ogbanje phenomenon so terrifying. Ogbanje are viewed as "mischievous beings who want to torment their earthly families with the promise of healthy children, only to destroy that promise later with sickness and premature death" (Bastian 119). To illustrate the degree of fear associated with ogbanje, Chidi T. Maduka notes that "in Igbo language the word *ogbanje* can be used metaphorically to designate any person who in a given situation behaves in a weird, capricious, callous or even sadistic way" (18). This then is what confronts Sethe upon Beloved's return from the dead—a sadistic child.

Although Beloved comes back as a fully dressed woman walking out of the water, her return is typically seen as a rebirth of sorts. Although she is described as a woman, her actions seem more like a child—she has difficulty holding her head up and staying awake and even more intriguing—she "had new skin, lineless and smooth" (Morrison, *Beloved* 61). The association with childbirth is solidified with Sethe's reaction upon seeing Beloved—her bladder fills and she voids what seems like an endless amount of fluid. Sethe thinks to herself that she's carrying on like a horse, but then it dawns on her that it was "more like flooding the boat when Denver was born" (61). Morrison tells Carabi, "Obviously I wanted Sethe to be reexperiencing [*sic*] birth" (Carabi 39). However, other aspects of the water imagery seem to be less obvious. Morrison continues, "The other part has to do with the African conviction regarding reincarnation. It is believed that, in particular, children or young people who die uneasily return out of the water in forms of members of your family. Water is a dangerous and haunted place because spirits dwell in it" (39). Although I am not familiar with Morrison's reference to young people returning out of water, I associate Beloved's return via water with the Kalûnga line. According to the Kongo cosmogram, the Kalûnga line separates the physical world from the spiritual world. Kalûnga, "meaning ocean, is a door and a wall between those two worlds" (Fu-Kiau 20–21). Thus an endless body of water separates the physical and spiritual world, so Beloved's return to this world would mean passing through water.

The African inflections of Morrison's text have been recognized by a number of critics. La Vinia Delois Jennings, author of *Toni Morrison and the Idea of Africa*, asserts "Morrison's fiction exposes an African palimpsest upon which European-American culture superimposes itself. Lying latent under that super imposition, and at times commingled with interpolations from indigenous peoples' beliefs, are decipherable, identifiably Black, traditional, cosmological inscriptions thought lost to the North American experience" (2). For example, In *Africanism and Authenticity in African-American Women's Novels*, Amy K. Levin connects Beloved to African initiation rites; however, her argument is based on a faulty description of Beloved's "pallid appearance as she rises from the water, dressed in white" (66). Levin argues, "Dressed in white, also the color of death and ancestors in many African societies, Beloved is closely connected to the past. In this context, Beloved's surfacing may be read as an ironic signification not only on the Christian ritual of baptism but also on West African initiations, for she is being initiated into the cruelty and savagery of a racist American society" (66). Although this sounds plausible, the argument does not hold up when one considers the fact that Beloved was not wearing a white dress, but a black dress and rather than being pallid she is described as "gilded and shining" (61, 76).[2] Holland also makes connections between Beloved and African traditions by linking Beloved to a belief in lower Zaire that suggests " 'deceased ancestors become white creatures called *bakula* who inhabit villages of the dead located under river beds or lake bottoms; they may return from this underworld to mingle with the living without being seen and can direct the course of the living' " (54). However, noting that Morrison's bakulu is " 'Thunderblack and glistening,' " Holland moves on to suggest that Beloved is also modeled after the orisha, Oshun, the Yoruban " 'divinity of the rivers. . . . she controls all that makes life worth living, such as love and marriage, children, money, and pleasure . . .' " (55). Okonkwo notes various African diasporic mythologies which critics have pointed to as the source for Beloved include the Zairean bakulu, the Sierra Leonean Mende spirit myth, Haitian/Afro-Caribbean religion, Yoruba *Ájẹ́* and Obatala and abiku. However, like myself, he credits Beloved's source with ogbanje although he does it on the basis of Morrison's "expressed aesthetic and philosophic debt to Achebe"[3] rather than Kongo cosmology (*Spirit* 157–58).

Like Jennings, I note the significance of the Yowa, the Kongo cosmogram in Morrison's novel. According to Jennings, "Morrison turns to the most discernible African symbol in the Americas, the cross within a circle, which survived the Middle Passage and the Transatlantic Slave Trade. She uses it as the substructure for her literary landscapes and interior spaces, and as a geometric figure performed by or inscribed on the bodies of her characters" (2). Of course the most explicit example of this in the text is the circle and cross mark on Sethe's mother; however, I contend that the water from which Beloved emerges also is emblematic of the Yowa as it reflects the Kalûnga line and is used to show that Beloved has emerged from the realm of the Musoni—the realm of the ancestors. This fact is supported by the knowledge that Beloved comes from the spirit world. Although Sethe is slow to recognize it, it becomes increasingly clear that Beloved has been here before and she has brought those memories of past lives with her.

Perhaps the first indication to the inhabitants of 124 Bluestone that Beloved came from the spiritual plane is Beloved's comment, " 'This place is heavy' " (Morrison, *Beloved* 65). Beloved spends her first few days at Bluestone sleeping as she adjusts to her new environment. Part of this adjustment is the heaviness of the physical world. As Beloved adjusts to her new surroundings, she begins to ask questions about Sethe's past; however, the questions themselves reveal knowledge she should not have, such as the fact that Sethe had earrings that looked like diamonds. These same earrings were dangled before her "crawling-already? baby." Beloved's knowledge of things such as this as well as the scar on her neck allows Denver to put the pieces together and assume that Beloved is indeed the "crawling-already? baby"—her dead sister returned from the grave. Thus, Denver can say as a matter of fact that their dog, Here Boy, would not be back. Here Boy had already stopped entering the house after the ghost slammed him against a wall so hard that two of his legs were broken and an eye dislocated. Hence, his disappearance may be associated with Beloved's appearance. Denver's supposition regarding Beloved's identity becomes clear when she asks Beloved, " 'What's it like over there, where you were before?' " (88). Beloved describes being curled up in a fetal position in a hot cramped place surrounded by people—some of whom are dead. Without missing a beat, Denver asks, " 'You see Jesus? Baby Suggs?' " (88). For Denver, the notion that Beloved has come from the dead and that she is her deceased sister reborn seems completely plausible.

Although Elizabeth House maintains "evidence throughout the book suggests that the girl is not a supernatural being of any kind but simply a young woman who has herself suffered the horrors of slavery" (117), most critics tend to interpret Beloved as Sethe's deceased daughter and something more. For example, Angelita Reyes comments on "Beloved's post-natal link to the spirit world (death) and to the middle crossing of her ancestors who were brought into American slavery . . ." ("Rereading" 466). Similarly, Susan Bowers acknowledges, "But Beloved is much more than Sethe's resurrected daughter. She is the embodiment of the collective pain and rage of the millions of slaves who died on the Middle Passage and suffered the tortures of slavery" (34). Both of these readings of Beloved take into account her description of a Middle Passage experience and her apparent relation to Sethe. This dual positioning is commented on by Morrison in an interview with Marsha Darling,

"She is a spirit on one hand, literally she is what Sethe thinks she is, her child returned to her from the dead. And she must function like that in the text. She is also another kind of dead which is not spiritual but flesh, which is, a survivor from the true factual slave ship" (247). Christian comments, "I was struck by Morrison's representation of the character of Beloved as an embodied spirit, a spirit that presents itself as a body. In the Caribbean, spirits are everywhere, are naturally in the world, and are not ghosts in the horror-genre sense of that term" ("Fixing" 9). Christian goes on to note the presence of spirits in the wind, trees, waters, and rocks; however, Morrison's choice to embody her spirit calls attention to a significant aspect of African spirituality: "death does not represent the end of human existence, but rather a change in status" (Zahan, "Some" 10). With an embodied spirit, Morrison underscores the continuity between life and death.

Interestingly, Morrison's spirit is not merely the spirit of Sethe's deceased daughter, but also a deceased Middle Passage survivor. This suggests that Sethe's daughter was perhaps herself a reincarnation of a Middle Passage survivor. According to Ogbu U. Kalu, author of "Ancestral Sprituality and Society in Africa," "the African perception of time is cyclical: life moves from birth to death, through the ancestral world to reincarnating birth" (55–56). Nevertheless, this dual positioning of Beloved as both deceased daughter and Middle Passage survivor suggests that she has emerged from the realm of the ancestors. In the introduction, I note that Fu-Kiau designates two stages that reflect the ancestral realm—the Luvèmba stage and the Musoni stage. The Luvèmba stage is the sphere of the living-dead, who are still remembered by those alive in the physical world, whereas the Musoni stage is peopled by spirits who are no longer remembered and thus are further removed from their descendants. However, as both Sethe's deceased daughter and an embodiment of the Middle Passage, Beloved is a manifestation of both of these stages. The fact that Morrison folds these two stages into one seems to be an example of syncretization. As I noted in the introduction, African American depictions of ancestors typically do not distinguish between the Luvèmba and the Musoni stages and instead depict a generic ancestral presence.

Comments by Sethe and Denver indicate that the baby ghost is clearly recognized as the dead daughter/dead sister and thus Sethe's child/Denver's sister is clearly remembered and maintains a place in the family. Yet, Morrison describes Beloved as "violently 'disremembered'" (Carabi 38). This notion of Beloved as disremembered is related to her association with the Middle Passage as those who perished in the Middle Passage are largely unknown and unremembered. In her interview with

Carabi, Morrison notes that she "wanted a baby in a human body, without past or future (having been killed so young), and also to be the embodiment of the past" (38). She goes on to state, "I wanted the association between the physical journey on the slave ships and the grave to be very strong" (39). Morrison is able to create this association through a character who can move back and forth across the Kalûnga line and converse with "those who have gone before."

In speaking of ancestors, Pobee uses the term, "those who have gone before," as all departed are not literal ancestors. However, we must also remember that all departed are not ancestral either. For example, Pobee warns, "The man who in life was morally bankrupt is disqualified from being an ancestor; so is the one who dies tragically. . . . The ancestor is the one who lived to a ripe old age and in an exemplary manner or did much to enhance the prestige and standing of the family, clan, and tribe" (8). In other words, everyone who dies is not in the position to pass on ancestral knowledge. The position of ancestor, like that of elder, must be achieved. Thus, as Fu-Kiau describes the movement from the Tukula position to Luvèmba, he notes that the change may be either positive or negative, "After his tukula step, man must descend into the deepest world. . . . The descent at ku mpèmba is to enter, positively or negatively, the process of change" (30). During the movement from ku nseke, the physical world, to ku mpèmba, the spiritual world, "the life/death struggle is experienced" (30). However, once one has moved from the physical world to the spiritual world this does not end one's connection to the physical world. Janheinz Jahn observes, "According to African philosophy, the departed are spiritual forces which can influence their living descendants" (110). This point is affirmed by Morrison in her interview with Darling when she observes, "The gap between Africa and Afro-America and the gap between the living and the dead and the gap between the past and the present does not exist' (247). The ogbanje figure is ideal for illustrating the continuity between Africans and African Americans, the living and the dead, and the past and present.

In her 1991 essay, "Mother Right/Write Revisited: *Beloved* and *Dessa Rose* and the Construction of Motherhood in Black Women's Fiction," Carole Boyce Davies notes that although several anthropological texts make reference to the abiku or ogbanje belief, to her knowledge, "no African feminist scholar or writer has fully explored the social, theoretical, gendered implications of the *abiku* or *ogbanje* for African women" (57). Although not an African feminist scholar, Bastian, writing in 2002, observes an increase in ogbanje narratives in Nigeria: "Although a comprehensive survey of all Nigerian fiction would demonstrate that the importance of spirit children is nothing new to this country's writers, it appears that there has been an escalation of published narratives that center on not-quite-human creatures like *ogbaanje*[4] in the past two decades" ("Irregular" 59). Although Bastian concerns herself with the representation of ogbanje in popular discourse as a means to understanding socioreligious systems, literary critics have started to make note of the ogbanje phenomenon outside of African literature. Thus scholars have begun to make connections between Beloved and ogbanje or abiku. Chikwenye Okonjo Ogunyemi's "An Abiku-Ogbanje Atlas: A Pre-Text for Rereading Soyinka's *Aké* and Morrison's *Beloved*" published in 2002 provides some indication of the appeal of the ogbanje/abiku figure. Ogunyemi asserts, "the abiku emerges as a perverse, ghostly intimation of a horrendous past, a critique of a tedious present, and a reminder of mortality. The abiku doubles as a signifier for social and spiritual unease" (664). What better figure for Morrison to use to address the "social and spiritual unease" of slavery? Teresa N. Washington's 2005 essay, "The Mother–Daughter Àjé Relationship in Toni Morrison's *Beloved*," focuses on Àjé, the Yoruba concept referring to a spiritual force believed to be inherent in Africana women; however, she also identifies Beloved as "the *àbikú* child of the Yoruba—the one born-to-die—who is slashed and scarred to prevent return, but re-enters, from the spirit realm, the traumatized womb for rebirth and perhaps a chance at terrestrial longevity" (180–81). However, it is Okonkwo's 2008 book, *A Spirit of Dialogue: Incarnations of Ọ́gbañje, the Born-to-Die, in African American Literature*, which points to the paradoxical nature of Beloved's ogbanje status. Okonkwo notes, "On one hand is her malevolence and, on the other, her positivist situation as an agitator, a trigger, a kind of change agent that helps set in motion Sethe's as well as Paul D's healing memories of their repressed pasts" (160). Like Okonkwo, I argue that Beloved is an ogbanje seeking revenge for her murder; however, in the process Beloved forces Sethe to face her past and thus positions Sethe to move forward with her life; however, I also note the beneficial ancestral presence of Baby Suggs.

According to Achebe, "The literal meaning of an ogbanje is . . . one who comes repeatedly or one who dies and comes again" (33). Thus, it is Beloved's apparent return from the dead that undergirds my contention that she is in fact an ogbanje. However, it is Beloved's determination to torment Sethe that confirms my assessment. The objective of the ogbanje "is to torment its parents by dying early in infancy or before it completes the legitimate life cycle. And as soon as it can, it comes back with the same personality to be born to the same woman. It thus repeats this ruthless cycle unless something desperate is done to arrest it" (33). Before moving forward with my argument about Beloved as an ogbanje, I would like to address an issue that other scholars seem to overlook. Within the African context, the ogbanje is described as dying early, but Sethe murders Beloved. I contend that this deviation in form is a syncretization, which allows Morrison to take into account the New World context and the history of infanticide associated with slavery. Critic, William R. Handley makes a similar argument, noting "*Beloved* bears the unmistakable marks of African cultural practice. Yet Morrison's novel is also an American story whose narration is both defined and limited by the historical losses of life, culture, and dignity wrought by slave traders and slave owners during and after the Middle Passage" (678). Whether Morrison is aware of the African belief in ogbanje or not, she is knowledgeable regarding other aspects of African philosophy. For example, in her interview with Darling, Morrison comments, "it was clear to me that it was not at all a violation of African religion and philosophy; it's very easy for a son or parent or a neighbor to appear in a child or in another person" (249). This remark suggests that Morrison is informed regarding some aspects of African religious beliefs, but perhaps does not feel the need to reproduce them exactly as long as she does not violate them. However, I am not as concerned with authorial intention as I am with the result and I contend that Morrison's work reflects Africanisms whether consciously or unconsciously employed. As with the other writers discussed in this book, Morrison's work is infused with aspects of Kongo cosmology, which is most evident in her use of an Ogbanje figure.

Bastian notes that "*Ogbaanje* are, first and foremost, what my Igbo friends would call (when feeling charitable) 'returning children'" ("Irregular" 59). And this is indeed what Beloved proves to be—Sethe's child returned from the dead. Both Denver and Sethe welcome her return; however, Beloved's mischievousness and desire for revenge soon become apparent. This malevolent aspect of Beloved's character is suggested by Bastian's fuller explanation of ogbanje: "Such a returning child embodies, in the human world, a mischievous, spiritual person—one who is interested in human life, who could almost be said to experiment with the idea of being human, but who is not him/herself human and who has little interest in committing to a human lineage" (59). This idea of experimenting with human life is reflected in Beloved's fear of exploding. When she loses her back tooth, she thinks, "Next would be her arm, her hand, a toe. Pieces of her would drop maybe one at a time, maybe all at once" (Morrison, *Beloved* 157). The difficulty Beloved has keeping her body together and her fear of exploding points to the idea of playing a human role rather than being human.[5] Beloved has taken on a human form to not only connect with her mother, but to seek revenge. She tells Denver that she has come to see Sethe's face, but her deeper motivation is revealed in her statements: " 'She left me behind. By myself' " and " 'She is the one. She is the one I need' " (89). These statements imply the obsessive attraction Beloved has for Sethe.

Beloved's craving for Sethe's attention also is apparent in the way in which she draws out stories regarding Sethe's life at Sweet Home. For example, Beloved asks Sethe to tell her about her diamonds. "Sethe learned the profound satisfaction Beloved got from storytelling. It amazed Sethe (as much as it pleased Beloved) because every mention of her past life hurt. Everything in it was painful or lost. She and Baby Suggs had agreed without saying so that it was unspeakable; to Denver's inquiries Sethe gave short replies or rambling incomplete reveries" (69). Thus, Beloved was able to draw out things from Sethe in a way Denver never could. This ability is in keeping with the traits attributed to abiku and ogbanje. For instance, Ogunyemi comments that the abiku "is wise beyond his years as he seeks to appropriate elder rights, the basis of parental authority. From hindsight, he knows what is missing from the past; with insight, he manipulates the present; and with foresight, he will disappear, then create and move on to a new place" (665–66). Because the abiku or ogbanje has been here before, he or she has special insight regarding the past that can then be manipulated. Consequently, Beloved is able to probe Sethe about her past, whereas Denver is relegated to one and two word responses. So when Denver hears Sethe's response to Beloved's question about her diamonds, she says she never saw her earrings and asks where they are now. But rather than a story, as Beloved receives, Sethe responds, " 'Gone,' . . . 'Long gone,' and she wouldn't say another word' " (Morrison, *Beloved* 71). Sethe would like to keep a lid of silence on her past, as this is more comfortable than confronting the trauma of slavery. In fact, Rody suggests:

> The novel's distinctive tone arises from the very difficulty of telling for those recovering from the traumas of slavery—witnessing the murder, torture, or sale of family and friends; being whipped, chained, led with an iron bit in the mouth, and housed in an underground "box"; being examined and cataloged in terms of "human" and "animal" characteristics, or forcibly "nursed" by white boys when one's breasts held milk for a baby. These experiences fragment and block the memories of Morrison's ex-slaves, whose stories are revealed in bits, out of sequence, in a painful eking out and holding back often rendered in spare synecdoche. . . . (99–100)

Hence, Sethe's reticence to share her stories about Sweet Home is Sethe's meager attempt to manage the pain associated with those memories. However, her attempt to repress the past although instinctive, is not psychologically healthy. In "Psychic Trauma and Its Reconstruction with Particular Reference to Postchildhood Trauma," Sidney S. Furst claims, "The massive repression which is sometimes resorted to in the attempt to overcome the effects of trauma almost invariably fails, and instead predisposes to repeated traumatization" (32). This indeed seems to be Sethe's condition more than a decade after escaping slavery.

Yet Beloved is able to entice Sethe to move beyond her protective shell of silence and to share some of her stories about her early years. Beloved's ability to coax Sethe into talking about the past may be ascribed to her precociousness. According to Achebe, "these spirit children are precocious and exhibit a pattern of behavior outside of the norm of their age group" (34). Thus when Beloved asks Sethe, " 'Your woman she never fix up your hair?' " (Morrison, *Beloved* 72), Sethe finds herself telling a story, which triggers a memory that she had all but forgotten. As she tells Beloved and Denver about her mother: She worked in the indigo fields, she only nursed her for a few weeks, she had a circle and cross burnt under her breast, and she was hung. In the midst of telling this story, Sethe remembers Nan pulling her from the pile of bodies before she could find her mother's mark. The power of this rememory is apparent in Sethe's flustered response as she tries to do something with her hands as she confronts "[s]omething privately shameful" (73). Prior to Beloved's arrival, Sethe tried to explain the power of rememory to Denver:

> "Where I was before I came here, that place is real. It's never going away. Even if the whole farm—every tree and grass blade of it dies. The picture is still there and what's more, if you go there—you who never was there—if you go there and stand in the place where it was, it will happen again; it will be there for you, waiting for you. So, Denver, you can't never go there. Never. Because even though it's all over—over and done with—it's going to always be there waiting for you. That's how come I had to get all my children out. No matter what." (43–44)

It is during this conversation that mother and daughter confirm that " 'nothing ever dies' " (44). Not only does nothing ever die, but memories also do not stay buried.

In *Quiet as it's Kept: Shame, Trauma, and Race in the Novels of Toni Morrison*, Bouson asserts, "Sethe's account of her 'rememory'—that is, her uncontrolled remembering and reliving of emotionally painful experiences—recalls descriptions of a visual form of memory that trauma investigators refer to as traumatic memory" (135). Thus many of these rememories are not narrative memories, which Sethe can form into words, but yet they play an important role in her psyche. Thus, Sethe does not share the memory triggered by the story, but in fact sees the memory "getting clear and clearer as she folded and refolded damp laundry" (Morrison, *Beloved* 73). According to Bouson, "Because traumatic memories, unlike normal or so called narrative memories, are not readily incorporated into existing mental categories and schemes, victims of trauma find it difficult to assimilate and articulate what has happened to them" (135). Sethe had forgotten what Nan had told her as well as the language it had been told in, but "the message—that was and had been there all along" (Morrison, *Beloved* 74). Nan told Sethe about how she and her mother had been taken many times by the crew, but her mother only put her arms around the black man: " 'She threw them all away but you. The one from the crew she threw away on the island. The others from more whites she also threw away. Without names, she threw them. You she gave the name of the black man' " (74). Sethe is described as having been unimpressed by the story as a child and angry as an adult, but I contend that Sethe's inherited story of infanticide is crucial to Morrison's reworking of ogbanje in *Beloved*.

However, in order to understand Sethe's inherited story of infanticide, one must better understand her relationship with her mother. Although Sethe's mother worked in the fields and did not sleep with Sethe most nights, she made a point of showing her the mark burnt into her skin: " 'This is your ma'am. This,' and she pointed. 'I am the only one got this mark now. The rest dead. If something happens to me and you can't tell me by my face, you can know me by this mark' " (72). Upon hearing this, Sethe is concerned that she will not be recognized and wants to be marked too. Her mother responds by slapping her face. Sethe says, "I didn't understand it then. Not till I had a mark of my own" (73). The mark to which Sethe refers is the tree planted on her back when the boys whip her for telling on them for stealing her milk. Significantly, both her mark and her mother's mark are connected in some way to lactation and thus to motherhood. Thus Sethe's later understanding of her mother's slap may be attributed not only to her scar but also to her maternal role. In reference to *Beloved*, Carol E. Henderson states, "The stories behind the wounds on the psyches of many of these characters are as important as the scars evident on the flesh itself. Freedom for these individuals rests on tracing the multiple figurations of the scar—from its fleshly denotation to its cerebral connotation" (85). Much critical attention has been devoted to the significance of Sethe's mark, but not nearly as much to her mother's mark.

In Chapter 3, I discuss Ayo's scars as an example of archival memory. Michael Kreyling makes a similar point in *The South That Wasn't There: Postsouthern Memory and History* when he states, "With no other means of recording 'data,' the slave body itself became an archive" (29). Sethe's mother points out her mark to Sethe so that she may be identified, but what else does this mark tell us about Sethe's mother? Mae Henderson remarks "her mother had transformed a mark of mutilation, a sign of diminished humanity, into a sign of recognition and identity" ("Toni" 95). This reconfiguring of the slaveholder's mark seems to be in keeping with the type of resistance that might have gotten Sethe's mother hung. Yet Boyce Davies reads this mark as African scarification rather than the slaveholder's brand; she notes, "One thesis holds that African peoples, during the period of slave trafficking, deliberately inscribed ethnic identities on faces and bodies" ("Mother" 48). This thesis is particularly attractive in this setting because the mark resembles the Kongo cosmogram, yet this does not take into account the slap Sethe receives when she asks to be marked as well. Perhaps the slap is in response to an African symbol being denigrated as a brand to mark slave ownership—something far removed from its African purpose. Regardless of how we read the mark, the slap tells us that this is not what Sethe's mother wanted for her daughter. Kreyling observes, "The scar that marks the white man's possession and the breast of her mother are nearly conflated in Sethe's memory, and carry in the novel the heaviest burden of the particular suffering and identity of the woman enslaved" (38). If one considers the slap and the mark together, one might say that the slap is indicative of the way in which the New World has ruptured an African identity. In other words, Sethe's mother does not want Sethe to be marked with this African symbol because in the New World setting the meaning has been reconstituted as a symbol of ownership. This mark is not what Sethe's mother wants for her child.

The conflation of Sethe's mother's mark with her maternity is suggestive for our reading of infanticide. According to literary critic Gurleen Grewel, "Infanticide, Sethe's raw act of defense, runs counter to the slave community's response of resistance, namely, their determined effort to keep alive family ties despite the master's attempt to sunder them" (156–57). Despite Grewel's assertion, Morrison's novel suggests that Sethe's act was not without precedent—her own mother committed infanticide in response to her rape by the crew and other whites. Even Ella "had delivered, but would not nurse, a hairy white thing, fathered by 'the lowest yet.' It lived five days never making a sound" (305). Ella and Sethe's mother commit infanticide with children born of rape, whereas Sethe kills out of love. Each of these women rejected the role that *partus sequitur ventrem* required of them—they would not pass on the condition of slavery to their offspring, either because they would not raise children who were the product of rape or because they did not want the children they loved to be enslaved. In choosing to commit infanticide, these women refused to allow their wombs to be used for the good of the slave master.

This then leads to the crux of the story—was Sethe justified—was this the right thing to do? Sethe is subjected to the judgment of the community, but really only Beloved can answer this question of whether Sethe's actions were appropriate. In her interview with Carabi, Morrison observes, Sethe "tried very hard to say: 'This is the right thing to do.' And she was not repentant at all, but in the face of that child—not the neighbors, not Paul D—but in the face of that child she would have to explain and explain—and she could never explain enough. Now she is not so sure of her deed" (87). Because of the ogbanje's ability to traverse the Kalûnga line, it is the perfect tool for exploring this complex question. Yes, Sethe acted out of love, but Beloved questions whether she had the right to act.

Beloved's return seems motivated by love for her mother, but also longing and perhaps even shame. In fact I would argue that Beloved's emotions are a heightened form of the "[s]omething privately shameful that had seeped into a slit in [Sethe's] mind right behind the slap on her face and the circled cross" (Morrison, *Beloved* 73). Readers are not told what inspired this sense of shame in Sethe, but one might surmise that the shame might be connected to the thought that her mother might have been involved in an escape attempt without her. Thus, the shame would be attributed to her sense of abandonment. In her essay, "Nameless Ghosts: Possession and Dispossession in *Beloved*," Deborah Horvitz addresses Sethe's sense of desertion, "her memories of Ma'am are buried not only because their relationship was vague and their contact prohibited but also because those recollections are inextricably woven with feelings of painful abandonment. If Sethe remembers her mother, she must also remember that she believes her mother deserted her" (95).[6] Beloved too feels abandoned by her mother, but to a greater degree, knowing that her own mother had slit her throat. This knowledge then engenders a love/hate relationship, which proves to be both beneficial and dangerous for Sethe.

Beloved's threat to Sethe's safety is confirmed by the choking episode. While in the Clearing with Denver and Beloved watching her from the trees, Sethe feels fingers first massaging her neck and then choking her. Denver runs to Sethe when she falls from her seat on the rock, thrashing her legs and clawing at her throat. Beloved follows after Denver and massages Sethe's neck and kisses her bruises, but Denver realizes that Beloved had choked her in the first place. In response to Denver's accusation that she made Sethe choke, Beloved replies, " 'I fixed it, didn't I? Didn't I fix her neck?' " (119). Beloved's act of first choking and then kissing Sethe's neck is indicative of this love–hate relationship. She loves her mother, but she wants to punish her for leaving her.

Beloved is described as only having eyes for Sethe. Morrison says Beloved "is insatiable. Sethe could never give her enough. She represents 350 years of indifference, so it would take her 350 years to fill her up" (Carabi 87). And Sethe tries as best as she can to satisfy Beloved. In fact, her actions are in line with Ogunyemi's description of parental responses to abiku: "desperate parents resort to bribery in an attempt at a democratic solution—for him to choose to live" (664). The partiality Sethe shows toward Beloved increased once she saw and fingered the scar under Beloved's chin—from that point on it was as if only she and Beloved existed. Sethe spends so much time playing games with Beloved that she goes to work later and later and eventually loses her job. Denver reflects on this change in her mother, "And instead of looking for another job, Sethe played all the harder with Beloved, who never got enough of anything: lullabies, new stitches, the bottom of the cake bowl, the top of the milk. If the hen had only two eggs, she got both. It was as though her mother had lost her mind . . ." (Morrison, *Beloved* 282). Denver's fear that Sethe has lost her mind is in response to Sethe's determination to do anything to please Beloved. Sethe does this as a means to make amends, but Achebe notes, "a mother would be prepared to infringe rules and break societal taboos on behalf of her ogbanje child if only by so doing she could preserve the life of her child" (34). Sethe seems to believe that if she makes Beloved happy with her games and treats, Beloved will not leave her and this will make up for having cut her throat. For Sethe, this becomes more important than going to work and earning a living.

Since it is clear to Denver that Beloved and Sethe were not interested in her, she merely watches rather than joining in the games. However, she is on the alert for any sign that her mother "would kill again. But it was Beloved who made demands. Anything she wanted she got, and when Sethe ran out of things to give her, Beloved invented desire" (Morrison, *Beloved* 283). It is evident that Sethe is seeking to make amends for taking her daughter's life, but Beloved can never be fully compensated:

> She took the best of everything—first. The best chair, the biggest piece, the prettiest plate, the brightest ribbon for her hair, and the more she took, the more Sethe began to talk, explain, describe how much she had suffered, been through for her children, waving away flies in grape arbors, crawling on her knees to a lean-to. None of which made the impression it was supposed to. Beloved accused her of leaving her behind. (284)

Sethe pleaded for forgiveness in vain. Ogunyemi writes, "The quarrel between parent and child is metaphysical and mutually destructive" (665). We see this as Denver describes broken plates and windows as Beloved raged any time Sethe tried to assert her maternal authority: "little by little it dawned on Denver that if Sethe didn't wake up one morning and pick up a knife, Beloved might" (Morrison, *Beloved* 285). Sethe has lost all control of her relationship with Beloved and has essentially abdicated her maternal role.

This exchange of roles is reflected in Ogunyemi's depiction of the abiku, "The child's desire for attention keeps parent and child intensely invested in each other. Though the parent is initially in control, as the situation worsens, s/he cedes authority to the child, who then enslaves the parent" (666). Sethe's subjugation to Beloved is evident in the way she serves Beloved. Denver is ashamed and pained to see her mother carrying Beloved's night bucket and "pick-eating around the edges of the table and stove: the hominy that stuck on the bottom; the crusts and rinds and peelings of things" (Morrison, *Beloved* 285). As Beloved's stomach is growing fat, Sethe is shrinking before Denver's eyes—even the flesh between her forefinger and thumb began to fade. It is this reversal in body size that has led some critics to describe Beloved as a vampire. Harris says of Beloved, "Like a vampire feeding vicariously, she becomes plump in direct proportion to Sethe's increasing gauntness" (*Fiction* 157). However, Ogunyemi places this role reversal within the ogbanje sphere, "Beloved returns to institute justice by dismantling Sethe's parental authority, reducing Sethe to the role of a child. At the core of the power shift is ogbanje's refusal to be contained, to remain at the assigned place—that of ghost. Beloved is rememory made flesh" (674). As rememory made flesh, Beloved forces Sethe to confront painful memories she has repressed. While this is clearly a painful process, it is also a necessary one.

This need to confront the past is made palpable when Denver recognizes that she must "leave the yard; step off the edge of the world, leave behind and go ask somebody for help" (Morrison, *Beloved* 286). Denver comes to this realization after Sethe spit up something she had not eaten. This incident quickly moves her from protecting Beloved to protecting her mother. Realizing her mother was in need of help, Denver knows she must take action, but it is Baby Suggs who empowers her to take that first step. As she stands on the porch, she remembers Baby Suggs telling Sethe, " 'There's more of us they drowned than there is all of them ever lived from the start of time. Lay down your sword. This ain't a battle; it's a rout' " (287). In the face of this memory, Denver is paralyzed until she hears Baby Suggs laugh, " 'You mean I never told you nothing about Carolina? About your daddy?' " (287). Although Baby Suggs' laugh is crystal clear to Denver, she is actually dead at this moment and serving as an ancestral presence to guide her granddaughter in her time of need. She reaches out from the dead to suggest that there are positive memories to combat the negative ones. Baby Suggs asks, " 'You don't remember nothing about how come I walk the way I do and about your mother's feet, not to speak of her back? I never told you all that? Is that why you can't walk down the steps?" (288). Baby Suggs realizes that in agreeing with Sethe that some things were unspeakable, she had deprived Denver of essential knowledge about her past that might empower her later. Thus in not talking about Sethe's feet, they protected Denver from the pain of slavery, but they also hid from her the power of self-determination. The women may have been ashamed of the beatings that led to Baby Suggs' misshapen hip and Sethe's scarred back, but Baby Suggs now recognizes that these are not necessarily badges of shame, but symbols of survival as she tells Denver to go on out the yard.

With this admonishment to leave the yard, Baby Suggs provides the benevolent, instructive, and protective qualities one might expect from an ancestor. Although Linda Krumholz in "The Ghosts of Slavery: Historical Recovery in Toni Morrison's *Beloved*," describes Baby Suggs as a ritual model rather than an ancestral presence, she recognizes her positive influence: "Although Baby Suggs gave up struggling at the end of her life, her knowledge and spirit, and the knowledge of the past, make possible Denver's emergence into the world. With understanding comes the power to endure and to change" (92). With Baby Suggs' encouragement and guidance Denver finds her way to the home of her former teacher, Mrs. Lady Jones. Although she has not seen her in years, Lady Jones immediately recognizes her, but more significantly she says of Denver, "[e]verybody's child was in that face," suggesting a sense of belonging between Denver and the black community of Cincinnati (Morrison, *Beloved* 290). This recognition of belonging is significant because Sethe had separated herself and her family from the rest of the community after her imprisonment, but Lady Jones recognizes Denver as one of their own. This inclusion of Denver within Cincinnati's black community is also reflective of the communal nature of African societies, which "elevate community over the individual" and "recognize the intricate and mutual reliance of self and the collective" (Okonkwo, "Critical" 656). By leaving her yard, Denver fosters a reunion between her family and the community. This reunion is possible because of Denver's emergence as someone who is keenly attuned to ancestral presence.

Prior to the white men coming into Baby Suggs' yard, Denver's family had been integral members of the black community: "124 had been a cheerful, buzzing house where Baby Suggs, holy, loved, cautioned, fed, chastised and soothed" (Morrison, *Beloved* 103). Baby Suggs was an unchurched preacher who preached in the Clearing, an open space deep in the woods. Arlene R. Keizer says of Baby Suggs' preaching in the Clearing, "Though not African by birth, Baby Suggs creates her own syncretic folk religious practice, based on both West African and Christian spiritual traditions" (37). Her services in the Clearing entailed crying, laughing, singing, and dancing, in many ways echoing the Ring Shout and Big Drum ceremonies described in Marshall's *Praisesong for the Widow*. In fact, Jennings identifies the Clearing, along with "[t]he brand under Ma'am's breast, the 'boxwood brushes, planted in a ring' where Denver plays, the chokecherry tree cicatrix on Sethe's back" as "other cross and circle signages" (197). In the Clearing, Baby Suggs admonishes:

> "we flesh; flesh that weeps, laughs; flesh that dances on bare feet in grass. Love it. Love it hard. Yonder they do not love your flesh. They despise it. They don't love your eyes; they'd just as soon pick em out. No more do they love the skin on your back. Yonder they flay it. And O my people they do not love your hands. Those they only use, tie, bind, chop off and leave empty. Love your hands! Love them. Raise them up and kiss them." (103)

This is essentially a message of self-love in the face of hatred. She is saying that they must not look for love and affirmation from others, but must give it to themselves despite what others might say. This is the same philosophy that guides her advice to Denver—there is no defense, know it, and go on out the yard.

Therese E. Higgins describes Baby Suggs "as the ancestor who gives Denver the courage and the impetus to fight back, to become the strong, reliable woman that Baby Suggs, in freedom might have been"; however, I contend that Baby Suggs was not teaching Denver how to fight back but how to survive (40). For Baby Suggs, there was no defense, which implies that there is no battle plan. What she offers instead is self-love—the requirement for survival. In fact, it is the need to survive that first inspires Denver to seek help, but when she falters Baby Suggs provides the necessary reassurance. Denver is initially motivated by concerns for her mother, but later she realizes the importance of her own survival: "Somebody had to be saved, but unless Denver got work, there would be no one to save, no one to come home to, and no Denver either. It was a new thought, having a self to look out for and preserve" (Morrison, *Beloved* 297). This new thought signals a change in Denver's perspective and in her interactions with the community. In fact, I would argue that Denver's contact with her ancestor, Baby Suggs, has helped to move her forward toward elder status.

According to Bowers, Denver's "efforts lead to everyone's salvation: the reunion of the community. It begins with gifts of food accompanied by the givers' names, but culminates in the women coming to the yard of 124 to exorcise Beloved" (38). With Denver's departure from her yard and reincorporation into the community came the news: "Sethe's dead daughter, the one whose throat she cut, had come back to fix her. Sethe was worn down, speckled, dying, spinning, changing shapes and generally bedeviled" (Morrison, *Beloved* 300). Although some of the women believed Sethe was getting what she deserved, Ella convinced the women to rescue Sethe. Ella's response is guided by her understanding of the relationship between the past and the present and the living and the dead: "As long as the ghost showed out from its ghostly place—shaking stuff, crying, smashing and such—Ella respected it. But if it took flesh and came in her world, well, the shoe was on the other foot. She didn't mind a little communication between the two worlds, but this was an invasion" (302). By becoming flesh, Beloved has overstepped the boundaries of the departed—she is moving between the realm of the living and the dead; she is an ogbanje.

Consequently, Ella leads thirty women in an exorcism of what they believe to be an unnatural presence. Achebe notes ogbanje "is a perversion of that natural life pattern which gives hope of an auspicious life after death" (33). Ella and the other women respond to this perversion by gathering together symbols of Christian faith as well as other belief systems: "Some brought what they could and what they believed would work. Stuffed in apron pockets, strung around their necks, lying in the space between their breasts. Others brought Christian faith—as shield and sword. Most brought a little of both" (Morrison, *Beloved* 303). Morrison does not specify what is tucked in their pockets or strung around their necks, but the implication is that the "little of both" carried by the women represents an amalgamation of Christian and African beliefs. Jennings observes that this syncretization of religious beliefs is embedded in African American religious beliefs. According to Jennings, "West and Central African traditional beliefs amalgamated in the Caribbean and brought to the mainland of North America presently influence African Americans' religious beliefs and practices in ways of which African Americans are unaware" (80). The women did not gather with a coherent plan—some kneeled and prayed, others did not, but soon they broke into song. The song is depicted as "a wave of sound wide enough to sound deep water and knock the pods off chestnut trees. It broke over Sethe and she trembled like the baptized in its wash" (Morrison, *Beloved* 308). Krumholz describes the exorcism as "a purgation ritual, a baptismal cleansing and rebirth, and psychological clearing . . ." (90). For Krumholz, the ritual brings Sethe "back to the original scene of repression and enables her to relive it with a difference" (90). Thus, when Edward Bodwin enters the yard to pick up Denver for work, Sethe goes back in time to that other black hat entering her yard for "her best thing" (Morrison, *Beloved* 308). However, this time she uses the ice pick in her hand to lash out at Mr. Bodwin rather than attacking "her best thing."

All those years ago, Sethe was condemned for making what she thought was the only choice to protect those she loved, but now she believes she has been presented with the opportunity to rethink that choice. In *Race, Trauma, and Home in the Novels of Toni Morrison*, Evelyn Jaffe Schreiber argues, "Reliving traumatic memories is a prerequisite for living in the present" (42). With Bodwin's entrance into her yard, Sethe relives Schoolteacher's entrance in a similar black hat. Bouson observes, "Because Sethe, in this replay of the infanticide, attacks what she believes is the white perpetrator, this scene is often construed by critics as a therapeutic and self-healing reenactment of the original trauma of the infanticide in which the past is revised or reversed" (158). In fact, Harris contends "What Beloved could not see as a 'crawling-already?' baby, she is now able to see as an adult: that her mother's action, many years before an in its current duplicate, was indeed one of love" (163). Bouson notes that while the exorcism does suggest Sethe's deliverance from her haunted past, some commentators wonder about the redemption in attempted murder. She goes on to argue, "That Sethe's attack on Bodwin, which can be read as redemptive, is also an act of revenge points to the unresolved interracial conflict and shame-rage feelings that shape *Beloved*'s presentation of black-white relations" (158). However, Ogunyemi raises another issue regarding the exorcism: "Beloved's dubious disappearance repeats the patterns of the original ogbanje/abiku loss"[7] (676). Thus one is left to ask—is the exorcism a revision of the original loss or a repetition?

In the midst of Sethe's attack on Mr. Bodwin, Beloved disappears. Although several women were in the yard, no one knew what happened to Beloved—one moment they saw her and then they didn't. However, a boy does recall seeing a naked woman with "fish for hair" in the woods (Morrison, *Beloved* 315). This image of a woman with fish for hair immediately conjures up images of the water divinity, Mami Wata[8] who is sometimes "said to have a mermaid's tail" (Bastian, "Married" 123). In "Mami Water in African Religion and Spirituality," Kathleen O'Brien Wicker states, "Water divinities demonstrate by their very nature the divine, the human, and the natural worlds. They express the continuity of life among those not yet born, the living, and the living-timeless" (198–99). Although Beloved has been analyzed as a Mami Wata, I believe this is because of the tendency to conflate some aspects of ogbanje with Mami Wata.[9] For example, Okonwo explains that according to the Igbo creation myth there are two types of ogbanje: "one the 'Ogbanje-Elu' who inherit their qualifier Elu from the female deity of the forest/Ala named, Onabuluwa and, two, the 'Ogbanje-Mmiri,' associated with the River/Water deity called Nne Mmiri . . ." (*Spirit* 9). Although Okonwo refers to two types of ogbanje, Dr. O. Taiwo claims there are three main groups and several subgroups of ogbanje. His main groups include fire dwellers, sea dwellers, and land dwellers (178–80). His sea-dweller category seems akin to Okonwo's Ogbanje-Mmiri. Interestingly, by having Beloved appear to run through the woods with fish for hair, Morrison blends Ogbanje-Elu and Ogbanje-Mmiri or the land and sea dwellers.[10]

However, it is the fish for hair that confirms for me Beloved's inherent ogbanje status and the improbability that the cycle of premature death and return will be broken. Boyce Davies remarks, "In Yoruba cosmology, the *abiku* child eventually stays, when certain rituals and necessary passages have been accomplished" (*Black* 147). Taiwo outlines some of these rituals for ogbanje children. Water and fish are the greatest enemies of sea dwelling ogbanje because their "power lies in the electric fish." Thus, the purification ritual entails catching an electric fish. "It is believed that if he receives a shock in catching the fish, his supernatural powers are imparted to the fish. . . . After the purification, the child dreads the sea, swimming and the sight of live fish" (Taiwo

179). Therefore, if the naked woman with fish for hair is indeed Beloved, she does not seem to be displaying any repulsion towards fish, which suggests that she will not break her oath to Nne-Mmiri and abandon her status as ogbanje.

Before moving forward with my analysis of Beloved as an ogbanje, I should note that although the terms ogbanje and abiku are used interchangeably there are subtle differences.[11] In fact, Taiwo's essay, "Two Incantations to Abiku," is an analysis of two poems entitled "Abiku" written by J. P. Clak and Wole Soyinka, but he concludes his essay with a discussion of categories of Igbo ogbanje as though abiku and ogbanje are one and the same. Yet, Maduka warns that although "*Ogbanje* and *Abiku* are two words—the first Igbo and the second Yoruba—denoting the same reality . . . it is important to remember . . . that words designating a concept common to two languages do not have precisely the same semantic extension" (17).[12] In noting the difference between the Igbo o'gbañje and the Yoruba àbíkú, Okonkwo observes "unlike the journey-focus of Q'gbañje and its stress of Iyi Uwa, both of which are distinctly Igbo, àbíkú emphasizes mortality" (*Spirit* 17). I have elected to use the term *ogbanje* in reference to Beloved because Morrison appears to be emphasizing the movement back and forth between the living and the dead rather than a concern with mortality. I also contend that my selection of ogbanje rather than abiku is tied to what ultimately happens to Beloved.

Unlike the abiku child to whom Boyce Davies refers, Beloved does not stay; there is in fact no indication that the cycle of ogbanje has been broken. This exorcism may be no more successful than the one by Paul D, which led to Beloved's incarnation. Various critics have tried to make sense of Beloved's disappearance, but the focus has tended to be on its inexplicability. In " 'A Story to Pass On': Ghosts and the Significance of History in Toni Morrison's *Beloved*," Barbara Hill Rigney suggests, "The spirit of Beloved, thus, is relegated to the fringes of consciousness, to the watery essence from which she came, and to the world of myth that is the lost African identity" (233). According to Grewal, "Beloved goes as she comes; the unaccountability of her whereabouts, her physical absence, constitutes the experience of loss at the heart of slavery" (169). Grewal goes on to suggest that things have come full circle and that Beloved is gone because the past has now been confronted; however, I do not think the ending is as tidy as that. I suspect Beloved is merely gone for the moment. Toward the close of the novel, the reader is told, "By and by all trace is gone, and what is forgotten is not only the footprints but the water too and what it is down there. The rest is weather" (Morrison, *Beloved* 324). Initially, this may sound as if Beloved has all but disappeared, but the reference to weather here and a few lines later suggest that there is something more to this weather. Ogunyemi observes, "Besides being climatic, weather is a sign of instability—the inevitable shifts in a life" (676). Within Kongo cosmology, the inevitable shifts in life involve the cycle of birth, life, death, and rebirth. Thus, I like Okonkwo believe "at the end of the narrative Beloved becomes an un-born-in-waiting . . ." (159). In fact, Caroline Rody points out "various suggestions open the possibility that the naked pregnant 'wild woman' of the woods rumored to have given birth to Joe Trace is the woman of the same description last seen running toward the stream behind 124 in *Beloved*" (100). However, Rody also notes that these readings do not factor in the fact that Beloved was pregnant in 1874, while Joe was born in 1873.[13] While it would be nice to know what happens to Beloved, I suspect her future or futures will remain as mysterious as Sethe's.

Although some commentators read the closing pages of *Beloved* as very affirming for Sethe's future, I suggest the closing is more ambiguous and that Sethe's future hinges on her willingness to listen to ancestral wisdom. Grewal asserts, "On the metaphorical level, Beloved is gone because the past she represents has been confronted. Events have come full circle, and Sethe has been saved. In facing the past, Sethe emerges, released from it into the present" (169). Morrison actually confirms this reading of the ending in her interview with Carabi when asked about Beloved's disappearance, "Beloved has no place there now. Sethe is now going to concentrate on taking care of herself, the beloved that is inside her, which is her. She is the beloved, not the child. The past is returned and buried again or gone" (87). This indeed sounds as if Sethe has been saved, but I am troubled by this description of the past. This notion that the past might be buried again does not sound any different from the repressed past readers encountered at the opening of the novel. Schreiber notes that "*Beloved* raises the question of how to recover from trauma . . ." (32). The answer is certainly not to bury the past. In fact, the inability to bury the past is evident in Morrison's concept of "rememory." According to Schreiber, "What Morrison calls 'rememory,' the intrusive, uncontrollable repetition of cultural trauma, prevents the erasure of past trauma. Although Sethe would like to forget the painful past, she can only moderate her 'rememories,' not control them" (39). Sethe has already said that nothing ever dies, so I suspect that there is more to Beloved's disappearance than the past being gone.

This suspicion regarding the past's disappearance and Sethe's salvation is amplified by the image of Sethe in bed questioning whether she is indeed her own best thing. After the exorcism, Beloved is gone and Sethe is supposedly saved, but Denver tells Paul D that she thinks she has lost her mother. When Paul D goes to visit Sethe, 124 is strangely quiet: "Something is missing from 124. Something larger than the people who lived there. Something more than Beloved or the red light" (Morrison, *Beloved* 319). Although Paul D cannot put his finger on what's missing, the utter lifelessness of the home seems to be shouting at him. What makes this particularly eerie is that the house is not empty. Sethe is actually quietly humming and singing in Baby Suggs' old bed. Upon finding Sethe, Paul D fears that Sethe has taken to Baby Suggs' bed to die.

It is clear that Sethe is consumed with grief about losing Beloved yet again, and does not seem to see herself as beloved or her own best thing. Achebe reminds us, "apart from the sudden, mysterious, and seemingly inexplicable deaths of ogbanjes, they are also thought to be callous and chillingly indifferent to the hurt they cause others, particularly their mothers" (34). The exorcism meant to save Sethe has sent her to bed with no plans to get up again. However, Paul D intervenes by reminding Sethe, " 'You your best thing, Sethe. You are' " (Morrison, *Beloved* 322). I argue that this notion that she is her own best thing is merely a re-articulation of what Baby Suggs preached for years in the Clearing. Baby Suggs admonished them to love their flesh: " 'You got to love it, you!" (104). One might wonder why it was difficult for Sethe to absorb this lesson from an elder she respected, but I contend that this resistance is related to her relationship with her own mother. Literary scholar Angelyn Mitchell argues, "Most of Sethe's traumas produced by slavery, reside in the construct of motherhood: she is prevented from knowing her mother, she watches her mother murdered; she is beaten while she is pregnant; she gives birth in slavery and while escaping; and she murders her daughter to save her" (99). However, I would contend that what is more disturbing than finding her dead mother is suspecting that her mother elected to flee without her. Mitchell remarks, "Sethe wants to believe that her mother was not caught trying to escape without her, and it is possible that she was lynched for an act unrelated to escape. But if Sethe's mother was escaping without Sethe, then the notion of enslaved mother as self-sacrificing is exploded" (98). Mitchell argues that "The impressionable Sethe reads her mother's life as a discourse of resistance. In the short time they are together, Sethe learns from her mother the value of the self" (100–01). Although Sethe may have gained the strength to resist slavery from her mother, the second lesson does not seem to have held. To learn this lesson would mean to accept that her mother valued herself more than Sethe. Any time Sethe broaches the thought of her mother leaving her, she becomes upset. Thus, for Sethe to love her flesh, to love herself would mean to forgive her mother for abandoning her. I suspect it is her inability to forgive her own mother which makes Sethe particularly susceptible to Beloved's abuse—Sethe does not really want forgiveness because she cannot forgive herself.

Sethe did not learn this lesson of self-love while Baby Suggs lived, but perhaps, like Denver, she will learn the lesson now that Baby Suggs is in the realm of the ancestors. Perhaps she will make the link between the loving massages to her neck she received from beyond the grave, Baby Suggs' admonition to love your flesh, and Paul D's assertion that she is her own best thing. Morrison has shown that communication between the living and the dead is accepted by both Sethe and Denver; however, I am proposing that in addition to direct contact, Baby Suggs works through Paul D to deliver her message. Prior to the choking incident, Sethe actually calls on Baby Suggs, "Just the fingers, she thought. Just let me feel your fingers again on the back of my neck and I will lay it all down . . ." (112). Like Denver, Sethe has focused on only one part of Baby Suggs' message—the fact that they are outnumbered and thus should not even fight. It is this thought that almost prevents Denver from leaving her porch, but Baby Suggs then realizes that she needs to know more about her past in order to move forward, so she tells her about Carolina and her father. Denver is receptive to Baby Suggs' other worldly conversation and it provides the impetus for her to leave the porch. The advice was unsought, but well received. Sethe, on the other hand, actively seeks Baby Suggs' counsel: "Baby Suggs' long-distance love was equal to any skin-close love she had known. The desire, let alone the gesture, to meet her needs was good enough to lift her spirits to the place where she could take the next step: ask for some clarifying word; some advice . . ." (112). Sethe recognizes Baby Suggs' wisdom and desires to benefit from it. And although Sethe believes Baby Suggs' long-distance love to be equal to any skin-close love, I contend that Baby Suggs uses skin-close love to get her message across. Sethe lovingly remembers:

> . . . the touch of those fingers that she knew better than her own. They had bathed her in sections, wrapped her womb, combed her hair, oiled her nipples, stitched her clothes, cleaned her feet, greased her back and dropped just about anything they were doing to massage Sethe's nape when, especially in the early days, her spirits fell down under the weight of the things she remembered and those she did not: schoolteacher writing in ink she herself had made while his nephews played on her. . . . (116–17)

Paul D echoes the care and concern showed by Baby Suggs when he offers to run a bath for Sethe and rub her feet.

Initially, Sethe is hesitant to trust Paul D because the last time she saw him he was ready to count her feet. She had gone to the Clearing to get advice from Baby Suggs and had come away with the intention of telling him about killing her daughter. But before Sethe could share her story, Paul D confronted her with the newspaper clipping and she could not get her story out right. She tried to explain, but he told her, " 'You got two feet, Sethe, not four' . . . and right then a forest sprang up between them; trackless and quiet" (194). With this comment, Paul D aligned himself with schoolteacher who had documented her human characteristics alongside her animal traits. But now in this conversation with Sethe, Paul D is ready to listen, to put her story next to his. Schreiber suggests, "to live in the present, symbolic world, Sethe must reshape memory and tell a new story. Paul D and the community will help Sethe to remember her traumatic past and to learn to live with it in the present. Communal rememory transforms traumatic personal memory" (43). This is what Sethe had hoped for as she left the Clearing: "Her story was bearable because it was his as well—to tell, to refine and tell again" (Morrison, *Beloved* 116). Rody refers to this as "a mutual talking cure" ("Toni" 99). They can both move beyond their painful pasts by talking through their hurt. This time, Paul D has not come to sit in judgment, but to move forward as he tells her, " 'me and you, we got more yesterday than anybody. We need some kind of tomorrow" (322). Paul D has faced the past and is ready to move forward and hopes that Sethe is ready to do the same.[14] While Paul D offers Sethe "a mutual talking cure," I would suggest that whether Sethe accepts it or not is contingent on whether Sethe heeds the wisdom of her ancestor. She will need to see the connection between what Paul D is offering (she is her own best thing) and what Baby Suggs has preached (love her flesh).

Thus whether Sethe is indeed ready to leave the past behind and move forward will depend on how she responds to the admonishment: "It was not a story to pass on" (324). Numerous critics have commented on the ambiguity of this phrase, repeated three times in some form in the last two pages of the text. For example, Krumholz asserts, "This line recapitulates the tension between repression and rememory figured throughout the novel. In one reading, the story is not one to pass by or to pass over. At the same time, the more evident meaning is intensely ironic—'This is not a story to pass on,' and yet, as the novel shows us, it must be" (95). The story, like the ancestor's wisdom, must be taken into account. In her essay, "Rootedness: The Ancestor as Foundation," Morrison states, "When you kill the ancestor you kill yourself. I want to point out the dangers, to show that nice things don't always happen to the totally self-reliant if there is no conscious historical connection" (344). For the black community of Cincinnati, Sethe's great sin was her self-reliance. After committing infanticide, Sethe was led away to jail, but she was not dejected—her head was held high and her back straight. The community had been prepared to wrap her in its arms and steady her, but her stance told them that they were not needed or welcomed. Whether Sethe is truly saved at the close of the novel will depend on whether she has realized the need for community, including elder women like Ella and ancestors like Baby Suggs. If she can answer affirmatively that she is indeed her own best thing as her ancestor, Baby Suggs preached and her mother displayed, then Sethe will love herself enough to put the past behind her.

While Sethe's future hinges on her responsiveness to ancestral intercession, Baby Suggs, not Beloved, is the source of this beneficial, instructive, and protective ancestral presence. In "Ancestral Spirituality and Society in Africa," Ogbu U. Kalu notes, "Death is a mere passage from the human world to the spirit world. The passage enhances the spiritual powers so that one could now operate in the human environment and especially in the human family as a guardian, protective spirit/power/influence" (54). This is indeed the role Baby Suggs plays as she massages Sethe's neck and speaks to Denver from beyond the grave. Although Beloved also comes from the spirit realm, she is not an ancestor. Dominique Zahan cautions in "Some Reflections on African Spirituality," "It is important also to note that not all dead people automatically attain the status of ancestor. . . . The notion of ancestor implies the idea of selection. It is necessary that it correspond, before any other consideration, to a social model based on the idea of exemplification, in the strictest sense of the word" (11). While Beloved is not an ancestral presence, children are often seen as conduits for ancestral spirits. For example, Kalu observes, "The belief in reincarnation further confirms that ancestors do return through children" (55). Zahan further explicates this point, "In most African societies, it is thought that the newborn of both sexes, while being the result of the fertilization of woman by man, carry within them (in forms defined by each individual society) an ancestor" ("Some" 12). In the chapter which follows, "The Child Figure as a Means to Ancestral Knowledge in *Daughters of the Dust* and *A Sunday in June*," I examine the relationship between children and ancestors.

Part III Preface

The Child and Ancestor Bond

In the introduction, I noted the close association between the child and the ancestor, as reflected in beliefs regarding reincarnation; however, children also play an important role in remembering deceased parents. According to John Mbiti, "parents are remembered by their children when they die. Anyone who dies without leaving behind a child or close relative to remember him or pour out libations for him is a very unfortunate person" (*Introduction* 111). Mbiti also observes, "The life of the individual is extended beyond death by the fact of being married and bearing children, because these children survive him and remain a constant evidence that their father and mother once existed. The son or daughter subsequently keeps up the memory of the parents" (111). In fact, it is the act of being remembered that designates one as a living-dead rather than a spirit. Although the living dead are still viewed as members of their families, spirits have been forgotten: "After four or five generations, the living dead are finally forgotten personally because those who knew them while they were human beings will by then have died as well. Their spirits are consequently lost to human memory" (126). Thus, the ancestor must rely on the child to be remembered; however, the child may benefit from the wisdom of ancestors.

Mbiti describes the living-dead as "guardians of family affairs" due to their protective stance towards their living family members (*African* 82). According to Mbiti, "The departed do not grow spiritually towards or like God, though some may act as intermediaries between men and God and may have more power and knowledge than human beings" (160). Because of their more powerful position and greater knowledge, ancestors may be called on for assistance or they may choose to intercede on behalf of their living family. Although ancestors may contact anyone,

151

I contend that there is a special relationship between children and ancestors that makes children more amenable or receptive to the ancestors' wishes. According to Bunseki Fu-Kiau, the Luvèmba and Musoni stage precede the Kala stage. The Kala stage represents the "existence stage of life," and thus I have designated this position as that of the child. However, it is during the Luvèmba stage that one leaves the physical world and thus I associate this stage with that of the living-dead, while the Musoni stage is described as a stage of preparation for the Kala stage and thus I connect it with spirits. Fu-Kiau states that "The position of musoni is associated with the notion of ndoki, the knower of man's principles . . . or science of higher knowledge" (33). Thus, just at the point when no living person remembers them, those at the Musoni stage "become a true knower of what is marked on one's own mind and body" (33). It is this stage that prepares one for rebirth or the Kala stage. However, in the texts that I discuss here there does not seem to be a need for the fine distinction between the Luvèmba and Musoni stages, and thus I consider both as ancestors without regard to how long they have been deceased.

This book's analysis began at the peak of the life cycle with a discussion of the Tukula stage or elder and then moved on to ancestors and is closing with the child. By now it should be apparent that the texts are using an African sense of family, which is more expansive than one might ordinarily consider. Thus, "The idea of the family also extends to include the departed, as well as those who are about to be born" (Mbiti, *Introduction* 115). There is interaction between all of these members of the family. Elders call on ancestors. Ancestors reach out to elders, children, and the unborn. Children and the unborn turn to elders and ancestors for guidance. This final chapter addresses the often-overlooked role of children and the unborn in dispensing ancestral knowledge.

The Child Figure as a Means to Ancestral Knowledge in *Daughters of the Dust* and *A Sunday in June*

Although references are made to the elder and the ancestor, the focus of this chapter is the child figure. In the case of Julie Dash's *Daughters of the Dust*, the child figure is called forth as a means of bringing ancestral cultural healing to her parents and extended family. Although the children in Phyllis Alesia Perry's *A Sunday in June* are not called forth in the same manner, births are predicted by foremothers who seem to have a special bond with their descendants. While Mary Nell, Eva, and Grace are not called on a "spiritual mission," they, like the Unborn Child, exemplify the relationship between the ancestor and the child (Dash, *Daughters: Making* 134). In the case of both texts, the child figures serve as conduits between ancestors and the living, as ancestors attempt to resolve family problems.

According to Bunseki Fu-Kiau, "A human being's life is a continuous process of transformation, a going around and around. . . . The human being is kala-zima-kala, a living-dying-living being" (35). This circle of life and death is particularly apparent in the proximity of the ancestor and the child. On the Kongo cosmogram, the Musoni position immediately precedes the Kala position. Fu-Kiau refers to the Musoni stage as the first stage or "formation process" while the Kala stage refers to one's entry into the upper world (137–38). As noted in the introduction, the Musoni and the Luvèmba stages reflect the different stages of immortality, those departed who are still remembered and those no longer remembered. Although the cosmogram notes four specific stages, there is fluidity between these stages. Thus, Bonnie J. Barthold argues in *Black Time: Fiction of Africa, the Caribbean, and the United States*:

> birth implied a passage from the spirit world. Accordingly, the cyclic continuity between the two worlds was perhaps most vulnerable where issues of birth and death were involved. . . . The passage between the spirit world and the material world was at best risky, and if the rituals of birth and death were left unfulfilled, the cycle could be broken, leaving the spirits of the dead or the unborn to wander, angry with the human community whose ritual negligence had excluded them from the spiritual continuum of the living and the dead. (11–12)

Thus, there is no clean division between the living and the dead, but a much more interdependent relationship.

The continuity between the living and the dead also is evident in beliefs regarding reincarnation. African religious authority, John Mbiti notes, "Belief in reincarnation is reported among many African societies. This is, however, partial reincarnation in the sense that only some human features or characteristics of the living-dead are said to be 're-born' in some children" (*African* 159). This point is supported by Janheinz Jahn, who contends the following: "Thus the [life] force that goes on existing in the ancestors becomes active again in a living person. This has, however, nothing to do with transmigration . . . in which the soul is separated from the body and is born again in another body. For in Africa, in contrast to that doctrine, a dead person can be born again in several different individuals, for example in his grandchildren" (110–11). Although aspects of the living-dead may be reincarnated in descendants, the living-dead continues "to have his separate existence and does not cease to be" (Mbiti, *African* 159). Thus, Perry's Ayo may pass on a gift to her descendants while holding on to the ability to interact with them. In *Stigmata*, it is apparent that Ayo is clairvoyant—she predicts her own death, the birth of her grandchild, and her grandchild's gift. Ayo tells Joy about the granddaughter coming to take her place, "*She gon know thangs the one that's comin. She'll know things that knowin be a gift from me her family that's lost*" (Perry, *Stigmata* 34). Readers learn later that Grace's gift is the ability to see the dead and in the prequel, *A Sunday in June*, readers discover that Ayo's other granddaughters Mary Nell and Eva have inherited her clairvoyance as well.

Ayo's ability to predict the birth of her grandchild despite the apparent infertility of the long married couple in *Stigmata* and Nana's ability to call forth the Unborn Child in *Daughters of the Dust* indicate the investment of extended family in the birth of a child. According to Mbiti, "In African societies, the birth of a child is a process which begins long before the child's arrival in this world and continues long thereafter. It is not just a single event which can be recorded on a particular date. Nature brings the child into the world, but society creates the child into a social being, a corporate person" (*African* 107). In the introduction, I note the role that relatives—living and dead—play in the birth of child because of the connection between children and a community's potential. In the words of Minnie Ransom, " 'the chirren are our glory' " (Bambara, *Salt* 62). It is belief in the promise of the younger generation that inspires Minnie to continue with a challenging healing session. Although elders and ancestors are called on to provide cultural healing to the younger generation in Toni Cade Bambara's *The Salt Eaters*, we see the reverse at play in the following examples. In Dash and Perry's texts, it is the child who is called upon to provide healing due to the special connection between children and ancestors.

I should reiterate that although I have been addressing various life stages, each of these roles are part of a continuum and thus are not static. However, this is particularly evident when discussing the child figure, which we would typically associate with a set time period. Nevertheless, the discussion of these figures can become a bit complex in that a character may begin as a child and then age. In the case of Dash's film, the Unborn Child is depicted as a child of about seven or eight, but in fact has not been born at the time of the migration depicted in the film. However, she narrates the film as though looking back on a past event. In the case of Perry's texts, the child characters are children when first introduced, but they grow and mature. I have elected to treat them as child figures because it is my contention that their initial connection to ancestral figures is contingent on the fact that they are children at that moment and thus more receptive to their ancestors.

For example, according to Manthia Diawara's reading of *Daughters of the Dust*, the Unborn Child is an ancestral mediator:

> the ancestors in Nana's belief system just move to another world and watch over their living descendants. The children are the reincarnation of the ancestors, and this makes them precious to the adults whose fathers and grandfathers have joined the land of the ancestors. The Unborn Child in the film is one such reincarnation. She is doubled not only in

the figure of Grandma Nana herself, but also in the young
girl with tribal scars who appears with her mother in one of
the flashbacks. She travels through time, and she is present
at different settings in the film: we see her among the first
generation of Africans working with indigo dye, and we see
her in a 1902 setting among children playing in the sand.
Like the ancestors, her role is one of mediator in the family.
It is in this sense that Grandma Nana states that for Africans,
the ancestors and the children are the most sacred elements
of society. (16)

Through the character of the Unborn Child, viewers realize that worry
for one's family transcends earthly bonds—care and concern transcend
life and death. The Unborn Child, as the ultimate example of the circle
of life, has left the realm of the ancestors and is on the brink of joining
the living. Although she is yet to be born, the Unborn Child is already
anxious about her parents, Eula and Eli, and thus wants to arrive before
it is too late—she wants to assure her father that she is indeed his child
and not the product of her mother's rape. Using *Daughters of the Dust*
as my first example, I discuss the often-overlooked role the child may
play in the intercessions of elders and ancestors.

　　Although I draw on Kongo cosmology to analyze the child, elder,
and ancestor figures in these texts, I am generally quick to note that I am
not arguing that the women I am discussing have knowledge of Kongo
cosmology, but rather this uncanny reflection of Kongo cosmology in
their usage of elder, ancestor, and child figures is actually a reflection
of Diaspora retentions or Africanisms. However, as I noted in Chapter
1, this caveat is not necessary for *Daughters of the Dust*, which Dash
researched for many years. This research included the advice of Gullah
expert, Dr. Margaret Washington Creel as well as the collections of the
Schomburg Center for Research in Black Culture, the National Archives
in Washington, D.C., the Library of Congress, the Smithsonian, and
the Penn Center on St. Helena Island (Dash, "Making" 5–7). Most
importantly, she includes an explicit reference to Kongo cosmology—a
turtle that young boys paint with a circle and a cross during one of
the picnic scenes. Next to the stage directions, Dash has noted, "use
Ki-Kongo symbol" (Dash, *Daughters: Making* 147). Thus, it is clear
that Dash's use of elder, ancestor, and child figures are informed by
Kongo cosmology.

　　Daughters of the Dust is not your typical Hollywood film; in fact,
Bambara describes it as "oppositional cinema" ("Preface" xiii). She
observes that the "film begins with three injunctions to remember the

past: the *Black Gnostic* is quoted, the Ibo phrase for 'remember' is chanted, an elder's hand sculling the waters of time is repeated. Each of these moments suggest that the past has set the stage for what is about to unfold, or in the words of Viola, " 'What's past is prologue . . .' " (Dash, *Daughters: Making* 79). It is not long before the Ibo tale is recited and begins to function as both evidence of, and argument for, cultural continuity" (Bambara, "Preface" xii). *Daughters of the Dust* is about both the cultural continuity connecting "those who're across the sea" (Dash, *Daughters: Making* 94) and those who have come and gone from our world. This connection across generations is emphasized through Dash's depiction of children. For example, Bambara remarks that:

> A particularly breathtaking moment begins with a deep-focus shot of the beach. In the foreground are men in swallowtail coats and homburgs. Some are standing, others sitting. Two or three move across the picture plane, coattails buffeted by the breeze. They speak of the necessity of making right decisions for the sake of the children. Across a stretch of sand glinting in midground, the children play on the shore in the foreground. Several men turn to look at the children. In turning, their shoulders, hips, arms, form an open "door" through which the camera moves; maintaining a crisp focus as we approach the children. The frame rate changes just enough to underscore the children as the future. For a split second we seem to travel through time to a realm where children are eternally valid and are eternally the right reason for right action. (xv)

Yet, even before this scene viewers are clued into the importance of children through the selection of the Unborn Child as a narrator. She tells viewers, "My story begins on the eve of my family's migration North. My story begins before I was born" (Dash, *Daughters: Making* 80). Very quickly viewers realize that the Peazants are at a turning point with the prospect of migration destined to separate the extended family and the brewing fissure between Eli and Eula threatening their marriage. However, it is also clear that help is on the way in the form of the Unborn Child, "Nana prayed and the old souls guided me into the New World" (80). Viewers then have their first indication that Nana called on the Unborn Child to heal this rift between her parents and within the Peazant family. Like the healing in Bambara's *The Salt Eaters*, this is a communal act as elder and ancestors join forces to guide the child home, so that she can aid her parents and extended family.

Although this story begins before she was born, the Unborn Child has claimed it, "The Unborn Child speaks the story as her own, as the story she has already been born into. She is possessive about the story as evidenced by the plethora of 'my's': 'my family,' 'my story,' 'my great grandmother' " (Curry 350–51). Thus, the Unborn Child is not a disinterested observer, but a participant-observer—she is invested in the story that she narrates. The story that she is telling is about her family's future and she is a vital component of that future. Diawara asserts, "Grandma Nana argues that the womb is as sacred as the ancestors, and that the Unborn Child is sent by the ancestors, precisely at this critical juncture in Ibo Landing's history, to ensure survival . . ." (17). As an elder, Nana is able to serve as a conduit for communication with the ancestors and thus call for the assistance of the Unborn Child. In Chapter 1, I noted that Nana served as both elder and othermother for the extended Peazant family. In particular, I focused on Nana as othermother for Eula; however, literary critic Renée Curry notes this relationship between the Unborn Child and Nana: "Interestingly, the first specific relationship she discusses is that with her great grandmother, which supports her awareness of this significant othermother" (351). Even before her birth, a bond has been established between the Unborn Child and the family elder, which suggests that she is not entering the world as an individual but as a member of an established community—the Peazant family.

Although the Unborn Child is reflecting upon a past moment, the memories are still very fresh: "I can still see their faces, smell the oil in the wicker lamps. . . . I can still hear the voice of Auntie Haagar calling out for her daughters . . ." (Dash, *Daughters: Making* 81–82). Her memories are very tangible, as if the day is unfolding that very moment. Film critic, Jacqueline Bobo argues that time is fused:

> As the Unborn Child states that she remembers and recalls, the significance is that the past is fused with the present moment, for she is a new member of the Peazant family, summoned by one who was an active participant in that past. The suggestion is that it is necessary to cling to the parts of the past that are vital to understanding the present and that there is knowledge to be gained from those who have lived before. (149)

Although Bobo associates the Unborn Child with past and present, literary critic, Angeletta Gourdine identifies the Unborn Child as "an image of both present and future" (Gourdine 502). I suspect that this difference of opinion arises because the Unborn Child actually bridges the past, present, and future. She has just left the realm of the ancestors or the past and is about to be born into the present as a child and will hopefully have a future, which will allow her to grow and develop into an elder. In making her argument for the Unborn Child as a representation of the present and future, Gourdine draws on the iconography of the Unborn Child's clothing. Although she wears white, "her blue ribbon connects her to both Nana and Eula" (502). Throughout the film, Nana wears an Indigo blue dress, whereas Eula wore a royal blue skirt in a scene with Eli. According to Gourdine, "The blue ribbon marks her as an image of black women's blues memory, and it portends her continuation of the family legacy into the future, for her royal blue is generations from Nana's indigo" (502). Thus, the Unborn Child is building on the lessons of her elders and ancestors, as she continues the family's legacy.

Although the Unborn Child has not yet been born, she is bringing ancestral knowledge—the knowledge of the Peazant ancestors. As a child, she has come from the place where the ancestors reside and is thus uniquely positioned to share their knowledge. This special access to ancestral knowledge is reflected in the privileged position of children within the Peazant family. Bambara comments on the way in which the camera frames the children to indicate their importance and to suggest that the children are the future, but should viewers miss this moment the Unborn Child actually comments on the significance of children as she reflects on the day, "I remember how important the children were to the Peazant family . . ." (Dash, *Daughters: Making* 124). With this comment, Dash seeks to ensure that her message regarding the importance of children is not lost on viewers.

In addition to dialogue and images, Dash uses music to convey the messages of the film. Thus, particular music is associated with the Unborn Child to imply the gravity of her spiritual mission. According to Dash, John Barnes "wrote the Unborn Child's theme in the key of B, the key of Libra, representing balance and justice. 'This character was coming into the world to impart justice, a healing upon her father and her mother and her family'" (Dash, "Making" 16). In the notations on the script, Dash underscores the Unborn Child's role as someone turned to for succor. Dash has written, "The Unborn child = 'Elegba' (The one we appeal to [to] overcome indecision)" (*Daughters: Making* 99). Elegba is a Yoruba deity, who is considered "the keeper of the crossroads between the world of the living and that of the spirits" (Kaplan 518). This is a particularly apt association for a character who is herself in the process of crossing over from one realm to the other.

Because Nana recognizes the power of the ancestors, she seeks to tap into their power by calling on the Unborn Child. The Unborn Child tells us early on that her great-great-grandmother called her, but toward the end of the film she reminds the viewers again, "I remember the call of my great-great-grandmother. I remember the journey home" (Dash, *Daughters: Making* 137). With this repetition viewers are provided additional information—this journey is a homecoming. She recalls walking to the house where she would be born—the site that will complete the cycle of death and rebirth. This connection between death and rebirth is underscored by the fact that Eula feels the Unborn Child by her side and instinctively walks to the family graveyard (137). The Unborn Child also leads her father, Eli, to the graveyard. The time Eula and Eli spend with the Unborn Child in the graveyard confirms what Nana had tried to explain to Eli earlier that day when he found her by her husband's grave. She reminded him that the living are responsible for keeping in touch with the dead who continue to watch over their living family. Nana urged Eli to respect his ancestors, and then took the point further by connecting the ancestors and the womb, " 'Those in this grave, like those who're across the sea, they're with us. They're all the same. The ancestors and the womb are one. Call on your ancestors, Eli. Let them guide you. You need their strength' " (94–95). Nana attempted to allay Eli's concern that Eula is carrying the rapist's child rather than his. As I noted in Chapter 1, she tells him that he " 'won't ever have a baby that wasn't sent to' " him (94). For Nana, the ancestors send all children. I read this claim by Nana as an intriguing revision of *partus sequitur ventrem*—the child follows the condition of the mother. During slavery, female slaves were in the unenviable position of determining the slave status of their children; however, contemporary black women artists seem intent on creating a different relationship with the womb. With this statement, Nana not only claims a maternal connection for the mother, but a familial relationship for the extended family.

However, despite Nana's effort to reassure him and offer him guidance, Eli is too furious to listen to his great-grandmother. Eli's resistance to his great-grandmother's advice seems in part a gendered response. As I observed in Chapter 2, women are typically associated with culture bearing—maintaining cultural traditions. Barthold contends, "In traditional Africa, women were the biological embodiment of the mythic cycle, by virtue of procreation and childbirth" (100). Thus as a woman, Nana has a perspective, which Eli does not share. I would also suggest that he cannot fathom the ancestors sending him a baby because he still thinks of Eula as his property. Eli tells Nana, "This happened to my wife. My wife! I don't feel like she's mine anymore. When I look at her, I feel I don't want her anymore." But Nana admonishes him, "You can't give back what you never owned. Eula never belonged to you, she married you" (Dash, *Daughters: Making* 95). He, like other members of the family, must stop viewing Eula as damaged goods in order to fully appreciate the child she is carrying.

Eli cannot accept his great-grandmother's message, but when his Unborn Child intervenes, he is able to understand. The Unborn Child is "traveling on a spiritual mission;" she has been called to provide cultural healing to the Peazant family (134). The Unborn Child is able to provide this healing during a private moment after leading her parents to the family graveyard to commune with their ancestors. While in the graveyard, Eula recounts the Ibo legend to the Unborn Child. According to Bambara, Eula "draws strength from the tale. And through Eula, the relatives are drawn into a healing circle and mend their rifts" ("Preface" xiii). An immediate example of this healing effect is seen as Eli actually walks on the water towards a rotting figurehead during Eula's recitation of the legend:

> The floating figure is a visual reminder of African heritage, and the pride of a legendary group of Africans who refused to be enslaved. Dash visually reinforces Eli's connection with this mythical past: As Eula tells the story, Eli walks out toward the floating figure on the surface of the water, like the legendary Ibo. Coming to know the spirit of his ancestors, as Nana urged him to, eventually leads him to decide not to leave the island for the mainland. (Brouwer 9)

As I commented in my discussion of Nana as an elder and culture bearer in Chapter 1, Nana had told Eli, " 'Call on those old Africans, Eli. They'll come to you when you least expect them. They'll hug you up quick and soft like the warm sweet wind. Let those old souls come into your heart, Eli. Let them touch you with the hands of time. Let them feed your head with wisdom that ain't from this day and time' " (Dash, *Daughters: Making* 97). In telling Eli to allow the ancestors to "feed [his] head with wisdom," Nana implies the importance of ancestral memory. The importance of memory is suggested from the lines of text which open the film, "Gullah communities recalled, remembered and recollected much of what their ancestors brought with them from Africa" (*Daughters*). In her narration, the Unborn Child recalls and remembers various aspects of her family's history, signaling the importance of memory. Nana's injunction to Eli to call on his ancestors points to her recognition of the important role memory plays in identity formation. For Nana, part of Eli's identity is based on his ancestors. Kathleen Brogan asserts, "Social or collective memory functions first and foremost to support the identity of the group. . . . Memory confirms who we are" (130). For Eli, part of knowing who he is means calling on his ancestors and the tale of Ibo Landing.

In calling on his ancestors, Eli is able to connect to the power of the Ibo legend. According to Brouwer, "through his experience of the ways of the ancestors, encouraged by Nana and mysteriously led by his daughter, and through his moment of realization while walking on the water in the presence of the Ibo icon, Eli comes to understand that he and Eula must not leave the island, the center of their existence" (10). In her interview with bell hooks, Dash comments on the Ibo Landing myth, stating, "there are two myths and one reality, I guess" (hooks and Dash 29). Dash notes that there are accounts of Ibos walking or flying back to Africa, "And then there is the story—the truth or the myth—of them walking into the water and drowning themselves in front of the captors." According to her research, crew members had nervous breakdowns, "Watching the Ibo men and women and children in shackles, walking into the water and holding themselves under the water until they in fact drowned" (29–30). Dash references both myths and the reality in her film through Eula's recitation and Bilal's interview with Mr. Snead.

While Eula's account of the Ibo legend reiterates Paule Marshall's depiction in *Praisesong for the Widow*, Bilal's eyewitness account tells a different story. He tells Mr. Snead that he arrived at Ibo Landing with the Ibo, " 'Some say the Ibo flew back home to Africa. Some say they all joined hands and walked on top of the water. But, Mister, I was there. Those Ibo, men, women, and children, a hundred or more shackled in iron . . . when they went down in that water, they never come up. Ain't nobody can walk on water' " (Dash, *Daughters: Making* 152). Initially, one might wonder why Dash includes this counter narrative in her film, but she seems to be tapping into "the ancestral presence in those waters," just as Bambara desired that we would in her interview with Zala Chandler. Dash, like Bambara, recognizes the power in "All those African bones in the briny deep. All those people who said 'no' and jumped ship" (Chandler 348). In other words, the power of the myth does not reside in whether the Ibo walked, flew, or drowned—the power resides in the very fact of their resistance and it is this power that will sustain Eli and his family. Eli has been touched by his ancestors and he realizes the importance of remaining on the island and maintaining his cultural roots, "The warning is not uttered, but implicit: To leave is to risk disconnection, decentering, marginalization" (Brouwer 10). During their time in the family graveyard, Eli and Eula have the opportunity to reconnect with their ancestors with the assistance of their Unborn Child. By leading them to the graveyard, the Unborn Child allows Eli and Eula to remember their legendary ancestors—the Ibo. By the end of the film, Eli and Eula have decided to stay on the island with Yellow Mary and Nana Peazant, rather than migrating north with the rest of the family. As I observed in Chapter 1, The Unborn Child closes the film with a voice over, "We remained behind, growing older, wiser, stronger" (Dash, *Daughters: Making* 164). However, it is clear that this strength and wisdom was not the result of their individual capabilities, but rather the result of the collective strength and wisdom of their ancestors made accessible by their Unborn Child.

Although I suspect that Dash's depiction of the Unborn Child is informed by some knowledge of Kongo cosmology, I would not make that argument regarding Perry's child figures yet her depiction of the life cycle is certainly in concert with the belief in the continuity of life which is central to Kongo cosmology. Whether Perry is knowledgeable regarding African beliefs about death is not certain, but her child figures, like Dash's Unborn Child, have similar abilities to tap into ancestral powers. "African peoples believe that death is not the end of human life. A person continues to exist in the hereafter. This continuation of life beyond death is recognized through a very widespread practice of remembering the departed, which is found throughout Africa" (Mbiti, *Introduction* 128). Not only is this practice found throughout Africa, but throughout the African Diaspora. For example, La Vinia Delois Jennings in her study of Africanisms in Toni Morrison's literature argues "that identifiable West and Central African traditional cosmologies that entered the New World through Voudoun in the Caribbean, Voodoo in the United States, and Candomblé in Brazil continue to inform, to varying degrees, the thoughts and actions of the Black diaspora of the Americas" (22). Thus traditional African cosmologies such as Kongo cosmology are very much present in the New World.

Kongo beliefs regarding death are certainly reflected in Perry's texts, as her child characters appear to serve as conduits for the ancestors. This seems to be particularly the case for Grace, Ayo's granddaughter, who is able to see and actually inhabit her foremother's life at times. In *Stigmata*, Perry explores the trials of an adult Grace who fears for her sanity as she grapples with these experiences, but in *A Sunday in June*, Perry delves into Grace's childhood and her first encounter with Ayo. Grace's childhood experiences with Ayo are corroborated by her sisters Mary Nell and Eva, who see or sense Ayo at various times. Although the focus of my discussion is Grace, I should note that in *Stigmata*, her granddaughter, Lizzie, is 14 when she receives Grace's trunk and begins to have visions of Grace and Ayo. In both of these texts the ancestral figures reach out to children, not adults, which implies that children may be more inclined to heed the ancestral call than adults. Thus, for my second example, I argue that when looked at together, Perry's novels suggest that children may be a source of healing due to their proximity to the ancestors.

A *Sunday in June* opens in February 1915, when Grace is approximately 15 years old. Grace is described as being intrigued by her grandmother from Africa, but now when she looks at her grandmother's picture, "she no longer felt as if Bessie's smile was a happy one. Her mouth was a little twisted, Grace could see, as if she was tasting bad fruit. And in her eyes was a deep longing that Bessie seemed to be giving to Grace with just that glance" (Perry, *Sunday* 8). This is our first indication of a connection between Bessie and Grace. Grace could feel Bessie's longing, pain, helplessness, and anger in her glance, but she could not understand what Bessie longed to share. Bessie had to reach out in a more tangible manner to get Grace's attention, so she visits Grace as a younger version of herself. The blue-clad girl seems out of place in Johnson's Creek with her shroud-like dress wrapped around her and bare feet, but her mysterious nature is heightened by the fact that Grace sees her clearly while Etta Mae does not see anyone. In fact, as Grace decides against her better judgment to follow the blue-clad girl, she thinks: "Best to let that, whatever *that* was, just turn the corner and leave . . ." (11). Her reference to the blue-clad girl as "that" indicates that Grace suspected early on that she was no ordinary girl. However, she cannot resist following her and finds herself at Grandma Bessie's old house. In the house, Grace finds a trunk with Bessie's quilt and a diary which Ayo dictated to Joy about her life. After contact with Ayo's artifacts, Grace begins to experience visitations of sorts from Ayo. According to Mbiti, "manifestations of the living dead are said to occur in dreams, visions, possessions and certain illnesses or mental disturbances. In dreams and visions, people claim to encounter the spirit of the living dead, to talk to it, and to receive certain instructions or requests from it" (*Introduction* 126). Grace's experiences after reading her grandmother's diary appear to take each of these forms—dreams, visions, possessions, and she even begins to believe she is mentally disturbed.

Grace's response to her visitations runs counter to Adama and Naomi Doumbia's account of spirit visitation among the Mande. Spirit visitation is encouraged by the Mande, "as the whole community prospers when a spirit descends upon one of us. They provide healing and impart knowledge for those of us present" (Doumbia and Doumbia 6).

This, however, is not Grace's attitude as she has not slept through the night "since she'd held those diary pages in her hands. Not since the girl in the blue dress had led her down the road. A door had opened for her that day. At night, she was often visited by strange dreams . . ." (Perry, *Sunday* 62–63). Grace does not understand why the dead are not dead. In one of her conversations with Ayo, she tells her, " 'The dead should stay dead, you hear me?!' " (67). As a child, Grace might be more receptive to Ayo, but initially she is no more encouraging than her mother Joy had been years before. This resistance on the part of Grace and Joy may be due in part to their New World location. Unlike their African foremother, Grace and Joy are African Americans and not fully cognizant of traditional African belief systems. Jennings remarks, "time, diasporic displacement, and the domination of Christianity have over-written African Americans' active cultural remembrance and acceptance of African religious beliefs, practices, and roles that continue subliminally in Black communities, complicating and conflating the sacred and the profane" (25). Perhaps it is the subliminal presence of these beliefs that leads Grace to follow the blue-clad girl, but the lack of active cultural remembrance of African religious beliefs makes Ayo's visits disturbing.

Grace does not understand and in fact resents Ayo's visits, but Ayo has a story to tell. According to Jennings, "Disturbing, posthumous visitations, mainly with the oldest living elders, may take place in order for the departed to resolve current family issues, to express dissatisfaction with improper burial, or to demonstrate unrest from pre- or post-mortem offenses" (87). Because elders help to maintain family order, one might expect them to be subject to these visitations, but I contend that because adults can be resistant to visitations that they do not understand children are also subject to these visitations as depicted in Perry's novels. Ayo does not visit Grace to complain about her treatment, but to set the record straight regarding her history. One of the key components of Ayo's story is her name. Grace knows Ayo as Grandma Bessie, but Ayo insists that she be recognized as Ayo. When describing the day she was taken from her family, Ayo sobs, "*I los' so much that day*" (Perry, *Sunday* 67). One of these things was her name. In visiting Grace, Ayo reclaims her name and other aspects of her story.

Joy says of her mother's story: " 'It's too hard a tale. . . . Grandma Bessie had a hard time her whole life. . . . She had nothin' but horror to tell. The tellin' of it lifted a burden from her after she was old, but for us now, it be best to forget it all. That slav'ry stuff ain't nothin' to dwell on' " (30). Joy listened to her mother's story long enough to record it in the diary, but then she was done with it. Although Joy insists Ayo's story is nothing to dwell on, it is clear that Ayo will not rest until her story is shared. Although *Stigmata* provides more insight regarding Ayo's desire to remember and record her story, *A Sunday in June* focuses on Grace's ambivalent response to sharing her grandmother's slavery experience. She is torn between wanting to understand and wanting to protect her own psyche: "If only she could get close enough she'd understand everything. But would that understanding free her or kill her?" (179). As a teenager, Grace is unprepared for the enormity of her grandmother's story and even as she grows into young adulthood Grace feels incapable of grappling with her foremother's painful legacy. Grace seeks advice from Willow, her grandmother's friend, who advises her to open herself up and really listen to Bessie because she must be trying to tell her something. However, Grace is afraid to truly open herself to this ancestral call: " 'If I listen, I lose myself, Miz Willow. I get lost in there with all them voices and visions. If I pay attention to her, there won't be any of me left. I know it' " (259). Although Grace hears Ayo's call, she is unprepared to provide the connection that Ayo seeks.

Ayo will not be content with merely passing along a simple instruction to Grace; she wants to pass on a legacy. For Ayo, telling her story allows her to work through the trauma of her enslavement. Although, Ayo's enslavement was surely physically debilitating, trauma authority Cathy Caruth asserts that "*trauma* is understood as a wound inflicted not upon the body but upon the mind" (*Unclaimed* 3). This psychological wound has impacted her identity and the significance that Ayo places on memory. According to Jeffrey C. Alexander in "Toward a Theory of Cultural Trauma," experiencing trauma entails a revision of collective identity. "This identity revision means that there will be a searching re-remembering of the collective past, for memory is not only social and fluid but deeply connected to the contemporary sense of the self. Identities are continuously constructed and secured not only by facing the present and future but also by reconstructing the collectivity's earlier life" (22).

Ayo's own rehearsal of her individual memories and concern regarding her descendants' understanding of her history is just one strand of this shared slave past. She wants her descendants to know her true story as this is an essential element in the reconstruction of the collectivity's earlier life. This becomes particularly apparent when Grace is pregnant with Sarah. Although Ayo had been gone during most of the pregnancy, she reappears as Grace's delivery date approaches. Grace tries to shut out Ayo's memories, but Ayo advises her: "*She'll remember. If you show her,* Ayo whispered. *Mama and me carrying the basket. The market and him what carried me off. The ship on the water*" (Perry, *Sunday* 291). Ayo does not just want Grace to know her story, but her great-granddaughter, Sarah, as well. Shortly after that visitation, Grace is compelled to create a picture quilt based on images she receives from Ayo. Grace is 34 years old when Ayo begins "speaking again, this time through the cloth, giving her those horrible pictures to show to the world" (292). This quilt will be Ayo's means of passing down her story to her descendants. The quilt then will operate as a site of memory to ward off the possibility of amnesia.

However, by the time she is 40 the nature of Ayo's visitations have intensified to the point that Grace actually exhibits Ayo's scars from slavery, as if Ayo has not only passed down her memories, but her physical traits as well. Recall, that I mentioned in Chapter 3 that according to Mbiti the belief in partial reincarnation means that "aspects of their personalities or physical characteristics are 're-born' in their descendants" (*African* 130). Eva noticed a scar around Grace's wrist and asks her whether George has seen it. Grace explains, " 'he think I got it tangled in some barbed wire. But Ayo got it on that slave ship. That and more" (Perry, *Sunday* 317). Over the years, Ayo's visitations have escalated from dreams to full-scale possession, as if Grace inhabits her foremother's life. When confiding in Willow, Grace noted that she had been hearing voices since she was 12 or 13, " 'It started out with just dreams. These days, I get it all,' Grace said. 'The voices, the visions, the dreams. Sometimes I walk out my front door and into whole 'nother place, Willow. One day I ain't gonna be able to get back' " (259). By the time Grace was 40, she was afraid that she was mentally disturbed: "It was all leading to the crazy house, one way or the other" (316). Because of what she calls the "sickness in my mind," Grace leaves her husband, George, and her children (323). She thinks by leaving Alabama she can leave Ayo, but shortly after her arrival in Detroit her ankle began to bleed from one of Ayo's wounds: " 'No! I didn't leave my home and my husband and . . .' her voice broke on a sob, 'my chillum for this! You 'supposed to be gone. Gone! Left back there in Alabama. Hoverin' 'round your grave or somethin'. Not here! How far I got to go?' " (326–27). Grace tries to escape Ayo and her horrific memories, but there is no escaping the past—Ayo is determined that her legacy of slavery be transmitted to the next generation. For Ayo, this means being the subject of her history rather than its object and for that difference she will reach out to her descendants.

Although Ayo chooses Grace, her eldest granddaughter, as the person to visit and speak to directly, she also appears to share her gift of clairvoyance with her other granddaughters, Mary Nell and Eva. According to Mbiti, "It is held in all African societies that there is power in the universe, and that it comes from God" (*Introduction* 41–42). Spirits and some people have access to this mystical power which allows them "to see the departed, hear certain voices, see certain sights . . . have visions . . . foretell certain things before they happen, communicate with the invisible world . . ." (42). Whereas Grace is able to see the departed, hear voices, have visions, and communicate with the invisible world, her younger sisters see sights, have visions, and foretell the future. As a young child of about seven, Eva tries to make sense of the dreams she and her sisters experience. She tells Grace, " 'Mary Nell say our dreams mean the devil is here, tryin' to do his work. But it don't feel bad to me. Magic. Maybe you got magic like us. I don't think it's bad" (Perry, *Sunday* 32). Grace, however, cannot be as accepting of their gifts as Eva, " 'No, Eva. I think maybe Mary Nell got it right this time. Maybe not *the* devil, but something. God cain't mean for us to be walkin' around with these burdens. Nah' " (32). When Ayo predicts Grace's birth, she tells Joy, *"when Im gone she come to take my place. She gon know things the one that's comin. She'll know things and that knowin be a gift from me her family that's lost"* (Perry, *Stigmata* 34). These comments by Ayo suggests that she sees Grace's visions and by extension Mary Nell and Eva's visions as a gift from her—an inheritance of sorts.

Mary Nell and Eva have had visions since they were children and these visions allow them to foretell the future. Thus they know Jug will die before the news reaches his mother, but they are not able to decipher the dreams that pertain to them or to fully understand the visions related to their sister. Although Eva does not know what is going on between Grace and Ayo, she can see enough to sense Ayo's presence. Consequently, when Grace talks and cries in her sleep Eva can calm her by saying, " 'It's fine for now. . . . She gone for a while' " (Perry, *Sunday* 70). Eva hasn't seen Ayo, but because of Grace's response she is able to surmise the problem.

Although Eva did not see Ayo that time, she does see her in a dream the next year. Earlier that day, Grace fainted from some type of attack and mumbled about being left to die and not wanting to be left. Joy tried to comfort her daughter by assuring Grace that she would never leave her, but Mary Nell predicted Grace's own departure: " 'She gon' leave you,' Mary Nell said softly, looking at Eva" (121). That same evening Eva dreams that she and Mary Nell see Grace at the train station with a young Ayo. This seems to be one of their shared dreams as Mary Nell recalls their dream when Grace flees town by train twenty years later: " 'You remember, Eva. . . . We saw her on the train. And that little girl was with her' " (324). Grace thought she could leave Ayo by leaving Alabama, but Mary Nell and Eva knew years before that Grace would not be able to discard Ayo that easily.

Ayo clearly feels a connection with Grace that exists beyond the realm of the living. If Ayo has indeed been partially reincarnated in Grace, then perhaps she sees herself in Grace and believes Grace is the ideal messenger. However, it should be recognized that Ayo's desire to tell her story is not just about history, it is about survival. According to Doumbia and Doumbia, "Our ancestors are the closest to us of all the intermediary spirits; they are our guardian spirits. Our ancestors maintain their role in our families and lives more significantly than when they were physically present. They are always available to us offering their guidance and protection" (9). For Ayo, sharing her story is her means of offering guidance and protection, but she must rely on Grace to assist her in communicating with her descendants. In Chapter 2, I noted the fluidity between the roles of ancestor and elder; however, the child also is an important component of the ancestral presence. Jennings defines ancestral presence as "a hybrid role of the two socio-religious roles . . . the living-dead ancestor followed by the elder, to mediate and naturalize the activities of the metaphysical in the physical realm" (84). Yet, this definition of ancestral presence does not fully take into account the African cyclical perception of time: "life moves from birth to death, through the ancestral world to reincarnating birth" (Kalu 55–56). When one recognizes the continuity of the life cycle from birth to death, then it is easy to appreciate the role of children as intercessors for elders and ancestors. It is in this role of intercessor or conduit of information that Grace takes on her healing function. However, we don't see this role truly fulfilled by Grace in *A Sunday in June* because she is still resisting Ayo's call, but we do see the possibility of the child's healing function in her sister Eva.

Eva, like Grace, shares some of her grandmother's characteristics but she is not the focus of Ayo's attention. However, by the end of the novel Eva is able to provide a degree of healing to her sister Mary Nell because of the intervention of the elder, Willow, who tries to mediate for Ayo. At the age of 13, Eva had been raped and impregnated by Lou Henry, her sister's husband, and hadn't been the same since. Thirteen years later, Willow tells Eva that she wants to wash her clean in the storm, " 'When people hurts you, they leaves a stain. I see it. I see it all over you. I see that man's evil self stand where you are, and you carry his sin 'round with you' " (Perry, *Sunday* 299). Willow believes that Eva's rape squeezed the life out of her and that she's become an old woman, but she uses the storm as an opportunity to rejuvenate Eva. She tells Eva:

"I been waiting for a day like this. A stormy day in May, in spring. May rain makes everything clean. It makes everything

grow. Wash the evil off your body and outta your heart, and
become a chile again. The little one needs someone who ain't
dead inside. My grandson he love you with all his heart and
he need you, the real you, the live one. Not this dead thing
that goes 'round walkin' and talkin' like a woman." (301)

Eva is hesitant regarding Willow's ritual, but does follow her instructions to undress in the rain. The reader is told, "It had been a long
time since Eva had been this open" (305). Eva seems to be overcome
by her memories, but Willow calms her as she "rocked her like a baby
there in the howling wind and rain" (305). She then tells Willow about
the Sunday in June when Lou Henry raped her. After recounting the
event and her inability to stop him, Willow enjoins her to stand up
and be a woman. This ritual is akin to the sponge bath that Avey
receives in *Praisesong* because it is in essence a rebirth. Afterward, Eva
is described as clean, wide open, different (307). The baptism has given
her a different perspective on life as she essentially reclaims her body—
her womb—from Lou Henry.

Willow's baptism seems to work, but what is particularly significant is that she seems to have been in concert with Ayo. After Eva
leaves, Willow murmurs to the deceased Ayo, " 'I don't know, Ayo,
my friend. . . . I think it took, but I don't know. May be I'll never
know if I helped her. But I did all I could. And she stronger than she
know, I think' " (308). Willow passes away shortly after Eva's baptism,
but as she closes her eyes she sees Grace who smiles back with Ayo's
smile that suggests that Ayo was working with Willow to bring peace to
Eva. Thus when Eva performs this same ritual with her sister Mary Nell
twenty-nine years later, she is passing along the same ancestral healing
that Ayo had shared with her. Grace will eventually be able to do the
same for her daughter Sarah, but only after her death. However, while
alive, Grace has an ambivalent response to Ayo's contact with her and
she has trouble balancing Ayo's desires with her fears.

Grace is frustrated because she wants Ayo to "Stay dead! Stay
dead!" (67). However, the problem is that Ayo has not yet reached the
final stage of death. Mbiti observes, "Death becomes, then, a gradual
process which is not completed until some years after the actual physical
death. At the moment of physical death the person becomes a living-
dead: he is neither alive physically, nor dead relative to the corporate
group" (154). Ayo is in this state of living death. Ayo tries to explain
her state to Grace in a brief conversation about sleep. Grace expresses
a desire to sleep and she hears a voice: "*Sleep. That for dead folk*" (64).
Grace realizes that sleep is not an escape from her visions. She continues

to hear Ayo's voice: "*Sleep ain't what you think it is. . . . It's only a place to wander. Sometimes a little trip teaches you something* (65). Although Ayo is trying to explain her situation to Grace, Grace resists the lesson because she just wants to be left alone. Eva, however, comes to relate to Ayo's situation after her rape because she feels like the walking dead: "She knew now how ghosts felt, dead but not free, silently angry at the living. That's why Grace had to speak with the spirits, why she and Mary Nell had to see the things they saw. And like the spirits, Eva was unable to banish emotion from a body that no longer belonged to this world" (173). Eva's interpretation of the emotions of ghosts differs from that of Mbiti who distinguishes between human spirits who died a long time ago (ghosts) and those who died recently (living dead) (*Introduction* 75–79). According to Mbiti, ghosts may "act in unpleasant ways towards people, and sometimes in beneficial ways" (77). However, "The living dead may also visit their surviving relatives in dreams or visions, or even openly, and make their wishes known" (78). I would argue that Ayo is not angry with her descendants, but she does want to make her wishes known. The fact that Eva perceives Ayo to be angry is indicative of what Jennings calls diasporic displacement. In other words, Perry is not writing novels which depict feature for feature traditional African religious beliefs; however, the presence of remnants of these beliefs or Africanisms is indicative of the African cosmological survivals, which like Ayo survived the horrors of slavery.

Ayo wants her story told and shared with her descendants. Her diary, her quilt, and now her haunting presence are her means of rewriting her enslavement. Ayo's diary begins with a reclamation of her identity: "*Bessie ain't my name she said. My name Ayo. . . . My name mean happiness she say. Joy. That why I name you that so I don't forget who I am and what I mean to this world*" (Perry, *Sunday* 16). These are not the words of an angry woman, but a determined woman—a woman determined to be remembered as she wishes to be remembered, not as others have identified her. Ayo cannot rest while her descendants think of her as Grandma Bessie because this is not who she is. Bessie is her slave name, while Ayo is her true name. The act of reciting her diary to Joy is not about recording history, but refuting history: "*I am Ayo. I remember. This is for those whose bones lay sleepin in the heart of mother ocean for those whose tomorrows I never knew who groaned and died in the dark damp aside of me. You rite this daughter for me and for them*" (27). Ayo is reclaiming her story, not only for herself, but for those who did not survive. This survivor's story is meant to be passed on, not to lie forgotten in the bottom of a trunk. Five years after leaving Johnson Creek, Grace finally realized that Ayo's story was indeed meant to be passed on, but she still felt burdened by her sickness. Rather than return home and share Ayo's story with her daughter Sarah, she sends home the quilt with Ayo's story on it asking her sisters to save it for her granddaughter. She writes: "*I feel`that others after us will need to know. Our grands maybe will need to get these things. Please leave these for my granddaughter. I know she ain't here yet. But I have faith that you and Eva will know when the time is right and when it is she will be waiting*" (330). Perry's *Stigmata* follows the story of Grace's grand-daughter, Lizzie, who receives the trunk with Ayo's diary and the quilt Grace made at the age of 34.

Like Ayo before her, Grace pins her hopes on a yet unborn granddaughter. As noted in the introduction, this project is particularly concerned with matrifocal relationships or the mother–child bond. In looking at relationships between mothers and daughters as well as the extended woman-centered networks of mothers, daughters, and other-mothers in the form of elders and ancestors, I am especially interested in the way writers such as Perry revisit and revise the history of *partus sequitur ventrem*. In Chapter 3, I discuss this in greater length in con-nection with Perry's *Stigmata*; however, I do wish to point out that the fact that Ayo and Grace look to their granddaughters to share their story is not happenstance. There are grandsons in the family, but as males they do not inherit the legacy of *partus sequitur ventrem*.

Thus, Grace reaches out to Lizzie both because she is female and because she is young. Grace seems to have known that the young Lizzie would be much more receptive to the ancestor's call than her mother. Despite Grace's desire to heal the wounds between herself and her child, she realizes that she cannot approach her directly. With the conclusion of *Stigmata*, we finally find the healing that Ayo initially sought. Grace and Lizzie together are able to bring a measure of closure to Ayo's story and to her descendants. Joy could not give her mother, Ayo, the satisfaction she craved and her descendant Sarah could not hear the story directly, but the intervention of the granddaughter and great-granddaughter, Grace and Lizzie, finally completes Ayo's story. Thus the implication seems to be that the young are more likely to hear the ancestor, while adults may tune them out.

This greater receptivity to the ancestor's call; however, does not mean that children are not resistant to what they hear—just that they can hear it in the first place. For example, Ayo has passed on the gift of clairvoyance to Mary Nell and Eva, but their mother Joy steadfastly denies her children's "reputed fortune-telling abilities" (1). Joy's denial of her children's gifts is in line with her earlier resistance to hearing her mother's story when she was still alive. Yet Ayo's ability to reach out to younger members of the family does not mean that these children easily accept her story or escape the pains of cultural trauma. According to Alexander, "Cultural trauma occurs when members of a collectivity feel they have been subjected to a horrendous event that leaves indelible marks upon their group consciousness, marking their memories forever and changing their future identity in fundamental and irrevocable ways" (1). Although Grace and Lizzie do not suffer the trauma of Ayo's enslavement, they inherit the cultural trauma of its legacy. Ron Eyerman argues: "slavery was traumatic in retrospect, and formed a 'primal scene' that could, potentially, unite all 'African Americans' in the United States, whether or not they had themselves been slaves or had any knowledge of or feeling of Africa. Slavery formed the root of an emergent collective identity through an equally emergent collective memory . . ." (60). Thus, Grace and Lizzie find themselves carrying the scars of their foremother's shackles even though they had never been enslaved. This stigmata is symbolic of the cultural trauma that Ayo's descendants must work through in order to heal the scars of slavery. Yet in reaching out across the grave Ayo does not merely transmit cultural trauma, she initiates ancestral healing to mend the bonds between Grace and Sarah which were negatively effected by Grace's initial handling of Ayo's traumatic story of enslavement. Ayo's story is not a happy one, but it is a necessary part of their family history and now that it is truly known her descendants can move on with their lives.

In Perry's novels and Dash's film a special relationship is depicted between child figures and ancestors. The connection between these figures seems to be related to their proximity on the life cycle. Because children are coming from where the ancestors are located, they often are seen as the ideal means for imparting the wisdom of the ancestors. However, the response of the child to the ancestors' call can vary greatly. Although the Unborn Child in Dash's film is quite willing to accept her role as intercessor, Perry's children are more ambivalent about their role. I would contend, however, that this difference is due to the fact that the Unborn Child has an elder, Nana, assisting her while Grace, Mary Nell, and Eva are left to their own devices. Willow attempts to step in and play the role of the elder in Ayo's absence, but it seems like this amounts to too little too late for these girls. And Lizzie in *Stigmata* lacks even a character like Willow to turn to—she has only her mother Sarah, who I would regard as a stunted elder and thus incapable of providing guidance. Although these child figures are not equally suited to their task of bringing ancestral healing, they are all called by the ancestors and to different degrees are able to serve as a conduit between the ancestors and the living.

Conclusion

Looking Back and Forward

The Ancestral Presence in Speculative Fiction

After reading novel after novel by black women writers in which ghosts narrated the stories or characters interacted with ghosts, I thought I might embark on a study of ghosts, but this has become so much more. Although I agree with Kathleen Brogan regarding the attraction of ghost stories for the types of narratives these artists wish to tell, there is much more going on in these texts. According to Brogan, "Stories of cultural haunting attempt to remap an often fragmented and inevitably changed memory to its new coordinates by conjuring ghosts who pass from the past into the present, from the old territory into the new. The ghosts bear witness to the rift that necessitates their presence, even as they often function to transmit a tradition threatened by accelerated or violent change" (130–31). However, these stories of cultural haunting also call attention to the continued presence of Africanisms within African American culture. In looking at the depiction of ghosts in these texts, it becomes increasingly clear that the dead are not dead. The deceased are maintaining a connection with the living that is reflective of African spirituality.

In text after text, I noted what I refer to as an uncanny connection to Kongo cosmology. However, this resemblance to Kongo cosmology is not inexplicable, but merely an example of Africanisms at work. Despite the forced separation from their homelands during the Transatlantic Slave Trade, Africans held onto aspects of their culture, which are now found in their descendants and referred to as Africanisms. Henry Louis Gates Jr. observed the following, "Violently and radically abstracted from their civilizations, these Africans nevertheless carried within them to the Western hemisphere aspects of their cultures that were meaningful, that could not be obliterated, and that they chose, by acts of will, not to forget: their music, . . . their myths, their institutional structures, their metaphysical systems of order" (3–4). Although these Africans were not stripped of their culture, they also were not able to transfer their culture wholesale to the New World, but instead created a new culture. Gates asserts:

> Slavery in the New World, a veritable seething cauldron of cross-cultural contact, however, did serve to create a dynamic of exchange and revision among previously isolated Black African cultures on a scale unprecedented in African history. Inadvertently, African slavery in the New World satisfied the preconditions for the emergence of a new African culture, a truly Pan-African culture fashioned as a colorful weave of linguistic, institutional, metaphysical, and formal threads. (4)

This Pan-African culture that Gates refers to explains the lack of one-to-one correspondence between Kongo cosmology and its representation in the texts I discuss. I argue that Toni Cade Bambara's *The Salt Eaters*, Paule Marshall's *Praisesong for the Widow*, Phyllis Alesia Perry's *Stigmata* and *A Sunday in June*, Toni Morrison's *Beloved*, and Julie Dash's film, *Daughters of the Dust* all reflect aspects of Kongo cosmology, but the depictions in their texts represent African survivals rather than a replication of Kongo cosmology.

In these texts, we see African survivals manifested in diverse ways. For example, Dash has clearly researched her film as purposefully drawn on Kongo cosmology, whereas Bambara and Morrison appear to be conversant regarding African spirituality, but it is unclear how much specific knowledge they might have regarding Kongo cosmology. Perry seems to indicate the least knowledge regarding African spirituality; however, she does acknowledge a connection between African American spirituality and African ancestors. Thus, the references to Kongo cosmology range from the explicit to the implicit. For example, the inclusion of the Kongo cosmogram painted on the turtle's back in Dash's film and burnt onto Sethe's mother in Morrison's *Beloved* are explicit referents to Kongo cosmology. Another physical manifestation of the cosmogram is found in Marshall's *Praisesong for the Widow* via the Ring Shout. The cosmogram's main component is the circle. According to Sterling Stuckey, "the circle ritual imported by Africans from the Congo region was so powerful in its elaboration of a religious vision that it contributed disproportionately to the centrality of the circle in slavery" (11). The circle is a key aspect of the healing session in Bambara's *The Salt*

Eaters. Perry also picks up on the importance of the circle in describing the life cycle. Ayo describes the circularity of life, "We are forever. Here at the bottom of heaven we live in the circle. We back and gone and back again" (Perry, *Stigmata* 7). Both of Perry's novels implicitly draw on the Kongo cosmogram's depiction of the circularity of life. Although all appear to draw on some notion of Kongo cosmology, with a diverse base of knowledge, one finds a varied representation of African survivals in their work. Yet, the presence of these African survivals suggests a continuum that speaks to the sustained importance of Kongo cosmology within African American culture. These texts indicate the persistence of an African worldview regarding the continuity of life that includes the living, the dead, and the unborn. Thus, whereas the focus of this study is the ancestral presence, the discussion could not be completed without some attention to elders and children and their interactions with ancestors.

I contend that each of these texts is in some way addressing the importance of ancestral healing, whether coming directly from an ancestor or via an elder or child, who is conversant with an ancestor. Thus, Marshall's Aunt Cuney comes from the grave to set Avey back on the right path—a path that acknowledges the ancestors; Bambara's Minnie Ransom provides much needed healing to Velma Henry, who has attempted to resist the ancestor's call; and Dash's Unborn Child can heal the rift between her parents and remind her father that they will never receive a child that the ancestors did not send. I also argue that these texts are particularly concerned with slavery and its aftermath, particularly in relation to women who suffered the additional ignominy of establishing the slave status of their issue through the practice of *partus sequitur ventrem*. This connection is particularly evident in contemporary novels of slavery, such as Morrison's *Beloved* in which Sethe opts to commit infanticide rather than have her child remanded to slavery, but the legacy of this practice is also apparent in texts set in post-emancipation periods. For example, Avey is traumatized by dreams of her children being killed during violence associated with the Civil Rights Movement, which feeds on her fear regarding her inability to protect and truly mother her children. This violation of the womb is returned to again and again by these artists as they seek ways to reclaim the wombs of their female characters.

This emphasis on women also may be tied to the important role of mothers. Dominique Zahan describes the mother as follows:

> a mediator, since the child perched on her hips is none other
> than an ancestor returned to the world of men through

her. Thus everything occurs as if woman were the crossroad
where future and past, death and life intersect. She results
from ambiguity, from that which is at once tomb and resur-
rection, decay and vitality. But she incarnates the junction,
the beginning and the end of the cycle of human existence.
(*Religion* 45)

Consequently, if one believes that an African cyclical view of life as
represented by the Kongo cosmogram continues to be influential within
African American culture, then one must attend to the powerful role
that the mother plays. Zahan makes a similar point, "Without woman
and the role she plays in the society of the living, the cult of ancestors
would probably have no reason for existence" ("Some" 14). Because
they bear children and thus make the future possible, women as mothers are essential. In their texts, Bambara, Marshall, Perry, Morrison, and
Dash have reclaimed this role for African American mothers. Rather than
the natal alienation implied by the practice of *partus sequitur ventrem*,
these artists are insisting on the connection between mothers and their
issue and even extending the mothering function to non-blood mothers or othermothers. I assert that these texts are feminist revisions of a
slave past, which draw on an ancestral presence to focus on a legacy of
survival and triumph rather than degradation and shame.

What then might the future hold for African American women's
texts? I suggest that black women's science fiction or speculative fiction is
the next field for significant literary analysis. For instance, Madhu Dubey
in "Becoming Animal in Black Women's Science Fiction" asserts "that
what is recently being marketed as the newly emergent phenomenon
of black women's science fiction shares common generic traits with
'mundane' or 'mainstream' black women's novels, such as Morrison's
own *Song of Solomon, Beloved,* or *Tar Baby;* Toni Cade Bambara's *The
Salt Eaters;* Ntosake Shange's *Sassafras, Cypress, and Indigo;* and Gloria
Naylor's *Mama Day,* to name just a few" (Dubey 35). Although science
fiction and speculative fiction are often used interchangeably, I prefer to
use Sandra Govan's more expansive definition of speculative fiction "as
the umbrella genre that shelters the subgenres of fantasy, science fiction,
utopian and dystopian fiction, supernatural fiction, and what has come
to be called by some critics fabulative fiction or fabulation" (683). The
broader term, *speculative fiction,* seems particularly appropriate because
"[t]he genres that compromise speculative fiction are so closely related
that authors may disagree with the categorization of their works, may
change genres from book to book, or may use elements of each in a
single novel" (Moore 335). However, despite the variations between

genres "each also shares in the basic premise underlying speculative fiction—the presentation of a changed, distorted, alternative reality from the reality readers know" (Govan 683). Ingrid Thaler, author of the 2010 monograph *Black Atlantic Speculative Fictions: Octavia E. Butler, Jewelle Gomez, and Nalo Hopkinson*, notes that black speculative fiction "has become more prominent over the last ten years. The mid- to late-1990s can be considered a watershed, resulting in both the critical reception of speculative texts by black authors, as well as an increasingly open marketplace, a stark contrast to the 1980s" (11). Thus, Tananarive Due's *The Between* (1995) is an ideal text to conclude this discussion which has been situated in the sociohistorical context of the 1980s and 1990s because Due was part of the black speculative fiction watershed moment of the mid- to late-1990s, but has continued to write prolifically. In many ways, Due allows us to look back and forward with regard to the future of black women's literature.

Although *The Between*, like many speculative novels, leads readers to consider future possibilities, it also is concerned with the past. In *Visions of the Third Millennium: Black Science Fiction Novelists Write the Future*, Sandra M. Grayson observes, "Memories of enslaved Africans in the Americas, a subtext in the novels selected for this study, link the past (of slavery in North America), current trends, and potential future trends. These connections indicate that the future is inextricably linked to past and present" (4). Grayson traces African influences in the texts of such writers as Octavia Butler, Nalo Hopkinson, LeVar Burton, Samuel Delany, Steven Barnes, Charles Saunders and Tananarive Due; although she does not address *The Between* specifically and instead looks at Due's treatment of ancient African nations in later novels, *My Soul to Keep* (1997) and *The Living Blood* (2001). Whereas Due's focus on immortals and the significance of ancient African nations is interesting, I am drawn to *The Between* because of its focus on a male narrator and its use of an ogbanje figure as both of these points provide interesting links to the texts of my study. As I noted in my discussion of Paule Marshall's *Praisesong for the Widow*, although my focus is on matri-lineal connections, Marshall's protagonist is left planning to share the story of Ibo Landing with her grandsons and her daughter's students rather than a daughter, granddaughter, or niece. Thus, although Avey's Aunt Cuney chose to focus her culture-bearing role on her niece to the exclusion of her nephews, Avey has revised this path to a more gender inclusive one that recognizes that both women and men have the responsibility of sharing familial stories and history. This recognition melds well with Due's focus on the relationship between Hilton and Nana. The strength of their bond is reflected in Nana's sacrifice of her own life to save Hilton from drowning; however, it becomes increasingly clear that Nana cheated death as Hilton was meant to die. As the novel ensues, Hilton begins to realize he was born to die. As an ogbanje, Hilton was not supposed to become an ancestor, which provides intriguing correlations with Toni Morrison's character, Beloved.

Due describes Hilton as "caught between life and death" (Due and Due 353), yet he seems nothing like the capricious Beloved, an ogbanje who desires to torment her mother. I contend that this difference between Hilton and Beloved is due to Hilton's ability to escape ogbanje status and seek ancestral rank as he strives to protect his family and preserve his lineage. In "Married in the Water: Spirit Kin and Other Afflictions of Modernity in Southeastern Nigeria," Misty L. Bastian states:

> If the *ogbanje* can be convinced to "stay," however, he or she can become fully human through marriage, bringing forth children for a human lineage, and taking part in the affairs of his or her human community. At death, the former *ogbanje* is enrolled in the ranks of the ancestors or human spirits—a fully realized person who has responsibility for the continuance of the lineage and who can eventually reincarnate as another human being. (123)

Because Nana died saving him, Hilton has sought to make her sacrifice worthwhile. I suggest that by marrying, bearing children, and dying to save their lives, Hilton, with Nana's help, extends ancestral protection to his family even if he did not achieve ancestor status himself.

Christopher N. Okonkwo's *A Spirit of Dialogue: Incarnations of Ọgbañje, the Born-to-Die, in African American Literature* provides the only in depth discussion of *The Between*, but his focus is on Hilton's ogbanje status rather than the relationship between Nana and Hilton, which facilitates ancestral healing. Like Baby Suggs in *Beloved*, Nana is a beneficial, instructive, and protective ancestral presence who ultimately guides Hilton back across the Kalûnga line once he completes his mission of preserving the familial lineage. "In Kongo cosmology, water is the imaginary boundary between the world of the living and that of the dead. It separates us from the land of the ancestors, *nsi a Kalunga*, but it also provides a passage to it" (Krüger-Kahloula 327). Although there is no direct reference to the Kongo cosmogram, such as Sethe's mother's mark in *Beloved*, the turtle's painted back in Julie Dash's *Daughters of the Dust*, or the Ring Shout in Paule Marshall's *Praisesong for the Widow*, the fact that Hilton was supposed to drown in an ocean is suggestive of the Kalûnga line and implicit with regard to the Kongo cosmogram. Due's novel, like Phyllis Alesia Perry's novels seems informed by an awareness of African cosmology and the circularity of the life cycle. In a 2004 interview with Yolanda Hood, Due acknowledges, "my books are research, research, research. I probably researched *The Between* less than anything else I've written, and only because I didn't know any better" (159). In talking about her 2003 novel, *The Good House*, with Dianne Glave, Due admitted wanting to "delve more deeply into the Afro-Caribbean magic systems" and that she had "been doing a great deal of reading about the Yoruba belief systems, vodou and Santeria" (704). This comment suggests that she has some prior knowledge regarding African cosmology on which she was basing her desire to "delve more deeply." This point is confirmed by Okonkwo who cites a private email communication between himself and Due in which she disclosed her familiarity with the born-to-die concept and its spread in West Africa while attending the University of Leeds as a graduate student (*Spirit* 202, note 11). Thus, I join Okonkwo in his assessment, "Due joins the practitioners of Afrofuturism who harness the potentials of the speculative mode and African diaspora spirituality and mythologies to represent black people's old and New World experiences" (89). Consequently, Due's *The Between* is an ideal text for looking back at African cosmology, while also looking forward regarding the legacy of the Civil Rights Movement.

As I noted in the introduction, all of the texts that I address here are responding to the legacy of slavery and its aftermath including the Civil Rights Movement. However, *The Between*'s 1995 publication came at a time when some might have been wondering just how far African Americans had come and what did the future hold. "The 1990s was a time when increased black racial and gendered shattering of the color, class, and professional bars, and those bars imports for racial membership, racial crossing and identity, agitated white supremacist resentment. It was an era when various 1960s civil rights gains were threatened or even stripped" (55). This is the sociocultural environment for what becomes a life and death battle, not only for Hilton James, but his children—the symbols of African American future possibilities. The novel unfolds through a series of flashbacks, nightmares, and the present tense organized into three main parts, a prologue, and epilogue. This arrangement is particularly well suited to display the relationship between past and present, ancestors and descendants.

The prologue opens in 1963 with the lines, "Hilton was seven when his grandmother died, and it was a bad time. But it was worse when she died again" (Due, *Between* 1). With these lines, Due establishes the ancestral presence of the text, Nana. After finding Nana dead on the floor, Hilton runs to a neighbor's home for help, but upon returning Nana is at the kitchen stove fixing supper. Although Nana claims to have possibly fainted, Hilton knows that her skin had been cold as death. Nana seeks to reassure him by saying, "Nana's not going to leave you" (3). However, this is not an empty promise, but recognition of the ancestor's eternal presence. As the novel continues, it becomes clear that Nana returned from the dead in order to save Hilton from drowning almost a year later and to eventually lead him back to her after he completes his mission of saving his own children.

Although initially it may seem as if Nana's act of saving Hilton from drowning was simple maternal instinct, I contend that Nana anticipated the danger and that she came back from the dead specifically to save her grandson. "Twice before, Nana had stayed home and his women cousins drove him to the reunions to meet his kin, but she decided to go this year" (4). I suspect Nana had a premonition or some other indication that something would go awry and that she needed to attend this year's reunion. This then is how Due sets the stage with her prologue that opens with Emily Dickinson's poem, "I Felt a Funeral, in my Brain," and closes with a recognition that "Sometimes the dead go unburied" (7) as Nana's body is never found. Nana's burial at sea conjures up associations with the victims of the Middle Passage; however, Nana is remembered as Grandma Kelly. Thus, the prologue provides the necessary background details of Hilton's life while also pointing to the significant subtext of death and remembrance.

Part I begins with Abena P. A. Busia's poem, "Exiles," which depicts the effects of our unburied dead. The implication is that the unburied dead are not at rest, but instead remain with us. Although we do not see Nana fighting with Hilton in his dreams as Aunt Cuney does with Avey, it is clear that Nana is not at rest as she appears to Hilton in his hallucinations and speaks to him. However, Nana's motivations are similar to Aunt Cuney's in that she is reaching out from her watery grave to help Hilton, not haunt him.

Since his near drowning, Hilton had bad dreams which tended to intensify just before his birthday. These nightmares seem to be Hilton's punishment for living beyond his intended time. In "*Ogbanje/ abiku* and Cultural Conceptualizations of Psychopathology in Nigeria," Sunday T. C. Ilechukwu presents a case study of patients at the Lagos University Teaching Hospital who described themselves as *ogbanje* or *abiku* and noted such symptoms as "visual hallucinations" and "vivid dreams about water and play" (244). This correlates well with Hilton's fragmented dreams of "*Choking. Water. Running*" (Due, *Between* 44).

According to Ilechukwu, the *ogbanje* has companions or cohort "said to communicate supernaturally, often contacting each other through hallucinatory experiences or dreams. They are said to use such media to . . . impose group discipline and punishment" (240). These are the voices that ask how many times Hilton can die and tell him to stop running. Because Nana prevented Hilton from dying at his appointed time, his companions who did indeed die at the appointed hour, have been tormenting him. Okonkwo explains:

> [a] subgroup member who, sidetracked by the lures and challenges of earthly life, reneges on this ostensibly cooperative arrangement by deciding to *stay* alive past the agreed death-/ return-date would be accordingly accosted by the complying counterparts with threats of sickness or accidents. The greater a member's obstinacy in conforming with the contract, the harsher and more regular the pestering from the complying preternatural members. (*Spirit* 10)

The fact that Nana also had bad dreams that began after her first death suggests that Nana may have violated expectations regarding her own designated time of death by returning from the dead to save Hilton from drowning at the family reunion. Although Nana is clearly not an ogbanje, the fact that she appears to have returned from the dead—the realm of the ancestors—suggests that she knows more than she shares with the young Hilton. Hilton is able to stop the bad dreams for five years after working with a psychologist to confront his guilt regarding Nana's death, but the dreams return along with hallucinations as Hilton can only deny death for so long.

Hilton's nightmares return at the same time his wife, Dede, a newly elected judge, begins to receive racist death threats. Hilton uses his wife's death threats as an explanation for the return of his dreams, but there seems to be more to this association. In fact, Due's use of racist death threats to move the plot forward seems connected to her notion that "history is real, and its effects still live and breathe among us" (Due, *Freedom* 354). Thus, although Thaler explains that black speculative fictions "move much further into areas of the fantastic and gothic—and beyond confrontations with the African American past" (10), this does not mean that the past is of no consequence. Okonkwo suggests that Due's novel reflects "on the related larger ambiguities of African American identity in America, a nation still troubled by the haunting memory and vestiges of slavery" (*Spirit* 91). This assessment seems supported by Due's comment, "Toni Morrison's *Beloved* (1987), to me, was just a masterpiece. It was, in novel form, the EXACT interpretation of the poison of slavery on the psychology of black people in this country. I had never seen it presented with such a brilliant metaphor before, but yes, we're all carrying around those ghosts" (Glave 696). Yet, in *The Between* Due moves beyond the ghosts of slavery to contemplate an African American community caught between the painful past of slavery and promised post-racial social society that was to be the fruits of the Civil Rights Movement. Thus just as Hilton is caught between life and death, African Americans are caught between the past and an imagined future.

Throughout the text, Hilton struggles with his memory of Nana because his memories are shrouded in fear; however, she is truly an ancestral figure providing a protective shield over her descendants. Okonkwo observes, "In intervening twice in Hilton's death, Nana exemplifies those endearing attributes of the outraged mother in African American letters" (*Spirit* 97). Joanne M. Braxton's "Ancestral Presence: The Outraged Mother Figure in Contemporary Afra-American Writing" notes that "[t]he ancestral figure most common in the work of contemporary Black women writers is an outraged mother" (300). According to Braxton, "The outraged mother embodies the values of sacrifice, nurturance, and personal courage—values necessary to an endangered group" (300). Certainly, these characteristics are at play when Nana strips off her dress and jumps in the ocean to rescue her grandson from an undertow. Nana's actions link her to the female protagonists Gina Wisker addresses in " 'Your Buried Ghosts Have a Way of Tripping You Up': Revisioning and Mothering in African-American and Afro-Caribbean Women's Speculative Horror." According to Wisker, "African-American and Afro-Caribbean women's speculative Gothic horror explores the duties of care that mothers and grandmothers have for the next generation, which needs to recuperate the past and revision the future" (73). However, what becomes increasingly clear is that these maternal duties do not end with the grave as these women ancestors do what is necessary to provide healthy futures for their descendants.

For Nana, her goal is to help Hilton protect his children, but then also to guide him to the spirit realm, so that he too may find peace. Nana's mission is implied by the closing words of Part I and the opening of Part II. Part I concludes with one of Hilton's dreams as he is tormented by voices asking, " '*Do you think you can keep dying forever?*' " (Due, *Between* 88). He is accosted by sundry voices—"*strangers and loved ones, the remembered, the forgotten*"—the voices of the Luvèmba and the Musoni, the living dead and the spirits (88). These voices are not merely disconcerting, but painful as they are described as piercing his skin. Hilton begs for peace, but through the cacophony of voices he hears Nana's kind voice, " '*Hilton, there's no peace where you're at,*' *she says, her words laden with the sadness of a dozen lifetimes*" (88). Nana's sadness regarding Hilton's lack of peace suggests that it is peace that she seeks to provide. Nana's role as protector is further alluded to by the Ghanaian proverb which introduces Part II of the novel: "Even a spirit looks after his child" (89). Nana is indeed a spirit, an ancestor, looking after her child.

As the story continues to unfold, Hilton's many near death experiences come to light—he was meant to die, but continued to live nonetheless. This cycle appears to have been set in motion by Nana who could not bear to allow her young grandson to drown, but upon further reflection she realizes her actions denied Hilton peace. In one of his dreams, Nana advises him, " '*Stop fighting, Hilton. It's wrong to fight,*' *Nana's voice says from all around him, a tunnel. 'I was wrong, too. I thought it was all for you, but I left you a curse, not a blessing*' " (128). Nana recognizes that Hilton cannot continue to stave off death and that he will only achieve peace once he accepts death, which is part of the natural cycle of life. In fact, Due has said that "the point of the book is that we must embrace our mortality" (Hood 162). Through Hilton, readers explore both the difficulties and the necessities of accepting all of life's stages, including death. Okonkwo observes, "In the anthropologic drama of the spirit child, the human baby, body, and world are cast as merely a shell, a temporary housing, for a displaced and alienated soul that yearns for and is at the same time under pressure to return home to kindred and kinship" (*Spirit* 92). Hilton is being called home to the realm of the spirits; however, the presence of his wife and children in the physical world complicate Hilton's return to the spiritual world. The danger surrounding his children is suggested by a bizarre dream in which Hilton is tormented by images of himself:

> "*You can't keep hiding,*" *says the Hilton figure at the bureau.* "*You don't belong here. You remind me of a tree knocked over in a storm, its exposed roots gnarled and shriveled black—*"

> "*That keeps dropping seedlings,*" *sighs the Hilton figure in the chair, grim-faced, flipping through Dede's legal pad.*

> "*What's another name for a dead tree?*" *calls the horrid Hilton figure in the bathroom.*

> "*Firewood,*" *says Hilton at the bureau.*

> *"Kindling," says the Hilton in the chair, his face filled with menace. "So how do you like that? A dead tree dropping seedlings. Everything is growing wild, no control. And your hiding is all for nothing, mind you, because those seedlings will choke soon enough. We've found someone to do some weeding."* (Due, *Between* 126)

The reference to Hilton's children as kindling implies the precariousness of their existence, which is further amplified by the threat of Charles Ray Goode—the white supremacist sending threats to Dede and her family.

Just as Nana comes to recognize the reckless nature of her actions and the curse she sets in motion, Hilton's Ghanaian mother-in-law, Kessie, also seems to sense something in connection to her grandchildren. During a casual conversation with one of his wife's cousins at a party to celebrate Dede's judgeship, Hilton learns that Kaya is a "born-to-die name" meaning " 'Stay and don't go back' " (143, 144). He and Dede had planned to name her Imani, meaning faith, but Dede changed her name after her mother insisted on a name from Ghana. Kessie had also tried to name their son, Jamil, but Hilton resisted without knowing the significance of these names. It was not until the party years later that he learns from Kofi, "Many cultures have superstitions about children dying. You'd be surprised how prevalent they are. They have to do with spirits inhabiting the child and leaving the child to die, so we have traditional names meant to trick or implore the spirits, to keep the child alive. Symbolic names" (144). Ilechukwu explains, "The logic seems to be that the 'threat' of these children to die feeds off excessive parental solicitude and the group's investment in their offspring. Calling their bluff by emotion divestment (or a pretence of it) is expected to cut off this energy and so break the cycle" (251). The fact that Kessie is so insistent on a born-to-die name for her grandchildren despite not giving her daughter such a name suggests that she is not merely acting out of superstition, but instead senses some type of danger to these children.

The threat to Kaya and Jamil is implied by Charles Ray's threats, Hilton's dreams, and Mama Kessie's response to her grandchildren. Charles Ray does not merely threaten Dede for sending him to jail, but threatens her children as well; Hilton's dreams of his near death experiences include his children; and Kessie saw a death spirit over Kaya and felt it over Jamil. Because Hilton was supposed to die at the age of 7, Kaya and Jamil should never have been born. According to Okonkwo, "much of the seeming fantastical encounters in the story—Goode's death threats against both Dede and Hilton's mortality, marriage, parenthood, sanity, job, social performance, and identity—translate as parts of the physical, spiritual, and psychic hounding that an ábíkú suffers for refusing to repatriate home" (*Spirit* 98). Although Hilton's dreams and hallucinations resonate with the literature regarding depictions of ogbanje phenomenon, Due's ability to depict Hilton's slipping sense of reality is clearly an aspect of the speculative mode. Wisker observes that speculative horror "as a hybrid form . . . can take from a mixture of sources and roots, including mythology, fable, myth, and nightmare. It takes from Afro-Caribbean, African-American and African roots as easily as from those of white middle America . . ." (73). Due is drawing on African cosmology while also drawing on elements of the supernatural.

Okonkwo comments, "Due's depiction of Hilton as a born-to die who fathers two of his own kind discloses some literary license," but this is in fact the power of speculative fiction. Editors of *The Black Imagination, Science Fiction and the Speculative*, Sandra Jackson and Julie Moody-Freeman, provide an extensive definition of speculative fiction; nevertheless, I am particularly drawn to their remark that black writers "have explored—indeed speculated—not only different futures, but different pasts and presents of the societies and cultures in which they live in multifaceted ways" (2). This notion is especially instructive with regard to Due's deployment of the ogbanje. In Chapter 4, I argue that Morrison's use of an ogbanje character who is murdered rather than dying early was an syncretization that took into account Morrison's New World context as well as the history of infanticide during slavery; however, with regard to Due's inclusion of ogbanjes born to an ogbanje (Kaya and Jamil) readers are presented with an syncretization that allows for speculation about the future.

Okonkwo correctly notes that Hilton "is the most fully developed born-to-die figure in a narrative that features other 'living dead' " (*Spirit* 93). He identifies Marguerite who was also hounded by her spirit companions after surviving a tragic fall as well as Hilton's children, Kaya and Jamil. While the inclusion of Marguerite suggests that Hilton's experience is not unique, Kaya and Jamil's characters point toward future possibilities. Although it is clear that Hilton and Marguerite can only defy death for so long, the futures of Kaya and Jamil are less certain. Charles Ray threatens their lives, but they have lived longer than Mama Kessie expected. In fact, she assumes that she was wrong and dismisses her worries as superstitions, " 'Kaya and Jamil both lived. We've managed to trick the spirits. Through prayer? Through resolve? I don't know how or why, but they are both still here and here they'll stay" (Due, *Between* 147). The possibility of their survival is also suggested by a dream Kaya has as well as one of Hilton's dreams. Kaya tells her father about a strange dream in which a dead girl visits her and tells her she will be a famous doctor as long as she watches out for Charles Ray. Although Kaya does not fully understand the implications of her dream, it clarifies a few more things for her father. This then leads him to ask pointedly about his family during his next dream after being warned, " *'Everybody has to let go sometime'* " (170). Hilton implores them to leave Dede alone and he is assured, " *'Of course. Dede belongs here'* " (171). He then asks about Kaya and Jamil and is initially only greeted with silence until one of the Hilton figures responds, " *'What's done is done'* " (171). This response is rather ambiguous, but along with Kaya's dream and the voices Hilton hears after sacrificing himself to protect his children suggests that Kaya and Jamil have a different future than their father.

Their ancestor, Nana, who shows Hilton the way to save his children makes this different future possible. Part III of the novel focuses on the peaceful aspect of death and is appropriately introduced by lines from James Weldon Johnson's "Blessed Sleep." Although Hilton had been rather frightened of his memories of Nana, he now welcomes her dream visits and seeks her guidance. Hilton asks Nana to help him save his children, like she saved him. In showing him a vision of the garbage can, Nana prepares Hilton to save his children from the mail bomb sent by Charles Ray. However, this action will also come with a cost: " *'Once you open it, there's no more doorways,'* Nana says. *'Can't be no more. No more running, Hilton'* " (215). In other words, Hilton must sacrifice himself as Nana did for him—he must exchange his life for that of his children.

The fact that Hilton and his children will have different futures also is implied in a conversation with Kaya about how long Hilton will be at home. Okonkwo observes that the conversation "is bi-referential. On one hand, it alludes to Hilton's domestic presence. On the other, it points to his imminent 'departure,' which both Kaya and Dede apparently sense" (*Spirit* 101). It is during this conversation that Kaya gives her father a pin she received from her science teacher, "a winged staff with twin serpents entwined around it" (Due, *Between* 257). The pin is identified as a medical insignia, but it also plays on the image of the Mami Wata or Nne Mmiri, who controls the water entry to the physical world. Ogbanjes are said to have fallen victim to the enticements of Nne Mmiri or Onabuluwa who controls the land entry. "Artist impressions of *mammy water* show a dark oriental looking woman entwined with two large serpents" (Ilechukwu 240).[1] Okonkwo refers to the pin as "reminiscent of an ábíkú's protective fetish" and suggests that Kaya gave her father her good luck charm as part of a failed attempt to intervene in his departure and block his next death (*Spirit* 101). I differ from

Okonkwo's reading of this scene in that I see the giving of the pin to her father as Kaya's way of saying good bye as well as recognizing that while he is an ogbange pledged to Nne Mmiri that is not her future—she will remain behind and become a doctor. Kaya's statement, " 'I feel like everything is going to be different from now on' " (Due, *Between* 258) serves as a recognition that her father must leave while she remains behind.

Predictably, the day of reckoning is Hilton's birthday—he has stolen some thirty birthdays, but no more after today. Okonkwo also notes the significance of Hilton's birthday being on a Sunday, "this Sabbath marks a big day of rest for Hilton. It is the occasion of his reprieve from his tiresome time-travels: his earthly, spiritual, and psychological journeys, anxieties and ethereal visitations" (*Spirit* 101). It is on his birthday that Hilton saves his children from a bomb by putting the package in a garbage can and holding down the lid. Initially, he simply placed the package in the garbage and started to run after his children, but upon hearing a woman calling his name he returns to the garbage can. I contend that this unnamed woman is Nana leading Hilton home, across the Kalûnga line. Hilton dies smiling as he holds the garbage can, knowing that "this was where he was supposed to be, and this was what he was supposed to do" (Due, *Between* 271). According to Okonkwo, "Sunday, as the day of Hilton's passing, has a numerical significance. For as the week's seventh day, it retraces the prologue's seventh year when Hilton should have first died in 1963 and returned home. The date actuates its original purpose. It indirectly completes the circle and a life journey that began narratively at age seven" (*Spirit* 102). Like Nana, Hilton dies willingly, protecting those he loves.

The epilogue brings closure to the novel by confirming that Hilton has succeeded in protecting his children while speculating about the future of African Americans as represented by these children. Whereas the preceding chapter ended with the explosion from the mail bomb, the epilogue opens with a car crash and then transitions to his drowning as though Hilton is traveling in reverse through deaths until he travels back in time to his youth when he should have died from drowning. As Hilton breaks free from the water, he sees Nana beckoning to him from the shore, " *'You did good, Hilton,' Nana says, taking him in her arms. His head only reaches her waist and the folds of her dress there, sinking into her soft belly. He is smaller than he imagined next to her, but it is right this way'* " (Due, *Between* 273). As he goes in to have dinner with Nana, he hears voices, "they caught him, baby/we're okay, daddy" confirming the safety of the family he left behind (273). This is confirmed by the presence of Kaya's pin in his hand: "*Suddenly, his insides tremble with joy.*

He has done something, he's not sure what, to make everything all right" (273). Hilton does not fully remember Kaya, but he knows that she is a famous healer he once knew.

As I noted earlier, everyone who dies is not destined to be an ancestor, so I will not claim ancestor status for Hilton as it is not clear that he has achieved the necessary prerequisites such as "the attainment of a ripe old age, for this is a good indication that one has fulfilled one's destiny" (Lawson 62). However, I do think this is the case for Nana despite her lack of a proper burial. In "Ancestral Spirituality and Society in Africa," Ogbu U. Kalu asserts, "an ancestor must have lived a morally worthy life and must have died a good death" (57). I argue that this is indeed the case for Nana who risked her own life to save her grandson; however, Kalu also notes "those who died bad deaths or did not get fitting burials do not reincarnate and, indeed, turn into malevolent spirits which hound their progeny for failing to bury them properly" (57–58). Nana was not buried properly, as her body was lost in the ocean, but she does not accost Hilton like a malevolent spirit as Beloved does with Sethe or Jay does with Avey. Nana does not hold Hilton responsible for her lack of burial, but instead seems bent on helping set things back on track after realizing that her act of love in saving Hilton from drowning also disrupted the established life cycle. Thus I maintain that it is Nana's ancestral presence that allows Hilton to set things right with his family and position his children to face the future.

Despite the danger of Charles Ray's racist assault, the novel concludes with his capture and the James' family's safety. Due's selection of a racist for her villain suggests "that despite racial and social integration race and racism continue to matter in late-twentieth and early twenty-first century postmodern America" (Okonkwo 104). However, the future that Antoinette predicts for Kaya of being a famous doctor is not restricted by race or racism. Thus, Due speculates about a future in which a black girl child from "what is now ostensibly a single black female-headed household, an urban black family that Moynihan would likely have 'studied,' statisticized, and pathologized" can grow up to become a famous doctor (104). Thus, threading together elements of Kongo cosmology and the supernatural, Due imagines brighter prospects for future generations of African Americans. Although we have yet to achieve a post-racial society in which racism is nonexistent, perhaps we can imagine how to get there through the lens of black speculative fiction.

Notes

Introduction

1. *Daughters of the Dust* was written, directed, and produced by Julie Dash.

2. See Ashraf H. A. Rushdy, *Neo-Slave Narratives: Studies in the Social Logic of a Literary Form* (New York: Oxford UP, 1999), *Remembering Generations: Race and Family in Contemporary African American Fiction* (Chapel Hill: U of North Carolina P, 2001), and "The Neo-Slave Narrative," *The Cambridge Companion to The African American Novel*, ed., Maryemma Graham (Cambridge: Cambridge UP, 2004).

3. Although Reagan has been criticized with regard to social welfare, Hugh Heclo argues that Reagan's legacy is much more mixed and that the overall result "was to consolidate rather than roll back America's middle-class welfare state" (558). He further asserts that there was no Reagan Revolution against the welfare state. See Hugh Heclo, "The Mixed Legacies of Ronald Reagan," *Presidential Quarterly* 38.4 (2008): 555–74.

4. Barthold's emphasis on the Guinea Coast as the origin of most enslaved Africans is supported by the assessment of scholars: Sterling Stuckey, Philip Curtin, and James H. Rawley who contend that the majority of slaves came from the central and western regions of Africa. See Sterling Stuckey, *Slave Culture: Nationalist Theory & The Foundations of Black America* (New York: Oxford UP, 1987), Philip Curtin, *The Atlantic Slave Trade* (Madison: U of Wisconsin P, 1969), and James H. Rawley, *The Transatlantic Slave Trade* (New York: W. W. Norton, 1981).

5. Although I discuss African religion and culture, it is important to remember that Africa is a vast continent with much variety, and thus I am limiting my comments to overarching generalities. However, I do think it is possible to look to shared customs and traditions of Western Africa and surmise that many of these were represented in the views of Africans forcibly removed and enslaved in the New World.

6. I should note that I have chosen the term *ancestors* to describe the spirits and living dead present in these texts because they are indeed related to

one or more characters in the text. However, Mbiti argues against the use of "ancestral spirits" or "ancestors" as these terms are unnecessarily limiting since some spirits and living-dead are not actually ancestors (*African* 83–84).

7. According to Thompson and Cornet, "Philip Curtin has estimated that fully one-third of United States blacks are of Kongo and Angola ancestry . . ." (32).

8. See Melville J. Herskovits, *The Myth of the Negro Past* (Boston: Beacon Press, 1941), Winifred Kellersberger Vass, *The Bantu Speaking Heritage of the United States* (Los Angeles: UCLA, Center for Afro-American Studies, 1979), Roger Abrahams and John Szwed, *After Africa* (New Haven: Yale University Press, 1983), Sterling Stuckey, *Slave Culture: Nationalist Theory and the Foundations of Black America* (New York: Oxford University Press, 1987), Margaret Washington Creel, *"A Peculiar People": Slave Religion and Community-Culture Among the Gullahs* (New York: New York University Press, 1988), and Joseph E. Holloway, *Africanisms in American Culture* 2nd ed. (Bloomington: Indiana University Press, 2005) among others.

9. See Figure 1. The Kalûnga line separates the physical world, ku nseke, from the spiritual world, ku mpèmba. Kala is the first position, followed by Tukula, Luvèmba, and Musoni.

10. *African Cosmology of the Bântu-Kôngo: Tying the Spiritual Knot: Principles of Life & Living* was published under the name, Kimbwandende Kia Bunseki Fu-Kiau; however, he refers to himself as Fu-Kiau Bunseki.

11. Although some trace Kongo crosses to the crucifix, Thompson and Cornet note that "it is the consensus of a variety of scholars who have studied the motif in cultural context, that the sign of the four moments of the sun predates the coming of the Portuguese" (44).

12. See Thompson and Cornet pages 27–28 and Fu-Kiau pages 20–21.

13. See Fu-Kiau 139.

14. In *Introduction to African Religion*, Mbiti notes that spirits or ghosts sometimes "act in unpleasant ways towards people, and sometimes in beneficial ways" (77).

15. Because there is not this distinction between the living-dead and spirits within African American communities, I have not created separate categories as Fu-Kiau does with the Luvèmba and Musoni stages and instead think of both stages as indicative of the ancestral role.

16. Ancestor veneration is an expression of respect, not to be confused with ancestor worship. Practitioners show respect and admiration for their ancestors, but they do not worship them as gods. In fact, Fairley notes that ministers she interviewed believe that ancestral dreams are "examples of the Christian God providing information to the living through their ancestors" (551).

17. Holloway actually resists designating the ancestral presence as beneficial. She states, "Sometimes the presence is meditative and instructive, sometimes it is meditative and condemnatory, sometimes it is meditative and silent" (115).

18. In November 2007, Gates introduced his own company, AfricanDNA (Gibson 20).

Part I Preface

1. Although Dove discusses motherhood within the framework of Cheikh Anta Diop's cradle theory, which suggests that the Southern cradle, Africa, produced matriarchal societies rather than the patriarchal societies of the northern cradle, her description of the role and high regard placed on motherhood is in line with descriptions of matrifocal societies. See Dove 3–4.

Chapter 1

1. See John S. Mbiti's *African Religions and Philosophy.* 2nd ed. (Oxford: Heinemann, 1990) and Janheinz Jahn's *Muntu: An Outline of The New African Culture.* 1958. (New York: Grove Press, 1961).

2. The correct spelling is Dataw Island; however, Dash spells it Dahtaw in *Daughters of the Dust: The Making of an African American Woman's Film.* Wright only cites the DVD in her sources, so she may have relied only on what she heard. Dataw Island is one of the South Carolina Sea Islands in Beaufort County, South Carolina just east of Beaufort.

3. Generally spelled, Egungun, this is a reference to the collective spirit of the ancestors.

4. Bambara noted that she had three working titles: "In the Last Quarter," "The Seven Sisters," and "The Salt Eaters" ("What" 165–66).

Chapter 2

1. Although Jane Olmsted refers to a celebration for the "Old People," in the text they are referred to as "Long-time People" or "Old Parents." See Marshall, *Praisesong for the Widow* p. 165.

2. Henry Louis Gates observes that the Yoruba trickster, Esu-Elegbara recurs frequently in black mythology in Africa, the Caribbean, and South America; however, he is known by various names in the New World, such as Exu in Brazil, Echu-Elegua in Cuba, Papa Legba in Haiti, and Papa Legba in the United States. See *The Signifying Monkey: A Theory of African-American Literary Criticism* (New York: Oxford UP, 1988).

Chapter 3

1. Much of Grace's story is depicted in the prequel, *A Sunday in June,* which I discuss in Chapter 5.

2. I prefer to use the broader terminology, *contemporary novels of slavery* because neo-slave narratives often reference a more specific genre as defined by Ashraf H.A. Rushdy—they "assume the form, adopt the conventions, and

take on the first-person voice of the ante-bellum slave narrative." See Rushdy's *Neo-Slave Narratives: Studies in the Social Logic of a Literary Form* (New York: Oxford UP, 1999). Other terminology for these types of narratives includes liberatory narratives as coined by Angelyn Mitchell. See *The Freedom To Remember: Narrative, Slavery, and Gender in Contemporary Black Women's Fiction* (New Brunswick: Rutgers UP, 2002) and postmodern slave narrative coined by A. Timothy Spaulding. See *Re-Forming the Past: History, The Fantastic, and the Postmodern Slave Narrative* (Columbus: Ohio State UP, 2005).

3. See *The Soul's Journey into God; The Tree of life; The Life of Saint Francis* by Saint Bonaventure. Translated by Ewert Cousins. (Mahwah, NJ: The Paulist Press, 1978).

4. The *maternal introject* is a psychological term to refer to the part of one's mother that lives in one's psyche.

5. Marlo David's reminder that Ayo means Joy in Yoruba made me think of the significance of Ayo's choice in naming her daughter.

6. I can't help but note allusions to the Trinity in that Lizzie represents three persons in one body. Perry seems to have revised the notion of Father, Son, and Holy Spirit to that of great-great-grandmother, grandmother, and granddaughter. Ayo, like the Father, also sends her other two persons to reach others, such as Sarah.

7. Comments by Dan Kenzie in our spring 2011 English 696/American Studies 650 course, Ancestral Presence in twentieth-century African American Novels has led me to rethink this point, as Dan noted Lizzie's greater success in working through her ancestral visitations than her grandmother, Grace.

8. Later in the interview, Perry observes, "And I would say that in this country, black rural Southern culture is the foundation of all the other variations of black culture that you see in the United States, even though you can say that its foundation is West Africa" (Duboin, "Confronting" 649).

Chapter 4

1. See John S. Mbiti *African Religions and Philosophy* and *Introduction to African Religion*.

2. Denver actually sees a white dress kneeling down next to Sethe in Baby Suggs's room. She assumes from this that the baby ghost has plans.

3. Okonkwo is referring to Chinua Achebe's *Things Fall Apart*.

4. Just as there are different terms for this concept—ogbanje and abiku—there also are variant spellings: ogbaanje, o'gbañje, àbikú and àbíkú

5. Thanks to Nancy J. Peterson for pointing out the connection between Beloved's strange behavior regarding her tooth and experimenting with being human.

6. Horvitz actually reads Beloved as both Sethe's murdered 2-year-old daughter and her African mother who are part of a cycle of mother–daughter loss and perceived abandonment.

7. A similar point is made by Levin who notes, "in interpreting the novel's conclusion as a kind of victory for the community, it is tempting to ignore or deny the fact that the infanticide is repeated" (136).

8. Mami Wata has several variant spellings: Mami Wota, Mammy Watta, Mammy Water, and Mami Water.

9. See Ousseynou B. Traoré's "Mythic Structures of Ethnic Memory in *Beloved*: The Mammy Watta and Middle Passage Paradigms" in Geneviève Fabre and Claudine Raynaud's "*Beloved, She's Mine*": *Essais sur Beloved de Toni Morrison*. 77–89.

10. Okonkwo comments, "Beloved's spiritual ingress and egress into the human realm are associated with water, trees, and woods, recalling . . . the Igbo deities Nne Mmiri's and Onabuluwa's cosmic checkpoints" (*Spirit* 159).

11. Christie Achebe states, "The Igbo call it 'ogbanje' the Efiks 'ekabasi' and the Yorubas 'abiku,' and so the variant names multiply for the many ethnic groups in the country" (32).

12. In Maduka's discussion of ogbanje and abiku in the work of Chinua Achebe, J. P. Clark and Wole Soyinka, he notes that Achebe is Igbo, whereas Clark and Soyinka are Yoruba.

13. See Caroline Rody, *The Daughter's Return: African-American and Caribbean Women's Fictions of History*, page 225, note 18. See also Sarah Appleton Aguiar, "Everywhere and Nowhere': Beloved's 'Wild" Legacy in Toni Morrison's *Jazz*." *Notes on Contemporary Literature* 25.4 (1995): 11–12, Deborah E. McDowell, "Harlem Nocturne," Review of *Jazz* by Toni Morrison. *Women's Review of Books* 11.9 (1992): 1, 3–5, and Paula Gallant Eckard, *Maternal Body and Voice in Toni Morrison, Bobbie Ann Mason, and Lee Smith*.

14. See Bowers and Grewal for discussions of the healing influence of Beloved on Paul D.

Conclusion

1. Mami Wata has several variant spellings: Mami Wota, Mammy Watta, Mammy Water, and Mami Water. For additional information about Mami Wata, see Chapter 4 regarding Beloved and Mami Wata.

Bibliography

Abrahams, Roger and John Szwed. *After Africa*. New Haven: Yale University Press, 1983. Print.

Achebe, Chinua. *Things Fall Apart*. 1958. New York: Anchor Books, 1994. Print.

Achebe, Christie C. "Literary Insights into the 'Ogbanje' Phenomenon." *Journal of African Studies*. 7.1 (1980): 31–38. *ProQuest*. Web. 3 May 2010.

Aguiar, Sarah Appleton. "Everywhere and Nowhere': Beloved's 'Wild" Legacy in Toni Morrison's *Jazz*." *Notes on Contemporary Literature* 25.4 (1995): 11–12. Print.

Alexander, Jeffrey C. "Toward a Theory of Cultural Trauma and Collective Identity." *Cultural Truama and Collective Identity*. Jeffrey C. Alexander, Ron Eyerman, Bernhard Giesen, Neil J. Smelser, and Pietr Sztompka. Berkeley: UC P, 2004. 1–30. Print.

Alwes, Derek. "The Burden of Liberty: Choice in Toni Morrison's *Jazz* and Toni Cade Bambara's *The Salt Eaters*." *African American Review* 30.3 (1996): 353–65. *JSTOR*. Web. 2 August 2001.

Ansa, Tina McElroy. *The Hand I Fan With*. New York: Doubleday, 1996. Print.

———. *Ugly Ways: A Novel*. New York: Harcourt Brace & Co., 1993. Print.

———. *You Know Better: A Novel*. New York: W. Morrow, 2002. Print.

Baker, Houston A. and Charlotte Pierce-Baker. "Patches: Quilts and Community in Alice Walker's 'Everyday Use.'" *"Everyday Use" Alice Walker*. Ed. Barbara Christian. New Brunswick, Rutgers UP, 1994. 149–65. Print.

Bambara, Toni Cade. "Preface." *Daughters of the Dust: The Making of an African American Woman's Film*. New York: New Press, 1992. xi–xvi. Print.

———. "Reading the Signs, Empowering the Eye: *Daughters of the Dust* and the Black Independent Cinema Movement." *Black American Cinema*. Ed. Manthia Diawara. New York: Routledge, 1993. 118–44. Print.

———. *The Salt Eaters*. New York: Vintage Books, 1980. Print.

———. "What It Is I Think I'm Doing Anyhow." *The Writer on Her Work*. Ed. Janet Sternburg. New York: W.W. Norton, 1980. 153–68. Print.

Barthold, Bonnie J. *Black Time: Fiction of Africa, the Caribbean, and the United States*. New Haven: Yale UP, 1981. Print.

Bastian, Misty L. "Irregular Visitors: Narratives About Ogbanje (Spirit Children) in Southern Nigerian Popular Writing." *Readings in African Popular*

Fiction. Bloomington: International African Institute in association with Indiana UP, 2002. 59–66. Print.

———. "Married in the Water: Spirit Kin and Other Afflictions of Modernity in Southeastern Nigeria." *Journal of Religion in Africa* 27.2 (1997): 116–34. JSTOR. Web. 25 July 2011.

Bentley, Nancy. "The Fourth Dimension: Kinlessness and African American Narrative." *Critical Inquiry* 35.2 (2009): 270–92. JSTOR. Web. 2 May 2012.

Bettanin, Guiliano. "Memory Work in Octavia Butler's *Kindred* and Women's Neo-slave Narratives." *Cultural Memory and Multiple Identities*. Eds. Rüdiger Kunow and Wilfried Raussert. Berlin: Lit Verlag, 2008. 91–107. Print.

Bilby, Kenneth M. and Kimbwandende Kia Bunseki. *Kumina: A Kongo-based Tradition in the New World*. Bruxelles: Centre d'etude et de documentation africaines, CEDAF, 1983. Print.

Bobo, Jacqueline. *Black Women As Cultural Readers*. New York: Columbia UP, 1995. Print.

Bonaventure, Saint. *The Soul's Journey into God; The Tree of life; The Life of Saint Francis*. Trans. Ewert Cousins. Mahwah, NJ: The Paulist P, 1978.

Bouson, J. Brooks. *Quiet as it's Kept: Shame, Trauma, and Race in the Novels of Toni Morrison*. Albany: SUNY P, 2000. Print.

Bowers, Susan. "*Beloved* and the New Apocalypse." *Modern Critical Interpretations: Toni Morrison's Beloved*. Ed. Harold Bloom. Philadelphia: Chelsea House Publishers, 1999. 27–43. Print.

Braxton, Joanne M. "The Outraged Mother Figure in Contemporary Afra-American Writing." *Wild Women In The Whirlwind: Afra-American Culture and The Contemporary Literary Renaissance*. Eds. Joanne M. Braxton and Andrée Nicola McLaughlin. New Brunswick, N.J.: Rutgers UP, 1990. 299–315. Print.

Brogan, Kathleen. *Cultural Haunting: Ghosts and Ethnicity in Recent American Literature*. Charlottesville: UP of Virginia, 1998. Print.

Brøndum, Lene. " 'The Persistence of Tradition': The Retelling of Sea Islands Culture in Works by Julie Dash, Gloria Naylor, and Paule Marshall." *Black Imagination and the Middle Passage*. Eds. Maria Diedrich, Henry Louis Gates Jr., and Carl Pederson. New York: Oxford UP, 1999. 153–63. Print.

Brouwer, Joel R. "Repositioning: Center and Margin in Julie Dash's *Daughters of the Dust*." *African American Review* 29.1 (1995): 5–16. JSTOR. Web. 27 February 2009.

Brown, Laura S. "Not Outside the Range: One Feminist Perspective on Psychic Trauma." *Trauma: Explorations in Memory*. Ed. Cathy Caruth. Baltimore: John Hopkins UP, 1995. 100–12. Print.

Brown-Hinds, Paulette. "In the Spirit: Dance as Healing Ritual in Paule Marshall's *Praisesong for the Widow*." *Religion and Literature*. 27.1 (1995): 107–17. Print.

Busia, Abena P. A. "What Is Your Nation?: Reconnecting Africa and Her Diaspora through Paule Marshall's *Praisesong for the Widow*." *Changing Our Own Words: Essays on Criticism, Theory, and Writing by Black Women*.

Ed. Cheryl A. Wall. New Brunswick: Rutgers UP, 1989. 196–211. Print.

Butler, Octavia. *Kindred*. Boston, Beacon Press, 1979. Print.

Carabi, Angels. "Interview with Toni Morrison." *Belles Lettres: A Review of Books by Women* 9.3 (1994): 38+. Print.

Caruth, Cathy. "Introduction." *Trauma: Explorations in Memory*. Ed. Cathy Caruth. Baltimore: John Hopkins UP, 1995. 3–12. Print.

———. *Unclaimed Experience: Trauma, Narrative, and History*. Baltimore: Johns Hopkins UP, 1996.

Chandler, Zala. "Voices Beyond the Veil: An Interview with Toni Cade Bambara and Sonia Sanchez." *Wild Women in the Whirlwind: Afra-American Culture and the Contemporary Literary Renaissance*. Eds. Joanne M. Braxton and Andrée Nicola McLaughlin. New Brunswick: Rutgers UP, 1990. 344–53. Print.

Christian, Barbara. "An Angle of Seeing: Motherhood in Buchi Emecheta's *The Joys of Motherhood* and Alice Walker's *Meridian*." *Black Feminist Criticism: Perspectives on Black Women Writers*. New York: Pergamon P, 1985. 211–52. Print.

———. "Fixing Methodologies: *Beloved*." *Cultural Critique* 24 (1993): 5–15. *JSTOR*. Web. 23 Feb. 2009.

———. "Ritualistic Process and the Structure of Paule Marshall's *Praisesong for the Widow*." *Callaloo* 6.2 (1983): 74–84. Print.

Collier, Eugenia. "The Closing of the Circle: Movement from Division to Wholeness in Paule Marshall's Fiction." *Black Women Writers (1950–1980): A Critical Evaluation*. Ed. Mari Evans. Garden City, NY: Anchor Press/ Doubleday, 1984. 295–315. Print.

Collins, Janelle. "Generating Power: Fission, Fusion, and Postmodern Politics in Bambara's *The Salt Eaters*." *MELUS* 21.2 (1996): 35–47. *JSTOR*. Web. 10 September 2009.

Collins, Patricia Hill. *Black Feminist Thought: Knowledge, Consciousness, and the Politics of Empowerment*. New York: Routledge, 1991. Print.

Connor, Kimberly Rae. *Conversions and Visions: In the Writings of African-American Women*. Knoxville: U of Tennessee P, 1994. Print.

Cooper, J. California. *Family: A Novel*. New York: Doubleday, 1991. Print.

Couser, G. Thomas. "Oppression and Repression: Personal and Collective Memory in Paule Marshall's *Praisesong for the Widow* and Leslie Marmon Silko's *Ceremony*." *Memory and Cultural Politics: New Approaches to American Ethnic Literatures*. Eds. Amritjit Singh, Joseph T. Skerrett, Jr. and Robert E. Hogan. Boston: Northeastern UP, 1996. 106–20. Print.

Creel, Margaret Washington. *"A Peculiar People": Slave Religion and Community-Culture Among the Gullahs*. New York: New York University Press, 1988. Print.

Curry, Renée R. *"Daughters of the Dust*, the White Woman Viewer, and the Unborn Child." *Teaching What You're Not: Identity Politics in Higher Education*. Ed. Katherine J. Mayberry. New York: NYU Press, 1996. 335–56. Print.

Curtin, Philip. *The Atlantic Slave Trade*. Madison: U of Wisconsin P, 1969. Print.

Dance, Daryl Cumber. "Go Eena Kumbla: A Comparison of Erna Brodber's *Jane and Louisa Will Soon Come Home* and Toni Cade Bambara's *The Salt Eaters*." *Caribbean Women Writers: Essays from the First International Conference*. Ed. Selwyn R. Cudjoe. Wellesley: Calaloux, 1990. 169–84. Print.

Darling, Marsha. "In the Realm of Possibility: A Conversation with Toni Morrison." *Conversations with Toni Morrison*. Ed. Danille Taylor-Guthrie. Jackson: UP of Mississippi, 1994. 246–54. Print.

Dash, Julie. *Daughters of the Dust: The Making of an African American Woman's Film*. New York: New Press, 1992. Print.

———. "Making *Daughters of the Dust*." *Daughters of the Dust: The Making of an African American Woman's Film*. New York: New Press, 1992. 1–26. Print.

Daughters of the Dust. Dir. Julie Dash. Kino on Video, 1991. DVD.

Davidson, Cathy N. and E. M. Broner, eds. *The Lost Tradition: Mothers and Daughters in Literature*. New York: Frederick Ungar Publishing Company, 1980. Print.

Davies, Carole Boyce. *Black Women, Writing and Identity: Migrations of the Subject*. London: Routledge, 1994. Print.

———. "Mother Right/Write Revisited: *Beloved* and *Dessa Rose* and the Construction of Motherhood in Black Women's Fiction." *Narrating Mothers: Theorizing Maternal Subjectivies*. Eds. Brenda O. Daly and Maureen T. Reddy. Knoxville: U of Tennessee P, 1991. 44–57. Print.

Davis, Angela. "Sick and Tired of Being Sick and Tired: The Politics of Black Women's Health." *Women, Culture, & Politics*. Ed. Angela Davis. New York: Random House, 1989. 53–65. Print.

———. "Women in the 1980's: Setbacks and Victories." *Women, Culture, & Politics*. Ed. Angela Davis. New York: Random House, 1989. 91–94. Print.

Denniston, Dorothy Hamer. *The Fiction of Paule Marshall: Reconstructions of History, Culture, and Gender*. Knoxville: U of Tennessee P, 1995. Print.

De Veaux, Alexis. "Paule Marshall: In Celebration of Our Triumph." *Essence* May 1979: 70+. Print.

Diawara, Manthia. "Black American Cinema: The New Realism." *Black American Cinema*. Ed. Manthia Diawara. New York: Routledge, 1993. 3–25. Print.

Doumbia, Adama and Naomi Doumbia. *The Way of the Elders: West African Spirituality & Tradition*. St. Paul: Llewellyn Publications, 2004. Print.

Dove, Nah. *Afrikan Mothers: Bearers of Culture, Makers of Social Change*. Albany: SUNY, 1998. Print.

Doyle, Laura. *Bordering on the Body: The Racial Matrix of Modern Fiction and Culture*. New York: Oxford UP, 1994. Print.

Dubey, Madhu. "Becoming Animal in Black Women's Science Fiction." *Afro-Future Females: Black Writers Chart Science Fiction's Newest New-Wave Trajectory*. Columbus: The Ohio State UP, 2008. 31–51. Print.

Duboin, Corinne. "Trauma Narrative, Memorialization, and Mourning in Phyllis Alesia Perry's *Stigmata*." *Southern Literary Journal* 40.2 (2008): 284–304. *Project Muse*. Web. 1 September 2009.

Due, Tananarive. *The Between: A Novel.* New York: Harper Collins, 1995. Print.

Due, Tananarive and Patricia Stephens Due. *Freedom in the Family: A Mother–Daughter Memoir of the Fight for Civil Rights.* New York: Ballantine Books, 2003. Print.

Eckard, Paula Gallant. *Maternal Body and Voice in Toni Morrison, Bobbie Ann Mason, and Lee Smith.* Columbia: U of Missouri P, 2002. Print

Ela, Jean-Marc. "Ancestors and Christian Faith: An African Problem." *Liturgy and Cultural Religious Traditions.* Eds. Herman Schmidt and David Power. New York: The Seabury Press, 1977. Print.

Eyerman, Ron. "Cultural Trauma: Slavery and the Formation of African American Identity." *Cultural Trauma and Collective Identity.* Jeffrey C. Alexander, Ron Eyerman, Bernhard Giesen, Neil J. Smelser, and Pietr Sztompka. Berkeley: UC P, 2004. Print.

Fairley, Nancy J. "Dreaming Ancestors in Eastern Carolina." *Journal of Black Studies* 33.5 (2003): 545–61. *JSTOR.* Web. 22 June 2007.

Fu-Kiau, Kimbwandende Kia Bunseki. *African Cosmology of the Bãntu-Kôngo: Tying the Spritual Knot: Principles of Life and Living.* Brooklyn, NY: Athelia Henrietta Press, 2001.

Furst, Sidney S. "Psychic Trauma and Its Reconstruction with Particular Reference to Postchildhood Trauma." *The Reconstruction of Trauma: Its Significance in Clinical Work.* Ed. Arnold Rothstein, MD. Madison, CT: International Universities P, 1986. 29–39. Print.

Gabbin, Joanne V. "A Laying On of Hands: Black Women Writers Exploring the Roots of their Folk and Cultural Tradition." *Wild Women in the Whirlwind: Afra-American Culture and the Contemporary Literary Renaissance.* Eds. Joanne M. Braxton and Andrée Nicola McLaughlin. New Brunswick: Rutgers UP, 1990. 246–63. Print.

Gates, Jr., Henry Louis. *The Signifying Monkey: A Theory of African-American Literary Criticism.* New York: Oxford UP, 1988. Print.

———. "We Are All Africans." *Ebony.* Dec. 2007: 132–34, 136. *Wilson Web.* Web. 29 May 2012.

Gibson, Lydialyle. "Long Way Home." *Current.* Feb. 2008: 18–21. Print.

Glave, Dianne. " 'My Characters are Teaching Me to be Strong': An Interview with Tananarive Due." *African American Review* 38.4 (2004): 695–705. *JSTOR.* Web. 2 May 2012.

Gordon, Avery F. *Ghostly Matters: Haunting and the Sociological Imagination.* Minneapolis: U of Minnesota P, 1997. Print.

Gourdine, Angeletta K. M. "Fashioning the Body [as] Politic in Julie Dash's *Daughters of the Dust.*" *African American Review* 38.3 (2004): 499–511. *JSTOR.* Web. 27 February 2009.

Govan, Sandra Y. "Speculative Fiction." *The Oxford Companion to African American Literature.* Eds. William L. Andrews, Frances Smith Foster, and Trudier Harris. New York: Oxford UP, 1997. 683–7. Print.

Grayson, Sandra M. *Visions of the Third Millennium: Black Science Fiction Novelists Write the Future.* Trenton: Africa World P, 2005.

Grewel, Gurleen. "Memory and the Matrix of History: The Poetics of Loss and Recovery in Joy Kogawa's *Obasan* and Toni Morrison's *Beloved.*" *Memory and Cultural Politics: New Approaches to American Ethnic Literatures.* Eds. Amritjit Singh, Joseph T. Skerrett, Jr. and Robert E. Hogan. Boston: Northeastern UP, 1996. 140–74. Print.

Griffin, Farah Jasmine. *"Who Set You Flowin'?": The African-American Migration Narrative.* New York: Oxford UP, 1995. Print.

Handley, William R. "The House a Ghost Built: Nommo, Allegory, and the Ethics of Reading in Toni Morrison's *Beloved.*" *Contemporary Literature* 36.4 (1995): 676–701. *JSTOR.* Web. 25 July 2011.

Harris, Trudier. *Fiction and Folklore: The Novels of Toni Morrison.* Knoxville: U of Tennessee P, 1991. Print.

———. *Saints, Sinners, Saviors: Strong Black Women in African American Literature.* New York: Palgrave, 2001. Print.

Harrison, Elizabeth. "Intolerable Human Suffering and the Role of the Ancestor: Literary Criticism as a Means of Analysis." *Journal of Advanced Nursing* 32.3 (2000): 689–94. Print.

Hartman, Saidiya. *Lose Your Mother: A Journey Along the Atlantic Slave Route.* New York: Farrar, Straus and Giroux, 2008. Print.

Heclo, Hugh. "The Mixed Legacies of Ronald Reagan." *Presidential Quarterly* 38.4 (2008): 555–74. *JSTOR.* Web. 21 May 2012.

Henderson, Carol E. *Scarring the Black Body: Race and Representation in African American Literature.* Columbia: U of Missouri, 2002. Print.

Henderson, Mae G. "Toni Morrison's *Beloved*: Remembering the Body as Historical Text." *Toni Morrison's Beloved: A Casebook.* Eds. William L. Andrews and Nellie Y. McKay. NY: Oxford UP, 1999. 79–106. Print.

Henry, Annette. "The Politics of Unpredictability in Reading/Writing/Discussion Group With Girls From the Caribbean." *Theory into Practice* 40.3 (2001): 184–89. *JSTOR.* Web. 8 April 2010.

Herman, Judith. *Trauma and Recovery.* New York: Basic Books, 1992. Print.

Herskovits, Melville J. *The Myth of the Negro Past.* Boston: Beacon Press, 1941. Print.

Heyman, Richard. "Universalization and its Discontents: Morrison's *Song of Solomon*—A (W)hol(e)y Black Text." *African American Review* 29.3 (1995): 381–92. *JSTOR.* Web. 16 April 2002.

Higgins, Therese E. *Religiousity, Cosmology, and Folklore: The African Influence in the Novels of Toni Morrison.* New York: Routledge, 2001. Print.

Holland, Sharon Patricia. *Raising the Dead: Readings of Death and (Black) Subjectivity.* Durham: Duke, 2000. Print.

Holloway, Joseph E. "Introduction." *Africanisms in American Culture* 2nd ed. Ed. Joseph E. Holloway. Bloomington: Indiana UP, 2005. 1–17. Print.

Holloway, Karla F. C. *Moorings & Metaphors: Figures of Culture and Gender in Black Women's Literature.* New Brunswick: Rutgers UP, 1992. Print.

hooks, bell and Julie Dash. "Dialogue: Between Bell Hooks and Julie Dash." *Daughters of the Dust: The Making of an African American Woman's Film.*

Julie Dash with Toni Cade Bambara and bell hooks. New York: New Press, 1992. 26–67. Print.

Horvitz, Deborah. "Nameless Ghosts: Possession and Dispossession in *Beloved*." *Critical Essays on Toni Morrison's Beloved*. Ed. Barbara H. Solomon. New York: G. K. Hall & Co., 1998. 93–103. Print.

House, Elizabeth B. "Toni Morrison's Ghost: The Beloved Who Is Not Beloved." *Critical Essays on Toni Morrison's Beloved*. Ed. Barbara H. Solomon. New York: G. K. Hall & Co., 1998. 117–26. Print.

Hudson-Weems, Clenora. *Africana Womanist Literary Theory*. Trenton, NY: Africa World Press, 2004. Print.

Hull, Gloria T. " 'What It Is I Think She's Doing Anyhow': A Reading of Toni Cade Bambara's *The Salt Eaters*." *Conjuring: Black Women, Fiction, and Literary Tradition*. Eds. Marjorie Pryse and Hortense Spillers. Bloomington: Indiana UP, 1985. 216–32. Print.

Ikard, David. " 'So Much of What We Know Ain't So': The Other Gender in Toni Cade Bambara's *The Salt Eaters*." *Obsidian III: Literature in the African Diaspora* 4.1 (2002): 76–100. Print.

Ilechukwu, Sunday T. C. "*Ogbanje/abiku* and Cultural Conceptualizations." *Mental Health, Religion & Culture* 10.3 (2007): 239–55. *EBSCOhost*. Web. 5 June 2012.

Jackson, Sandra and Julie Moody-Freeman, eds. "Editorial Note: The Genre of Science Fiction and the Black Imagination." *The Black Imagination and the Speculative*. London: Routledge, 2011. 1–6. Print.

Jahn, Janheinz. *Muntu: An Outline of The New African Culture*. 1958. NY: Grove Press, 1961. Print.

Jennings, La Vinia Delois. *Toni Morrison and the Idea of Africa*. New York: Cambridge, 2008. Print.

Jones, Gayl. *Corregidora*. Boston, Beacon Press, 1975. Print.

Juneja, Renu and James Kingsland. "The Caribbean-American Connection: A Paradox of Success and Subversion." *Journal of American Culture* 21.3 (1998): 63–68. Print.

Kalu, Ogbu U. "Ancestral Sprituality and Society in Africa." *African Spirituality: Forms, Meanings, and Expressions*. Ed. Jacob K. Olupona. New York: The Crossroad Publishing Co., 2000. 54–84. Print.

Kammen, Michael. *In the Past Lane: Historical Perspectives on American Culture*. New York: Oxford UP, 1997. Print.

Kaplan, Sara Clarke. "Souls at the Crossroads, Africans on the Water: The Politics of Diasporic Melancholia." *Callaloo* 30.2 (2007): 511–26. Print.

Keizer, Arlene R. "*Beloved*: Ideologies in Conflict, Improvised Subjects." *African American Review* 33.1 (1999): 105–23. *EBSCO Host*. Web. 3 May 2010.

Kelley, Margot Anne. " 'Damballah is the First Law of Thermodynamics': Modes of Access to Toni Cade Bambara's *The Salt Eaters*." *African American Review* 27.3 (1993): 479–93. *JSTOR*. Web. 2 August 2001.

Kiely, Robert. "Further Considerations of the Holy Stigmata of St. Francis: Where Was Brother Leo?" *Religion and the Arts* 3.1 (1999): 20–40. Print.

Kopytoff, Igor. "Ancestors as Elders in Africa." *Perspectives on Africa: A Reader in Culture, History, and Representation*. Eds. Roy Richard Grinker and Christopher B. Steiner. Oxford and Cambridge: Blackwell Publishers, 1997. 412–21. Print.

Kreyling, Michael. *The South That Wasn't There: Postsouthern Memory and History*. Baton Rouge: LSU P, 2010. Print.

Krüger-Kahloula, Angelika. "Homage and Hegemony: African American Grave Inscription and Decoration." *Slavery in the Americas*. Ed. Wolfgang Binder. Wurzburg: Konigshausen & Neumann, 1993. 317–35. Print.

Krumholz, Linda. "The Ghosts of Slavery: Historical Recovery in Toni Morrison's *Beloved*." *Modern Critical Interpretations: Toni Morrison's Beloved*. Ed. Harold Bloom. Philadelphia: Chelsea House Publishers, 1999. 79–95. Print.

Kubitschek, Missy Dehn. *Claiming the Heritage: African-American Women Novelists and History*. Jackson: UP of Mississippi, 1991. Print.

———. "Paule Marshall's Women on Quest." *Black American Literature Forum* 21.1–2 (1987): 43–60. *JSTOR*. Web. 2 August 2001.

LaCapra, Dominick. *Writing History, Writing Trauma*. Baltimore: John Hopkins UP, 2001. Print.

Laub, Dori. "Bearing Witness or the Vicissitudes of Listening." *Testimony: Crises of Witnessing in Literature, Psychoanalysis, and History*. Eds. Shoshana Felman and Dori Laub. NY: Routledge, 1993. 57–74. Print.

Laub, Dori and Nanette C. Auerhahn. "Knowing and Not Knowing Massive Psychic Trauma: Forms of Traumatic Memory." *International Journal of Psychoanalysis* 74.2 (1993): 287–302. Print.

Lawson, Thomas E. *Religions of Africa, Traditions in Transformation*. New York: Harper Collins, 1985. Print.

LeClair, Thomas. " 'The Language Must Not Sweat': A Conversation with Toni Morrison." *The New Republic* 184.12 (1981): 25–29. Print.

Levin, Amy K. *Africanism and Authenticity in African-American Women's Novels*. Gainesville: UP of Florida, 2003. Print.

Long, Lisa. "A Relative Pain: The Rape of History in Octavia Butler's *Kindred* and Phyllis Alesia Perry's *Stigmata*." *College English* 64.4 (2002): 459–83. *JSTOR*. Web. 1 January 2009.

"Looking Back: Ronald Reagan, A Master of Racial Polarization." *The Journal of Blacks in Higher Education* 58 (2007/2008): 33–36. *JSTOR*. Web. 21 May 2012.

Maduka, Chidi T. "African Religious Beliefs in Literary Imagination: *Ogbanje* and *Abiku* in Chinua Achebe, J. P. Clark and Wole Soyinka." *Journal of Commonwealth Literature* 22.1 (1987): 17–30. Print.

Manns, Wilhemina. "Support Systems of Significant Others in Black Families." *Black Families*. Ed. Harriette McAdoo. Beverly Hills: Sage Publications, 1981. 238–51. Print.

Marni, Gauthier. *Amnesia and Redress in Contemporary American Fiction: Counterhistory*. New York: Palgrave Macmillan, 2011. eBook.

Marshall, Brenda. "The Gospel According to Pilate." *American Literature* 57.3 (1995): 486–89. *JSTOR*. Web. 19 April 2002.

Marshall, Paule. *Praisesong for the Widow*. New York: E.P. Dutton, 1984. Print.

Mbiti, John S. *African Religions and Philosophy*. 2nd ed. Oxford: Heinemann, 1990.

———. *Introduction to African Religion*. 2nd ed. Oxford: Heinemann, 1991.

McDowell, Deborah E. "Harlem Nocturne," Review of *Jazz* by Toni Morrison. *Women's Review of Books* 9.9 (1992): 1+. Print.

———. "Negotiating between Tenses: Witnessing Slavery after Freedom—*Dessa Rose*." *Slavery and the Literary Imagination*. Eds. Deborah E. McDowell and Arnold Rampersad. Baltimore: John Hopkins UP, 1989. 144–63. Print.

McKoy, Sheila Smith. "The Limbo Contest: Diaspora Temporality and its Reflection in *Praisesong for the Widow* and *Daughters of the Dust*." *Callaloo* 22.1 (1999): 208–22. *JSTOR*. Web. 27 February 2009.

Mellencamp, Patricia. "Haunted History: Tracey Moffatt and Julie Dash." *Discourse: Journal for Theoretical Studies in Media and Culture* 16.2 (1993): 127–63. Print.

Mitchell, Angelyn. *The Freedom to Remember: Narrative, Slavery, and Gender in Contemporary Black Women's Fiction*. New Brunswick: Rutgers, UP, 2002. Print.

Mobley, Marilyn Sanders. "A Different Remembering: Memory, History and Meaning in Toni Morrison's *Beloved*." *Modern Critical Interpretations: Toni Morrison's Beloved*. Ed. Harold Bloom. Philadelphia: Chelsea House Publishers, 1999. Print.

Moore, Kari. "Speculative Fiction." *African American Literature: A Guide to Reading Interests*. Westport: Libraries Unlimited, 2004. 335–74. Print.

Morrison, Toni. *Beloved*. 1987. New York: Vintage International, 2004. Print.

———. *Playing in the Dark: Whiteness and the Literary Imagination*. Cambridge: Harvard UP, 1990. Print.

———. "Rootedness: The Ancestor in Afro-American Fiction." *Black Women Writers at Work: A Critical Evaluation*. Ed. Mari Evans. Garden City, N.Y.: Anchor Press, 1984. 339–45. Print.

———. "The Site of Memory." *Inventing the Truth: The Art and Craft of Memoir*. Rev. and expanded 2nd ed. Ed. William Zinsser. Boston: Houghton Mifflin, 1995. 85–102. Print.

Nasta, Susheila, ed. *Motherlands: Black Women's Writing from Africa, the Caribbean and South Asia*. New Brunswick: Rutgers, 1991. Print.

Nora, Pierre. "Between Memory and History: *Les Lieux de Mémoire*." *Representations* 26 (1989): 7–24. *JSTOR*. Web. 6 August 2004.

Nunes, Ana. "From the Fantastic to Magic Realism: The Spectral Presence in Phyllis Perry's *Stigmata*." *Revisiting Slave Narratives II/Les Avatars Contemporains des re'cits d'esclaves II*. Ed. Judith Misrahi-Barak. Montpellier, France: Université Paul Valéry, 2007. 223–48. Print.

Ogunleye, Foluke. "Transcending the 'Dust': African American Filmmakers Preserving the 'Glimpse of the Eternal.'" *College Literature* 34.1 (2007): 156–73. Print.

Ogunyemi, Chikwenye Okonjo. "An Abiku-Ogbanje Atlas: A Pre-Text for Rereading Soyinka's *Aké* and Morrison's *Beloved*." *African American Review* 36.4 (2002): 663–78. *JSTOR*. Web. 22 Feb. 2010.

Okonkwo, Christopher N. "A Critical Divination: Reading Sula as Ogbanje-Abiku." *African American Review* 38.4 (2004): 651–68. *JSTOR*. 22 February 2010.

———. *A Spirit of Dialogue: Incarnations of O'gbañje, the Born-to-Die, in African American Literature*. Knoxville: U of Tennessee P, 2008. Print.

Olmsted, Jane. "The Pull to Memory and the Language of Place in Paule Marshall's *The Chosen Place, The Timeless People* and *Praisesong for the Widow*." *African American Review* 31.2 (1997): 249–67. *JSTOR*. Web. 2 August 2001.

O'Reilly, Kenneth. *Nixon's Piano: Presidents and Racial Politics from Washington to Clinton*. New York: The Free Press, 1995. Print.

Parrinder, Geoffrey. *Religion in Africa*. London: Pall Mall Press, 1969. Print.

Passalacqua, Camille. "Witnessing to Heal the Self in Gayle Jones's *Corregidora* and Phyllis Alesia Perry's *Stigmata*." *MELUS* 35.4 (2010): 139–63. *Project Muse*. Web. 13 April 2011.

Patton, Venetria K. *Women in Chains: The Legacy of Slavery in Black Women's Fiction*. Albany: SUNY P, 2000. Print.

Patterson, Orlando. *Slavery and Social Death: A Comparative Study*. Cambridge: Harvard UP, 1982. Print.

Perry, Phyllis Alesia. *Stigmata*. New York: Anchor Books, 1998. Print.

———. *A Sunday in June*. New York: Hyperion, 2004. Print.

Peterson, Nancy. *Against Amnesia: Contemporary Women Writers and the Crises of Historical Memory*. Philadelphia: U of Pennsylvania P, 2001. Print.

Pettis, Joyce. "Self Definition and Redefinition in Paule Marshall's *Praisesong for the Widow*." *Perspectives of Black Popular Culture*. Ed. Harry B. Shaw. Bowling Green: Bowling Green UP, 1990. 93–100. Print.

———. *Toward Wholeness in Paule Marshll's Fiction*. Charlottesville: UP of Virginia, 1995. Print.

Pobee, John. "Aspects of African Traditional Religion." *Sociological Analysis* 37.1 (1976): 1–18. Print.

Rawley, James H. *The Transatlantic Slave Trade*. New York: W. W. Norton, 1981. Print.

Reagon, Bernice Johnson. "African Diaspora Women: The Making of Cultural Workers." *Women in Africa and the African Diaspora*. Eds. Rosalyn Terborg-Penn and Andrea Benton Rushing. 2nd ed. Washington, DC: Howard UP, 1996. 263–75. Print

Reyes, Angelita. "Politics and Metaphors of Materialism in Paule Marshall's *Praisesong for the Widow* and Toni Morrison's *Tar Baby*." *Politics and the Muse: Studies in the Politics of Recent American Literature*. Ed. Adam J. Sorkin. Bowling Green: Bowling Green State U Popular P, 1989. 179–205. Print.

———. "Rereading a Nineteenth-Century Fugitive Slave Incident: From Toni Morrison's Margaret Garner's Dearly Beloved." *Annals of Scholarship* 7 (1990): 464–86. Print.

Rigney, Barbara Hill. " 'A Story to Pass On': Ghosts and the Significance of History in Toni Morrison's *Beloved*." *Haunting the House of Fiction: Feminist*

Perspectives on Ghost Stories by American Women. Eds. Lynette Carpenter and Wendy K. Kolmar. Knoxville: U of Tennessee P, 1991. 229–35. Print.

Rody, Caroline. *The Daughter's Return: African-American and Caribbean Women's Fiction of History*. Oxford: Oxford UP, 2001. Print.

———. "Toni Morrison's *Beloved*: History, 'Rememory,' and a 'Clamor for a Kiss.'" *American Literary History* 7.1 (1995): 92–119. *JSTOR*. Web. 20 April 2006.

Rogers, Susan. "Embodying Cultural Memory in Paule Marshall's *Praisesong for the Widow*." *African American Review* 34.1 (2000): 77–93. *JSTOR*. 3 August 2001.

Rushdy, Ashraf H. A. "The Neo-Slave Narrative." *The Cambridge Companion to The African American Novel*. Ed. Maryemma Graham. Cambridge: Cambridge UP, 2004. Print.

———. *Neo-Slave Narratives: Studies in the Social Logic of a Literary Form*. New York: Oxford UP, 1999. Print.

———. *Remembering Generations: Race and Family in Contemporary African American Fiction*. Chapel Hill: U of North Carolina P, 2001. Print.

Schreiber, Eveyln Jaffe. *Race, Trauma, and Home in the Novels of Toni Morrison*. Baton Rouge: LSU P, 2010. Print.

Sievers, Stefanie. "Embodied Memories-Sharable Stories? The Legacies of Slavery as a Problem of Representation in Phyllis Alesia Perry's *Stigmata*." *Monuments of the Black Atlantic: Slavery and Memory*. Eds. Joanne M. Braxton and Maria Diedrich. Münster, Germany: LIT, 2004. 131–39. Print.

Singh, Amritjit and Joseph T. Skerrett, eds. "Introduction." *Memory and Cultural Politics: New Approaches to American Ethnic Literatures*. Boston: Northeastern UP, 1996. Print.

Slattery, Dennis Patrick. *The Wounded Body: Remembering the Markings of Flesh*. Albany: SUNY P, 2000. Print.

Smith-Wright, Geraldine. "In Spite of the Klan: Ghosts in the Fiction of Black Women Writers." *Haunting the House of Fiction: Feminist Perspectives on Ghost Stories by American Women*. Knoxville: U of Tennessee P, 1991. Print.

Somé, Malidoma Patrice. *The Healing Wisdom of Africa: Finding Life Purpose Through Nature, Ritual, and Community*. New York: Penguin, 1998. Print.

———. *Of Water and the Spirit: Ritual, Magic, and Initiation in the Life of an African Shaman*. New York: Penguin, 1994. Print.

Spaulding, A. Timothy. *Re-Forming the Past: History, The Fantastic, and the Postmodern Slave Narrative*. Columbus: Ohio State UP, 2005. Print.

Spillers, Hortense. "Interstices: A Small Drama of Words." *Pleasure and Danger: Exploring Female Sexuality*. Ed. Carole S. Vance. Boston: Routledge and Kegan Paul, 1984. 73–100. Print.

———. "Mama's Baby, Papa's Maybe: An American Grammar Book." *Diacritics* 17.2 (1987): 65–81. *JSTOR*. Web. 22 June 2007.

Stanford, Ann Folwell. "Mechanisms of Disease: African-American Women Writers, Social Pathologies, and the Limits of Medicine." *NWSA Journal* 6.1 (1994): 28–47. *JSTOR*. Web. 10 September 2009.

Steady, Filomina Chioma. "The Black Woman Cross-Culturally: An Overview." *The Black Woman Cross Culturally*. Ed. Filomina Chioma Steady. Cambridge: Schenkman Publishing Company, Inc., 1981. 7–48. Print.

Stepto, Robert and Toni Morrison. " 'Intimate Things in Place': A Conversation with Toni Morrison." *The Massachusetts Review* 18.3 (1977): 473–89. *JSTOR*. Web. 20 July 2010.

Stuckey, Sterling. *Slave Culture: Nationalist Theory & The Foundations of Black America*. New York: Oxford UP, 1987. Print.

Taiwo, Oladele. "Two Incantations to 'Abiku.' " *Nigerian Writing: Nigeria as Seen by Her Own Writers as Well as by German Authors*. Eds. A. G. S. Momodu and Ulla Schild. Benin City, Nigeria: Bendel Book Depot and Tübingen, Germany: Horst Erdmann Verlag, 1976. 166–81. Print.

Tate, Greg. "A Word: From Greg Tate." *Daughters of the Dust: The Making of an African American Woman's Film*. Julie Dash with Toni Cade Bambara and bell hooks. New York: New Press, 1992. 69–71. Print.

Thaler, Ingrid. *Black Atlantic Speculative Fictions: Octavia E. Butler, Jewelle Gomez, and Nalo Hopkinson*. New York: Routledge, 2010. Print.

Thompson, Robert Farris and Joseph Cornet. *The Four Moments of the Sun: Kongo Art in Two Worlds*. Washington: National Gallery of Art, 1981.

Traoré, Ousseynou B. "Mythic Structures of Ethnic Memory in *Beloved*: The Mammy Watta and Middle Passage Paradigms." *"Beloved, She's Mine": Essais sur Beloved de Toni Morrison*. Eds. Geneviève Fabre and Claudine Raynaud. Paris: Cetanla, 1993. 77–89. Print.

Traylor, Eleanor W. "Music as Theme: the Jazz Mode in the Works of Toni Cade Bambara." *Black Women Writers (1950–1980): A Critical Evaluation*. Ed. Mari Evans. Garden City, NY: Anchor P, 1984. 58–70. Print.

Van der Kolk, Bessel and Onno Van der Hart. "The Intrusive Past: The Flexibility of Memory and the Engraving of Trauma." *American Imago* 48.4 (1991): 425–54. *ProQuest*. Web. 6 September 2009.

Vass, Winifred Kellersberger. *The Bantu Speaking Heritage of the United States*. Los Angeles: UCLA, Center for Afro-American Studies, 1979. Print.

Vickroy, Laurie. *Trauma and Survival in Contemporary Fiction*. Charlottesville and London: University of Virginia P, 2002. Print.

Walker, Alice. *In Search of Our Mothers' Gardens: Womanist Prose by Alice Walker*. San Diego: Harcourt Brace Jovanovich, 1983. Print.

Wall, Cheryl. "Toni's Obligato: Bambara and the African American Literary Tradition." *Savoring the Salt: The Legacy of Toni Cade Bambara*. Eds. Linda Janet Holmes and Cheryl Wall. Philadelphia: Temple UP, 2008. 27–42. Print.

Walters, Wendy W. " 'One of Dese Mornings, Bright and Fair,/ Take My Wings and Cleave De Air': The Legend of the Flying Africans and Diasporic Consciousness." *MELUS* 22.3 (1997): 3–29. *JSTOR*. Web. 14 July 2010.

Washington, Margaret. "Gullah Attitudes toward Life and Death." *Africanisms in American Culture*. Ed. Joseph E. Holloway. Bloomington: Indiana UP, 2005. 152–86. Print.

Washington, Teresa N. "The Mother–Daughter Àjé Relationship in Toni Morrison's *Beloved*." *African American Review* 39.1–2 (2005): 171–88. *JSTOR*. Web. 22 Feb. 2010.

White, Deborah Gray. "Female Slaves: Sex Roles and Status in the Antebellum Plantation South." *Journal of Family History* 8.3 (1983): 248–61. Print.

Wicker, Kathleen O'Brien. "Mami Water in African Religion and Spirituality." *African Spirituality: Forms, Meanings, and Expressions*. Ed. Jacob K. Olupona. New York: The Crossroad Publishing Co., 2000. 198–222. Print.

Wilentz, Gay. "Civilizations Underneath: African Heritage as Cultural Discourse in Toni Morrison's *Song of Solomon*." *African American Review* 26.1 (1992): 61–76. *JSTOR*. Web. 19 April 2002.

———. "If You Surrender to the Air: Folk Legends of Flight and Resistance." *MELUS* 16.1 (1989–90): 21–32. Print.

———. "Towards a Spiritual Middle Passage Back: Paule Marshall's Diasporic Vision in *Praisesong for the Widow*." *Obsidian II: Black Literature in Review* 5.3 (1990): 1–21. Print.

Williams, Patricia J. "Emotional Truth." *The Nation* 6 Mar. 2006: 14. *Academic Search Premier*. Web. 21 May 2012.

Willis, Susan. *Specifying: Black Women Writing the American Experience*. Madison: U of Wisconsin P, 1987. Print.

Wisker, Gina. " 'Your Buried Ghosts Have A Way of Tripping You Up': Revisioning and Mothering in African-American and Afro-Caribbean Women's Speculative Horror." *FemSpec* 6.1 (2005): 71–86. *Wilson Web*. Web. 16 May 2012.

Woolfork, Lisa. *Embodying American Slavery in Contemporary Culture*. Urbana: U of Illinois P, 2009. Print.

Wright, Nancy E. "Property Rights and Possession in *Daughters of the Dust*." *MELUS* 33.3 (2008): 11–25. Print.

Zahan, Dominique. *The Religion, Spirituality, and Thought of Traditional Africa*. Trans. Kate Ezra Martin and Lawrence M. Martin. Chicago: U of Chicago P, 1979. Print.

———. "Some Reflections on African Spirituality." *African Spirituality: Forms, Meanings, and Expressions*. Ed. Jacob K. Olupona. New York: The Crossroad Publishing Co., 2000. 3–25. Print.

Index

Abiku, 20–21, 121, 127, 130–31,
133, 138–39, 144–45, 182,
187–88, 194n, 195nn 11, 12
(*See also under* Child)
Achebe, Christie C., 21, 121, 131,
134, 138, 142, 147, 195n
African Cosmology, 23, 85, 181, 187
African Spirituality, 117, 124, 129,
175–76
African Survivals (*See* Africanisms)
Africanisms, 10–12, 23, 82, 118,
132, 156, 163, 171, 175–77
Alexander, Jeffrey C., 166, 173
Alwes, Derek, 42, 46, 51
Ancestor, 2–3, 6–11, 13–19, 21–
23, 27–29, 31, 33–50, 52–53
55–57, 60–63, 65, 68–69,
72–87, 90–92, 94, 96–97,
99–101, 104, 106–107, 111,
114, 117–21, 123–25, 127–30,
140, 142, 148–64, 169, 172–
73, 176–77, 180–85, 188,
190, 191n, 192nn 6, 16,
193n
   Malevolent Ancestor, 7, 20, 23,
   56–57, 69, 118, 121
Ancestral Call, 18, 20, 38, 44, 111,
164, 166
Ancestral Cultural Healing (*See*
Ancestral Healing)
Ancestral Figure (*See* Ancestral
Presence)

Ancestral Healing, 15, 23, 33, 48,
153, 170, 173, 177, 180
Ancestral Presence, 20, 22–23, 48,
57, 68, 87, 92, 118, 121–22,
129, 131, 140–41, 150, 155,
162, 164, 169, 177–78, 182,
184, 190, 192n, 194n
Ansa, Tina McElroy, 9, 20 (See also
*The Hand, Ugly Ways, You Know
Better*)
Auerhahn, Nanette, 101–102, 108

Baker, Houston, 110
Bambara, Toni Cade, 2, 6–7, 9, 14,
22, 31–33, 35, 40–43, 46, 48,
51–52, 63, 155–58, 161–62,
176–78, 193n (See also *The Salt
Eaters*)
Barnes, Steven, 179
Barthold, Bonnie, 9–10, 12, 93,
154, 160, 191n
Bastian, Misty L., 121, 126, 130–32,
144, 180
Beloved, 2–3, 5, 9–10, 12, 15,
20–23, 53, 55–57, 87, 112,
118–50, 176–78, 180, 183,
190, 194nn 5, 6, 195nn 9, 10,
13, 14 (*See also* Morrison)
   Abiku, 127, 131, 133, 138–39,
   144–45
   Ancestor, 55, 57, 123–24, 127–29,
   140, 142, 148–50

Beloved (continued)
  Child, 5, 15, 22, 125–27, 129,
    135–36, 140, 144, 146, 177
  Ghost, 119–25, 128–29, 139, 142,
    184, 194n
  Malevolent Ancestor, 20–21, 23,
    56–57
Bentley, Nancy, 5
Bettanin, Guiliano, 99
The Between, 23, 179–90 (*See also*
  Due)
  Abiku, 182, 187–88
  Ancestor, 180–83, 185, 188, 190
Bobo, Jacqueline, 34, 40, 158
Bouson, J. Brooks, 125, 135, 143
Bowers, Susan, 128, 142, 195n
Braxton, Joanne, 28, 184
Brogan, Kathleen, 41, 60, 62,
  68–69, 73, 122–24, 162, 175
Brøndum, Lene, 6–7, 66
Broner, E. M., 2
Brouwer, Joel, 39, 161–62
Brown, Laura S., 101
Brown-Hinds, Paulette, 81–84
Busia, Abena, 67, 72, 85–86, 90,
  182
Burton, LeVar, 179
Butler, Octavia, 9, 92–93, 99, 115,
  179

Carabi, Angels, 120, 122, 124, 126,
  129–30, 137–38, 146
Caruth, Cathy, 93–94, 101, 104,
  166
Chandler, Zala, 48, 162
Child, 1–2, 5–6, 16, 21, 28, 37–39,
  44–45, 71, 84, 95, 100, 102–
  103, 107, 118, 125–26, 129,
  132, 135–40, 146, 151–52,
  155–57, 159–61, 165, 168–69,
  172–73, 177, 185–86, 190
  Abiku Child, 131, 144–45
  Ogbanje Child, 138
  Child Figure, 11, 14–15, 20–23,
    34–35, 46, 153, 155–56, 163,
    173

Children, 9, 16, 21, 28, 35, 38,
  42, 46, 48, 51, 57, 62, 67, 74,
  79, 86, 90, 97, 102, 125–27,
  131–32, 134, 137, 139, 150–
  55, 157, 159, 162, 164–65,
  167, 169, 172–73, 177–78,
  180, 181–82, 184–90
  Ogbanje Children, 144
  Spirit Child, 21, 121, 185
  Spirit Children, 121, 131, 134
Christian, Barbara, 41, 67, 70–71, 73,
  76, 79–80, 84, 86, 124–25, 129
Circle Dance (*See* Ring Shout)
Civil Rights Movement, 3, 7, 23,
  60–61, 177, 181, 184
Collier, Eugenia, 76
Collins, Janelle, 52
Collins, Patricia Hill, 1, 41
Connor, Kimberly Rae, 63, 65, 74,
  83, 85
Cooper, J. California, 9 (See also
  Family)
Cornet, Joseph, 11, 14–15, 81,
  192nn 7, 11, 12
Corregidora, 91–92 (*See also* Jones)
Cosmogram, 12–14, 34, 81–82, 87,
  126–27, 136, 153–54, 176–78,
  180–81
Couser, G. Thomas, 60–61, 72
Creel, Margaret Washington, 18, 34,
  156, 192n (*See also* Washington,
  Margaret)
Culture Bearer, 16, 22, 27, 29, 31,
  35, 53, 60, 63, 74–75, 77, 79,
  85–86, 95, 97, 161
Curry, Renée, 158

Dance, Daryl Cumber, 44
Darling, Marsha, 128, 130, 132
Dash, Julie, 2, 6–7, 12, 22–24, 31,
  33–35, 37–39, 67, 76, 153,
  155–57, 159, 161–63, 173,
  176–78, 180, 191n, 193n (See
  also *Daughters of the Dust*)
Daughters of the Dust, 2–3, 12,
  15–16, 21–23, 27–28, 31–40,

44, 53, 67, 76, 150, 153–63,
176, 180, 191n, 193n (*See also*
Dash)
Ancestor, 31, 33, 35–40, 44, 53,
76, 155, 158–63
Child, 16, 21, 23, 35, 37–39,
153, 156, 159–61
Davidson, Cathy N., 2
Davies, Carole Boyce, 130, 136,
144–45
Davis, Angela, 8
Delany, Samuel, 179
De Veaux, Alexis, 65–66, 84
Denniston, Dorothy Hamer, 72
Diawara, Manthia, 36, 155, 158
Doumbia, Adama, 10, 31, 56, 92,
164, 169
Doumbia, Naomi, 10, 31, 56, 92,
164, 169
Dove, Nah, 27, 33, 193n
Doyle, Laura, 5, 7, 102
Dubey, Madhu, 178
Duboin, Corinne, 93, 107–10, 112,
114, 117, 194n
Due, Tananarive, 23, 179–85, 187–
88, 190 (See also *The Between,
The Good House, The Living
Blood, My Soul to Keep*)

Eckard, Paula Gallant, 125, 195n
Ela, Jean-Marc, 9, 36
Elders, 1–3, 8–9, 15–17, 19, 21–23,
27–29, 31–53, 55–57, 60,
63, 73–76, 80, 86, 114, 118,
123, 130, 133, 142, 147, 150,
152–53, 155–59, 161, 165,
169, 172–73, 177
Elder Figure, 7, 11, 14–16, 23,
34–35, 74, 76, 156
Eyerman, Ron, 90, 116, 173

Fairley, Nancy J., 18, 192n
Family 9 (*See also* Cooper)
Four Vees, 14–15, 86
Fu-Kiau, Bunseki, 14–15, 19–21, 28,
31, 55, 57, 86–87, 91, 121,

126, 129–30, 152–53, 192nn
10, 12, 13, 15
Furst, Sidney S., 102, 134

Gibson, Lydialyle, 23, 192n
Gabbin, Joanne V., 79
Gates, Jr., Henry Louis, 23–24, 77,
175–76, 192n, 193n
Ghost, 9, 41, 57, 59–60, 62, 69, 71,
90, 93, 96, 119–25, 128–29,
139, 142, 171, 175, 184, 192n,
194n
Glave, Dianne, 181, 184
Gordon, Avery F., 59–62, 71,
90–91, 93, 96, 122
Gourdine, Angeletta, 158–59
Govan, Sandra, 178–79
Grayson, Sandra M., 179
Grewel, Gurleen, 136
Griffin, Farah Jasmine, 19

The Hand I Fan With, 9, 20 (*See
also* Ansa)
Ancestor 20
Handley, William R., 132
Harris, Trudier, 42, 45, 48–49, 51,
119, 121, 125, 139, 143
Harrison, Elizabeth, 44, 47, 49
Hartman, Saidiya, 24
Henderson, Carol E., 102–104, 107,
135
Henderson, Mae, 123, 136
Henry, Annette, 35
Herman, Judith Lewis, 93–94, 103,
110–11, 117
Heyman, Richard, 84
Higgins, Therese E., 142
Hogan, Robert E., 56
Holland, Sharon, 6, 56, 125, 127
Holloway, Joseph E., 91, 192n
Holloway, Karla, 19, 43, 49, 192n
Hood, Yolanda, 181, 185
hooks, bell, 38, 67, 162
Hopkinson, Nalo, 179
Horvitz, Deborah, 137, 194n
House, Elizabeth, 128

Hudson-Weems, Clenora, 27
Hull, Gloria T., 219, 48, 52

Ibo, 39, 56, 61, 63–65, 72, 78, 85,
    116–17, 157, 161–63, 179
  Ibo Landing, 22, 32, 61–63,
    65–67, 71, 73, 85, 158, 162
Ikard, David, 43
Ilechukwu, Sunday T. C., 182–83,
    186, 188

Jackson, Sandra, 187
Jahn, Janheinz, 35–36, 130, 154,
    193n
Jennings, La Vinia Delois, 12–13,
    82, 126–27, 141, 143, 163,
    165, 169, 171
Jones, Gayle, 91–92 (See also
    Corregidora)
Juneja, Renu, 76, 82

Kala, 11, 14, 21, 28, 86, 152–53,
    192n
Kammen, Michael, 4
Kalu, Ogbu U., 129, 150, 169, 190
Kalûnga Line, 14, 91, 126–27, 130,
    137, 180–81, 189, 192n
Kaplan, Sarah Clarke, 39, 159
Kindred, 9, 92 (See also Butler)
  Ancestor, 9
Kingsland, James, 76, 82
Keizer, Arlene R., 141
Kelley, Margot Anne, 50
Kiely, Robert, 100
Kongo, 10–12, 14, 34, 55, 163,
    192nn 7, 11
  BaKongo, 11, 81, 98
  Cosmogram, 12, 34, 81–82, 87,
    126–27, 136, 153, 176–78,
    180–81
  Cosmology, 11–12, 14, 19, 23,
    34–35, 52, 55, 117–18, 127,
    132, 146, 156, 163, 175–77,
    180, 190
  Ki-kongo, 12, 35, 156
Kopytoff, Igor, 31, 118

Kreyling, Michael, 136
Krüger-Kahloula, Angelika, 180
Krumholz, Linda, 140, 143, 149
Kubitschek, Missy Dehn, 77, 84, 116

LaCapra, Dominick, 93
Laub, Dori, 94, 101–102, 108
Lawson, Thomas E., 57, 190
LeClair, Thomas, 123
Levin, Amy K., 127, 192n
Lieux de mémoire, 71, 83–84, 90,
    97, 107, 110
The Living Blood, 179 (See also Due)
Living-dead, 15, 17–18, 57, 96, 129,
    151–52, 154, 169, 192nn 6, 15
Long, Lisa, 93, 95–96, 104, 114–16
Luvèmba, 11, 14–15, 19, 86, 91,
    129–30, 152–53, 184, 192nn
    9, 15

Maduka, Chidi T., 126, 145, 195n
Mama Day, 178 (See also Naylor)
Mami Wata, 144–45, 188–89, 195nn
    8, 10, 1
Manns, Wilhemina, 16
Marni, Gauthier, 4–5
Marshall, Brenda, 74
Marshall, Paule, 2, 6–7, 9, 13, 22,
    53, 55–56, 59–60, 62–63,
    65–68, 70, 74–77, 81–87, 90,
    120, 141, 162, 176–80, 193n
    (See also Praisesong for the
    Widow)
Mbiti, John S., 10, 15, 17, 21, 35,
    41, 69, 89, 96, 100, 119–20,
    124, 151–52, 154–55, 163–64,
    167, 170–71, 192nn 6, 14,
    193n, 194n
McDowell, Deborah, 5, 195n
McKoy, Sheila Smith, 12, 37
Mellencamp, Patricia, 35
Memory, 1, 7, 17, 24, 49, 56,
    59–60, 62, 64, 69, 71, 73,
    78–81, 83–84, 90, 93–94,
    97–101, 104–105, 107, 109–10,
    114, 122, 124–25, 134–36,

140, 149, 151, 159, 161–62,
    166–67, 173, 175, 183–84
Middle Passage, 12, 23, 37, 48, 65,
    72–73, 78, 82, 84, 94–95, 98,
    102, 104, 123–24, 127–29,
    132, 182
Mitchell, Angelyn, 147, 194n
Mobley, Marilyn Sanders, 125
Moody-Freeman, Julie, 187
Morrison, Toni, 2–3, 6–7, 9, 16,
    20, 22, 28, 41, 53, 55–56, 74,
    92, 118–33, 135–38, 143–46,
    148, 163, 176–78, 180, 183,
    187 (See also *Beloved*, *Song of
    Solomon*, *Tar Baby*)
  Ancestor, 19–20, 47, 120, 124, 149
  Natally Dead, 3, 28
  Rememory, 56, 91, 104, 123,
    125, 134–35, 139, 146, 149
Moynihan, Daniel Patrick, 7, 190
Mud Mothers, 44–46, 49, 51, 53
Musoni, 11, 14–15, 21, 87, 127,
    129, 152–53, 184, 192nn 9, 15
My Soul to Keep, 179 (*See also* Due)

Nasta, Sushelia, 2
Naylor, Gloria, 178 (See also *Mama
    Day*)
Nne Mmiri (*See* Mami Wata)
Nora, Pierre, 71, 81, 83, 90, 97–98,
    107, 110
Nunes, Ana, 104, 110, 114

Ogbanje, 20–21, 23, 121, 126–27,
    130–33, 135, 137–39, 142,
    144–45, 147, 179–80, 182–83,
    187–88, 194n, 195nn 11, 12
    (*See also under* Child)
Ogunleye, Foluke, 39
Ogunyemi, Chikwenye Okonjo, 131,
    133, 138–39, 144, 146
Okonkwo, Christopher N., 121, 127,
    131, 141, 145–46, 180–81,
    183–90, 194n, 195n
Olmsted, Jane, 65, 71–73, 85, 193n
Onabuluwa (*See* Mami Wata)

O'Reilly, Kenneth, 7
Othermothers, 1–2, 16, 27–28, 31,
    40–42, 53, 55, 172, 178

Parrinder, Geoffrey, 55, 92, 100
Partus sequitur ventrem, 5–6, 23, 37,
    95, 137, 160, 172, 177–78
Passalacqua, Camille, 91, 94, 101,
    106, 112–13
Patterson, Orlando, 3, 95, 103
Patton, Venetria K., 5–6
Perry, Phyllis Alesia, 2, 6–7, 9,
    12–13, 22, 53, 55–56, 89–90,
    92, 94, 96, 98, 100, 104, 107,
    109, 113–15, 117–18, 120,
    153–55, 163–65, 171–73, 176–
    78, 181, 194nn 6, 8 (See also
    Stigmata, *A Sunday in June*)
Peterson, Nancy J., 4
Pettis, Joyce, 68, 75, 77–78, 80
Pierce-Baker, Charlotte, 110
Pobee, John, 62, 119–20, 130
Praisesong for the Widow, 2, 3, 9,
    13, 15, 28, 55–57, 59–87, 90,
    92, 95, 97, 116, 118, 120, 141,
    162, 176, 179–80, 193n (*See
    also* Marshall)
  Ancestor, 10, 28, 55, 60–62, 65,
    68–69, 72–87
  Beg Pardon, 13, 73, 79–80, 82–83
  Big Drum, 28, 75, 79, 81–85, 87,
    141
  Child, 63, 71, 79, 84
  Ghost, 60, 62, 69, 71
  Long-time People (*See* Old Parents)
  Old Parents, 72, 73, 76, 83, 87,
    193n
  Old People (*See* Old Parents)

Rich, Adrienne, 4
Reagan, Ronald, 4, 7–8, 191n
Reagon, Bernice Johnson, 27
Reincarnation, 35, 90, 92, 98,
    100–101, 113–15, 121, 126,
    129, 150–51, 154–55, 167
Reyes, Angelita, 70, 74, 75, 78, 128

Rigney, Barbara Hill, 145
Ring Shout, 13, 18, 79, 81–83, 87,
    141, 176, 180
Rody, Caroline, 123, 133, 146, 149,
    195n
Rogers, Susan, 78, 80, 85, 97
Rushdy, Ashraf H. A., 3, 7, 91, 122,
    191n, 193n, 194n

The Salt Eaters, 2–3, 9, 14–16, 22,
    27–28, 31–32, 40, 42–43, 53,
    155, 157, 176–78, 193n
    Ancestor, 22, 31, 40–43, 45,
    48–50, 52–53
    Child, 45
Sassafras, Cypress, and Indigo, 178
    (*See also* Shange)
Saunders, Charles, 179
Schreiber, Evelyn Jaffe, 143, 146, 149
Shange, Ntosake, 178 (See also
    Sassafras, Cypress, and Indigo)
Sievers, Stefanie, 105, 115
Singh, Amritjit, 56
Skerrett, Jr., Joseph T., 56
Slattery, Dennis, 104–105
Somé, Malidoma Patrice, 8–9, 16,
    21, 28, 38
Song of Solomon, 74, 178 (*See also*
    Morrison)
Smith-Wright, Geraldine, 69, 71,
    119–20
Spillers, Hortense, J. 6
Stack, Carol, 1
Stanford, Ann Folwell, 42, 47, 49, 59
Stepto, Robert, 16
Stigmata, 2, 3, 5, 9, 12–13, 15, 20,
    53, 55–57, 87, 89–118, 120,
    154–55, 163, 166, 172–73,
    176–77 (*See also* Perry)
    Child, 5, 95, 107
    Ghost, 90, 93, 96
Stuckey, Sterling, 13, 18, 81, 176,
    191n, 192n
Sudarkasa, Niara, 1
A Sunday in June, 2–3, 13, 21, 23,
    56, 153–54, 163–73, 176, 193n
    (*See also* Perry)

Ancestors, 21–22
    Child, 21–22, 165, 168

Taiwo, O., 144–45
Tanner, Nancy, 1
Tar Baby, 178 (*See also* Morrison)
Thaler, Ingrid, 179, 183
Thompson, Robert Farris, 11,
    14–15, 18, 81, 192nn 7, 11, 12
Trauma, 27, 67–68, 90, 93–94, 98,
    101–105, 108–109, 111, 113,
    116–17, 133–35, 143, 146–47,
    166, 173
Traylor, Eleanor, 46, 51
Tukula, 11, 14–15, 20, 28, 86, 130,
    152, 192n

Ugly Ways, 20 (*See also* Ansa)
    Malevolent ancestor, 20

Van der Hart, Onno, 105, 116
Van der Kolk, Bessel, 105, 116
Vickroy, Laurie, 104–105, 108

Walker, Alice, 2, 41
Wall, Cheryl, 50
Walters, Wendy W., 66–67
Washington, Margaret, 98 (*See* Creel,
    Margaret Washington)
Washington, Teresa N., 131
White, Deborah Gray, 1
Wicker, Kathleen O'Brien, 144
Wilentz, Gay, 56, 66, 73–74, 83,
    86
Williams, Patricia J., 24
Willis, Susan, 40–42, 47, 52
Wisker, Gina, 184, 187
Woolfork, Lisa, 94, 98, 109, 114
Wright, Nancy, 32, 35, 37, 40, 193n
Wright, Sarah, 41

You Know Better (*See also* Ansa) 20
    Ancestor, 20
Yowa (*See* Cosmogram)

Zahan, Dominique, 57, 63, 65, 69,
    129, 150, 177–78